Recommended Books in Spanish for Children and Young Adults, 1991–1995

Other Scarecrow Titles by Isabel Schon

Basic Collection of Children's Books in Spanish
A Bicultural Heritage
Books in Spanish for Children and Young Adults
Books in Spanish for Children and Young Adults, Series II
Books in Spanish for Children and Young Adults, Series III
Books in Spanish for Children and Young Adults, Series IV
Books in Spanish for Children and Young Adults, Series V
Books in Spanish for Children and Young Adults, Series VI
A Hispanic Heritage
A Hispanic Heritage, Series II
A Hispanic Heritage, Series III
A Hispanic Heritage, Series IV
A Latino Heritage, Series V
The Best of the Latino Heritage

Recommended Books in Spanish for Children and Young Adults, 1991–1995

Isabel Schon

The Scarecrow Press, Inc.
Lanham, Md., & London
1997

SCARECROW PRESS, INC.

Published in the United States of America
by Scarecrow Press, Inc.
4720 Boston Way
Lanham, Maryland 20706

4 Pleydell Gardens, Folkestone
Kent CT20 2DN, England

British Cataloguing-in-Publication Information Available

Library of Congress Cataloging-in-Publication Data

Schon, Isabel.
    Recommended books in Spanish for children and young adults,
1991–1995 / Isabel Schon.
        p.   cm.
    Includes indexes.
    ISBN 0–8108–3235–6 (cloth : alk. paper)
    1. Children's literature, Spanish—Bibliography. 2. Children's
literature, Spanish American—Bibliography. 3. Young adult literature,
Spanish—Bibliography. 4. Young adult literature, Spanish American—
Bibliography. 5. Children's literature—Translations into Spanish—
Bibliography. 6. Young adult literature—Translations into Spanish—
Bibliography. 7. Best books. 8. Children's libraries—Book lists. 9. School
libraries—Book lists. I. Title.
Z1037.7.S387   1997
[PN1009.A1]
011.62—dc20   96–32447

ISBN 0-8108-3235-6 (cloth : alk.paper)

♾™ The paper used in this publication meets the minimum requirements of
American National Standard for Information Sciences—Permanence of
Paper for Printed Library Materials, ANSI Z39.48–1984.
Manufactured in the United States of America.

Para mi familia

CONTENTS

INTRODUCTION

Recommended Books in Spanish for Children and Young Adults, whether used for the development and support of an existing library collection or for the creation of a new library serving Spanish-speaking young readers, includes 1,055 books in print that deserve to be read by Spanish-speaking children and young adults (or those who wish to learn Spanish). These books have been selected because of their quality of art and writing, presentation of material, and appeal to the intended audience, and are intended to support the informational, educational, recreational, and personal needs of Spanish speakers from preschool through the twelfth grade.

This book is arranged in the following sections: Reference Books; Nonfiction Books, which includes Religion, Social Science, Folklore, Language, Science and Technology, Health and Medicine, Cookery, The Arts, Arts and Crafts, Recreation and Sports, Literature, Poetry, Geography, History, and Biography; Publishers' Series; and Fiction Books, which includes Easy Books and General Fiction. Completing the volume is an appendix of dealers of books in Spanish, followed by author, title, and subject indexes.

Each book is listed under its main entry, which is usually the author. For some books, however, the main entry is under the title or series title.

To assist the non-Spanish-speaking selector, I have translated each title into English and provided an extensive annotation. Also, I have indicated a tentative grade level for each book, but the individual student's Spanish reading ability, interest, taste, and purpose should be the main criteria for determining the true level of each book. In addition, I have provided a price for each book. It is important to note, however, that prices of books in Spanish definitely will vary with dealer and time of purchase.

All of the books reviewed were still in print as of May 1996. Unfortunately, as any experienced teacher or librarian knows, it is impossible to determine with any degree of certainty the availability of books in Spanish. Selectors are encouraged to check with various dealers (in the United States and abroad) before assuming that a book is out of print.

The selector will note that most of the books were published in the United States, Spain, Mexico, Venezuela, and Argentina. These countries are now publishing the best books in Spanish for children and young adults.

Selectors will undoubtedly discover some gaps in this recommended collection of books in Spanish for children and young adults. Omission of some important topics is due to unavailability, nonexistence at the time of compilation, or by my own lack of awareness.

I wish to express my appreciation to the students and volunteers of the Center for the Study of Books in Spanish for Children and Adolescents, California State University, San Marcos, for their assistance; and to Ms. Jan Lenhert, Ms. Cathy Pullman, Ms. Maribel Corona, Mrs. Natalie Diamond, Ms. JanetLynn Mosemak, Ms. Lydia Neill, Ms. Leslie Sewall, Mrs. Adriana Valle-Rodríguez, and Mr. Ronald Villalta for their marvelous cooperation.

Isabel Schon, Ph.D.
Founding Faculty and Director
Center for the Study of Books in Spanish
    for Children and Adolescents
Centro para el Estudio de Libros Infantiles
    y Juveniles en Español
California State University, San Marcos
May 1996

REFERENCE

Ardley, Neil. *Diccionario de la ciencia. (Dictionary of Science)*
Translated by Ambrosio García. Barcelona: Plaza & Janés, 1994.
192p. ISBN: 84-226-4818-0. $29.95. Gr. 5-9.
   Arranged by themes, this dictionary explains important words,
terms, and concepts from the worlds of physics, chemistry,
technology, and mathematics. Originally published in 1993 by
Dorling Kindersley, London, it includes excellent, sharp color
photographs, drawings, and charts that add immensely to the more
than 2,000 concise definitions. The well-done index will be
appreciated by scientists-to-be.

Atlas geográfico. (Geographical Atlas) Madrid: Ediciones SM,
1994. 154p. ISBN: 84-348-4114-2. $22.00. Gr. 7-12.
   Beginning with the planet Earth, this well-designed atlas
examines the physical, political, social, and economic characteristics of the continents, countries, and regions of the world.
Easy-to-read charts, maps, and diagrams explore such aspects as
world weather, vegetation, population, and economic activities.
Unfortunately, it devotes one whole chapter to Spain—more than
fifty pages—and only five pages to North America, which includes
the United States.   Despite this caveat, this is one of the best
geographical atlases in the Spanish language.

Atlas geográfico mundial. (Geographic World Atlas) Madrid:
Editorial Everest, 1994. 152p. ISBN: 84-2412-5231. $24.95.
Gr. 5-10.
   Beginning with the Solar System, this Atlas introduces readers
to the Earth including time zones, weather, the evolution of
continents, water, vegetation, and countries with information on
population, languages, religion, and natural resources.   As an
inviting reference guide to the study of the world, this well-
designed, large-format will appeal to students.   A few caveats must
be noted: the index was not updated (e.g., It states *"Unión de
Repúblicas Socialistas Soviéticas"* instead of *"Rusia"*), and its

1

emphasis on Europe and Spain versus other countries makes it of special interest to students in Spain.

Atlas histórico. (Historical Atlas)   Barcelona: Editorial Marin/ Encyclopaedia Britannica, 1991.   294p.   ISBN: 84-7102-158-7. $175.00. Gr. 8-adult.

Through excellent, detailed chronological charts, graphs, and maps as well as photographs in color and a concise text, readers are exposed to the evolution of cultures from prehistoric times to 1990. This historical synthesis summarizes mankind's political events as well as artistic, scientific, and literary achievements. A well-done and most complete index adds to the value of this large-format publication.   Serious history students as well as historians-to-be will find this historical atlas a concise and useful aid.

Atlas histórico. (Historical Atlas)   Madrid: Ediciones SM, 1994. 153p. ISBN: 84-348-4115-0. $22.00. Gr. 7-12.

Arranged chronologically, this atlas provides an overview of political, social, economic, and cultural world events from prehistoric times up to the 1990s. Clear color charts, maps, drawings, photographs, and a brief text summarize important milestones in the history of humankind. Like other reference materials published in Spain, this atlas emphasizes Spanish history.   Even so, this is a useful and informative historical atlas.

Atlas Sopena del arte y los estilos, cómo conocerlos. (Sopena Atlas of Art and Style: How to Recognize Them)   Barcelona: Editorial Ramón Sopena, 1990. 120p. ISBN: 84-303-1100-9. $29.95. Gr. 7-12.

This attractive, large-format introduction to the history of art includes prehistoric, ancient, medieval, up to modern art. Easy-to-read explanations and excellent color photographs make this a most appealing way to learn about art through the ages. A well-done glossary adds further to the value of this reference source.

Atlas Sopena del cuerpo y la vida. (Sopena Atlas of the Human Body and Life) Barcelona: Editorial Ramón Sopena, 1989. 95p. ISBN: 84-303-1065-7. $23.95. Gr. 8-12.

Divided into forty-five two-page topics, this well-illustrated, large-format publication explains the function of the human body. Readers will find interesting information in the fields of anatomy, physiology, genetics, health, and disease with carefully-designed charts, drawings, and photographs in color. This is a basic guide to the study of the human body.

Aula: enciclopedia del estudiante. (Aula: Student's Encyclopedia)
Barcelona: Editorial Planeta-De Agostini, 1988. 10 vols. For the
series: ISBN: 84-395-0802-6. $350.00. Gr. 5-9.

Approximately 1,000 topics are described in this well-written,
ten-volume student encyclopedia. Young Spanish-speaking readers
will find the brevity of the articles with numerous color photographs, charts, and drawings on all disciplines, arranged in alphabetical order, most informative. Readers will note a strong
emphasis on Spanish or European culture, history, and traditions.
Despite this obvious limitation, this is a most useful and attractive
encyclopedia for Spanish-speaking students in the United States and
abroad.

Cabanne, Pierre. *Hombre, creación y arte, enciclopedia del arte:
enciclopedia del arte universal. (Man, Creation, and Art: Encyclopedia of World Art)* 5 vols. Barcelona: Editorial Argos-Vergara/
Encyclopaedia Britannica, 1989. ISBN: 84-7178-311-8. $385.00.
Gr. 8-adult.

Originally published in Paris, France, by Bordas under the title
Dictionnaire International des Arts, this encyclopedic dictionary is
intended to include all the world's knowledge in the fields of art
and aesthetics from its origins up to the present. Approximately
4,000 entries, which vary in length from one paragraph to six pages,
analyze the art, artists, art critics, museums, archaeological sites,
architecture, and other artistic expressions found around the world.
Outstanding photographs in color on every page add to the beauty
and usefulness of this work.

Campos, Juana G., and Ana Barella. *Diccionario de refranes Espasa.
(Espasa's Dictionary of Proverbs)* Madrid: Espasa Calpe, 1993.
399p. ISBN: 84-239-5984-8. $23.95. Gr. 9-adult.

This dictionary is an update of all the proverbs included in the
prestigious 18th edition of the *Diccionario de la lengua española*
as well as others included in well-known classic and contemporary
works by such authors as Juan de Valdéz, Miguel de Cervantes,
Hernán Núñez, Fernán Caballero, Benito Pérez Galdós, Camilo José
Cela, Miguel Delibes, and others. This is indeed a most complete
collection of popular Spanish expressions, locutions, maxims, and
aphorisms, including their definitions and modern interpretations.
A subject index adds to the usefulness of this dictionary.

Carwardine, Mark. *Atlas de los animales. (Animal Atlas)* ISBN:
950-11-0886-4.

Crocker, Mark. *Atlas del cuerpo humano. (Atlas of the Human Body)*
ISBN: 950-11-0888-0.

Nicolson, Iain. *Atlas del espacio.* *(Space Atlas)* ISBN: 950-11-0887-2.

Wood, Robert Muir. *Atlas de la prehistoria.* *(Prehistoric Atlas)* ISBN: 950-11-0889-9.

Ea. vol.: 64p. (Colección Atlas del Saber) Translated by Elida Marta Colella. Buenos Aires: Editorial Sigmar, 1992. $18.50. Gr. 6-10.

Readers will find much valuable information about animals, the human body, space, and prehistory in these well-organized atlases, originally published by Ilex Publishers, Oxford. Numerous excellent drawings, diagrams, tables and charts on every page and easy-to-understand explanations make the study of these topics a pure delight. Casual readers as well as serious students will appreciate the carefully prepared table of contents, facts and figures sections, glossaries, and subject indexes that make these atlases even more useful.

Corbeil, Jean-Claude, and Ariane Archambault. *The Facts on File English/Spanish Visual Dictionary.* New York: Facts on File, 1992. 924p. ISBN: 0-8160-1546-5. $39.95. Gr. 6-adult.

The main value of this English/Spanish visual dictionary is to assist the general reader in identifying a wide range of technical terms from various areas by providing graphic representations of essential features and noting their English and Spanish names. Over 3,000 illustrations, 25,000 words as well as useful indexes and tables in a wide range of areas such as food, furniture, clothing, communication, sports, energy, and others are included. It is important to note that this dictionary favors words used by the average person as opposed to terms used by specialists. Also, when various Spanish regionalisms are used, the editors selected the Spanish words used in Mexico. In the case of English, the dictionary provides British usage in italics and American usage in roman. Inexplicably, the English introduction does not mention the Spanish language at all, but insists on the French language—which is obviously where this introduction was previously used. This is a useful bilingual, visual dictionary; it is unfortunate that the editors didn't use the correct English introduction or correct a few typos in the Spanish preface.

Crónica de la técnica. *(Chronicle of Technology)* Barcelona: Plaza & Janés, 1989. 1035p. ISBN: 84-01-60791-4. $89.95. Gr. 7-adult.

This is an excellent chronicle that describes technological developments from their initial stages up to today. It includes chapters on the main historical periods of technological development, as well as chapters on specific technological areas such as electronics, automobiles, textiles, graphics, and others. Well-done appendices, a comprehensive subject index, and numerous black-and-white and color photographs on every page complement this attractive large-format chronicle.

Diccionario Anaya de la lengua. *(Anaya's Language Dictionary)*
Madrid: Grupo Anaya, 1991. 1079p. ISBN: 84-207-4148-5. $47.95. Gr. 7-12.

This Spanish language dictionary, especially designed for students, includes over 33,000 entries and one black-and-white photograph on every other page. Users will appreciate the clear, easy-to-read format and design. Also valuable to students are the appendices which include scientific and technical terms, grammar rules, irregular verbs, "language mistakes that should be avoided," common abbreviations, and others.

Diccionario básico del español de México. *(Basic Dictionary of the Spanish Language from Mexico)* Mexico: El Colegio de México, 1986. 565p. ISBN: 968-12-0286-4. pap. $18.00. Gr. 4-9.

The purpose of this dictionary is to assist students in Mexico in understanding their textbooks and school assignments and to intro-duce them to standard Spanish. It includes 7,000 entries selected from a basic vocabulary used in Mexico noting especially terms used in Mexican political and social history and natural sciences. It does not include regionalisms, popular expressions, or new words. Unfortunately the homely presentation—cheap paper, lack of graphics, plain cover, cluttered design—limits its appeal. Despite these limitations, a dictionary of Mexican Spanish should be as accessible to Spanish speakers in the United States as dictionaries of contemporary American English are to English speakers in the United States.

Diccionario de la lengua española (Dictionary of the Spanish Language) (Espasa de Bolsillo) Madrid: Editorial Espasa Calpe, 1993. 916p. ISBN: 84-239-5993-7. pap. $13.95. Gr. 7-adult.

This is indeed one of the best paperback dictionaries of the Spanish language with more than 35,000 entries and 70,000 definitions including new words, accessible definitions, and a well-organized appendix with examples of acceptable grammar usage. Students of the language as well as native speakers will appreciate this handy, easy-to-use Spanish dictionary.

Diccionario de sinónimos y antónimos. (Dictionary of Synonyms and Antonyms) (Espasa de Bolsillo)   Madrid: Editorial Espasa Calpe, 1994.   795p.   ISBN: 84-239-9204-7.   pap. $15.95.   Gr. 7-adult.

This easy-to-use paperback dictionary of Spanish synonyms and antonyms includes 18,000 entries and more than 90,000 words. As a quick-reference guide to assist Spanish speakers in their search for just the right word as they consider changes in the meaning of words, frequency of usage, and Spanish words particular to Spanish America, this paperback is a most welcome resource.

Diccionario didáctico de español: Elemental.   (Didactic Spanish Dictionary: Elementary) Madrid: Ediciones SM, 1994.   878p. ISBN: 84-348-4307-2.   pap. $24.75.   Gr. 4-7.

Designed especially for elementary-age students, this dictionary includes more than 25,000 definitions and 1,500 black-and-white and color drawings and photographs.   Students will appreciate the well-done introduction, the part-of-speech labels, and the simple definitions and illustrative examples. A few of the color illustrations may be too simple; nonetheless, this is a useful plastic-covered dictionary for students in the middle grades.

Diccionario didáctico de español: Intermedio.   (Didactic Spanish Dictionary: Intermediate) Madrid: Ediciones SM, 1993.   1296p. ISBN: 84-348-4112-6.   pap. $29.95.   Gr. 7-12.

Especially developed for junior and senior high students, this dictionary includes more than 100,000 definitions including neologisms and foreign words.   Users will appreciate the clear, brief definitions identified as to level of usage, the illustrative examples to help clarify meanings, and the design and type used, which facilitate ease of reading.

Diccionario enciclopédico: Enseñanza general básica.   (Encyclopedic Dictionary: Basic Education)   15 vols.   Barcelona: Multilibro, SA, 1988.   Distributed by Chicago: Encyclopaedia Britannica Educational Corporation.   ISBN: 0-8347-5189-5. $199.00.   Gr. 3-7.

Especially designed for elementary-age students, this easy-to-use encyclopedic dictionary includes over 10,000 entries with 2,000 color illustrations.   The brevity of each entry—one to two paragraphs—and the clear definitions/explanations make this an excellent introduction to the use of encyclopedias/dictionaries for students in the middle grades.

Diccionario enciclopédico Espasa.   (Espasa Encyclopedic Dictionary) Madrid: Espasa Calpe, 1995.   2 vols.   ISBN: 84-239-6171-0.   pap. $40.00.   Gr. 5-adult.

As an accessible, up-to-date paperback encyclopedic dictionary, this one is hard to beat. It includes 72,000 entries—12,500 biographical entries, and more than 8,000 black-and-white illustrations and maps. Users also will note regionalisms and colloquialisms from Hispanic America as well as numerous technical and scientific neologisms now employed by Spanish speakers worldwide. Some will object to its size—7 1/2 by 5 inches—and the two-volume format, but its currency compensates for these detractions.

Diccionario enciclopédico Salvat cuatro. *(Salvat Four Encyclopedic Dictionary)* Mexico: Hachette Latinoamérica, 1994. Distributed by Grolier. 4 vols. ISBN: 970-611-356-8. $99.00. Gr. 8-12.

More than 60,000 dictionary and encyclopedic entries are included in this attractively illustrated, four-volume encyclopedic dictionary. Numerous full color and black-and-white photographs, maps, and charts on every page make it especially appealing to reluctant users. Like other reference materials originally published in Europe, users will note greater emphasis on European countries and topics (i.e., the United States is discussed in three-and-a-half pages whereas Spain is discussed in eight pages).

Diccionario esencial de sinónimos y antónimos. *(Essential Dictionary of Synonyms and Antonyms)* Barcelona: Biblograf, 1992. 390p. ISBN: 84-7153-300-6. pap. $15.95. Gr. 6-adult.

This is a handy, portable Spanish dictionary which includes synonyms, antonyms, meanings, and usage notes. Students of the language as well as others will appreciate its conciseness and effectiveness.

Diccionario esencial Santillana de la lengua española. *(Essential Santillana Dictionary of the Spanish Language)* Madrid: Santillana, 1991. 1360p. ISBN: 84-294-3415-1. $25.00. Gr. 6-adult.

The purpose of this Spanish dictionary is to satisfy the linguistic needs of most users, especially students. It includes specialized terms as well as Americanisms and neologisms making this a useful, up-to-date reference source. A well-conceived grammar of the Spanish language is included as an appendix, adding to the value of this dictionary.

Diccionario Everest sinónimos y antónimos. *(Everest Dictionary of Synonyms and Antonyms)* Madrid: Editorial Everest, 1989. 638p. ISBN: 84-241-1501-5. $12.95. Gr. 5-adult.

This is an excellent dictionary that gives meanings, usage notes, synonyms, and antonyms in Spanish.

Diccionario ideológico de la lengua española (Ideological Dictionary of the Spanish Language) Barcelona: Bibliograf, 1995. 1625p. ISBN: 84-7153-812-1. $38.95. Gr. 8-adult.

Serious students of the Spanish language will find much use for this ideological dictionary. Arranged in five sections—from a general classification of ideas to an authoritative dictionary in alphabetical order—users will be able to find the exact word that expresses a particular idea.

Diccionario ilustrado Océano de la lengua española. (Océano's Illustrated Dictionary of the Spanish Language) Barcelona: Ediciones Océano, 1994. 1048p. ISBN: 84-494-00377-6. $39.00. Gr. 8-adult.

Spanish speakers in the Americas will especially value this comprehensive dictionary of the Spanish language with more than 60,000 entries and 200,000 meanings from both sides of the Atlantic, including neologisms and Latin American phrases and proverbs. The 500 black-and-white pictorial illustrations aren't particularly exciting, yet in some cases, they may contribute to clarifying meanings. Readers interested in words originating from or commonly used in Hispanic America will be more than pleased with this up-to-date dictionary of their language.

Diccionario moderno Larousse Grolier: español-inglés; inglés-español. (Modern Larousse Grolier Dictionary: Spanish-English; English-Spanish) 2 vols. Mexico: Ediciones Larousse/Distributed by Grolier Educational Corporation, 1984. ISBN: 968-33-0151-7. $99.00. Gr. 8-adult.

The main purpose of this bilingual (Spanish-English; English-Spanish) dictionary is "to gather together all the words, classic and modern, which go to make up the rich Anglo-Hispanic cultural heritage" including new technical and scientific terms as well as neologisms, foreign words in common use, and recent colloquialisms. This is a useful bilingual dictionary with the following limitations: It lists the British spelling and pronunciation variant first, followed by the American variant, which may confuse students in the United States. And, some modern words, such as "ecosystem" and "AIDS," are not included.

Diccionario Nauta de biografías. (Nauta Biographical Dictionary) Barcelona: Nauta, 1994. 1096p. ISBN: 84-278-1649-9. $33.95. Gr. 6-12.

Biographical entries for 3,887 outstanding men and women from biblical times up to the present are included in this one-volume dictionary. Students looking for concise information on artists, historical, and literary figures from around the world will find the biographical entries easy to read. Black-and-white photos (approximately one per page) enliven the design. Many users will be disappointed by the wide representation of religious figures—mostly historical—and the scarcity of contemporary scientists. And some adults will object to a color reproduction of Modigliani's "Nude." Perhaps this is not a first-choice purchase, but the selection of biographical dictionaries in Spanish is indeed limited.

Diccionario para la enseñanza de la lengua española. (Dictionary for the Teaching of the Spanish Language) Madrid: Bibliograf/ Universidad de Alcalá de Henares, 1995. 1248p. ISBN: 84-7153-813X. $29.95. Gr. 7-adult.

The purpose of this dictionary is to assist in the teaching and learning of the Spanish language. It includes more than 22,000 entries selected for frequency of usage. Students of the language will especially appreciate the syllabication and pronunciation of words, which are seldom given in Spanish-language dictionaries. In addition, it notes special difficulties for students of Spanish as a second language such as differences between *ser* and *estar*, *estar* and *haber*, and the use of prepositions.

Elliott, Jane, and Colin King. *Mi primera enciclopedia. (My First Encyclopedia)* Illus: Sylvia Tate. Madrid: Susaeta, 1989. 128p. ISBN: 84-305-1614-X. $12.50. Gr. 3-6.

Originally published by Usborne Publishing in Great Britain in 1986, this children's encyclopedia includes basic facts about our planet, nature, history, people, science, and technology. Each page is heavily illustrated with small, colorful drawings or maps pertaining to the topics discussed. The brief, simple explanations are indeed easy to understand. It also includes a well-done index. Some adults may be turned off by the often whimsical illustrations, yet they provide a lighthearted tone to these topics that may be just right for many youngsters.

Enciclopedia hispánica. (Hispanic Encyclopedia) 18 vols. Barcelona: Encyclopaedia Britannica Publishers, 1990. ISBN: 0-85229-532-4. $899.00. Gr. 8-adult.

Definitely one of the best general encyclopedias in the Spanish language with up-to-date entries on specific as well as generic information. It includes a fourteen-volume *Macropedia* with over 5,500 topics arranged in alphabetical order, a two-volume *Micropedia* with basic information on 30,000 entries, a *Temapedia* with thirty-nine general essays which classify knowledge, and a *Datapedia* that presents information in tables or charts.

Espasa escolar. (Students' Espasa) Madrid: Espasa-Calpe, 1991. 1063p. ISBN: 84-239-5918-X. $24.95. Gr. 6-12.

The main purpose of this updated, Spanish language student dictionary is to include new terms in the fields of science, technology, and education. It includes over 35,000 entries as well as numerous photographs, drawings, and charts. Its convenient size—approximately 5 by 8 inches—and two-color typeset make it easy to use in most settings.

Freedman, Alan. *Diccionario de computación. (Dictionary of Computing)* Translated by Gloria Elizabeth Rosas Lopetegui. Santafé de Bogota, Colombia: McGraw-Hill, 1994. 353p. ISBN: 958-600-203-9. pap. $14.95. Gr. 8-adult.

This is a most useful and up-to-date translation of *Computer Words You Gotta Know!* originally published by The Computer Language Company in 1993. More than 2,000 English computer-related terms are translated into Spanish and explained with clarity, precision, and a good sense of humor. Computer fans and others will appreciate the numerous black-and-white charts and drawings that help clarify meanings, with the exception of the photographs, which are much too dark and unclear. A list of Spanish terms with English translations is also included.

García-Pelayo y Gross, Ramón. *Pequeño Larousse ilustrado. (Small Illustrated Larousse)* Mexico: Ediciones Larousse, 1992. 1663p. ISBN: 970-607-156-3. $44.00. Gr. 6-adult.

The first part of this dictionary of the Spanish language includes frequently used vocabulary terms as well as neologisms in the fields of technology, economics, politics, and the social sciences. The second part includes entries from the fields of history, geography, the natural sciences, and the arts with biographical and geographical data. The most noteworthy aspects of this one-volume dictionary with 91,000 entries and 5,200 black-and-white illustrations are its currency and its inclusion of entries and information from Spain and Latin America, providing an overview of the Spanish-speaking world. It is unfortunate that the cheap paper and flimsy binding will disappoint many users.

Gran diccionario de Carlitos. (Carlitos' Big Dictionary) Illus: Charles M. Schulz, Barcelona: Ediciones Junior, Grupo Grijalbo-Mondadori, 1990. 3 vols. ISBN: 84-7419-396-6 for the 3 volumes. $37.95. Gr. 2-6.

This is basically a Spanish-language dictionary for children with 2,400 entries. In addition, it includes the English equivalent of each entry and approximately 800 photographs or cartoons in color by Charles Schulz. Some entries also include antonyms and synonyms. This is a most appealing and lively introduction to dictionaries as well as to words and their meaning.

Gran enciclopedia de España. (Great Encyclopedia of Spain)
Zaragoza: Enciclopedia de España, S.A., 1990-1994. 20 vols.
ISBN: 84-87544-01-0. $3600.00 (for the complete set); $125.00
per volume. Distributed by Carlos Grossi, Boston, MA. Gr. 10-
adult.

The purpose of this beautifully executed encyclopedia is to present a microcosm of the culture and people of Spain from a historical perspective. Serious students of Spanish civilization will find information about the people and places that have influenced its history. Entries vary in length from one paragraph to a few pages. Each page is illustrated with exquisite photographs and maps in color which highlight the beauty of Spanish art, architecture, and geographical features. It is important to note that as of May 1996 only the first seven of the planned twenty volumes have been printed. The following features limit this encyclopedia to the scholar: Small-size print, extensive use of abbreviations and lack of subheadings that make longer entries difficult to read. In addition, information is limited to Spain; so, for example, the entry on "Cuba" is limited to Cuba up to 1898 and "Barcelona" emphasizes the city's art and history and only includes a few paragraphs on Barcelona in the twentieth century—almost nothing about the 1980s and 1990s.

Gran enciclopedia interactiva. (Great Interactive Encyclopedia)
Madrid: Aglo S.A., 1991. 11 vols. ISBN: 84-7973-052-8.
$198.00. Gr. 9-adult.

Only serious students of history and geography, especially of Spain and Mexico, should attempt to use this interactive encyclopedia. The table of contents on each volume is the only guide that readers have to in-depth coverage of such areas as European history, contemporary Spain, geology, history of Mexico, and others. The lack of indexes make this encyclopedia difficult to use. However, readers who don't mind searching through eleven tables of contents will be rewarded with well-written, up-to-date information, numerous maps, charts, graphs, and well-selected photographs in color on world geography and history.

Gran enciclopedia visual 2000. (Great Visual Encyclopedia 2000)
Barcelona: Ediciones Océano, S.A., 1992. 16 vols. ISBN: 84-
7764-723-2. $625.00. Gr. 6-10.

The purpose of this visual encyclopedia, originally published by Tammi Publishers (Finland) and Lidman Production (Stockholm), is to provide information through the interrelation of text and numerous visual images. Hence, each entry of approximately one page in length includes one column of text that is further explained through attractive drawings, photographs, charts, maps, and/or diagrams. The result is an appealing and approachable large-format encyclopedia. As an overview to numerous topics, this may be a useful introduction to encyclopedias for those in search of high-interest, easy-to-use reference materials with the following limitations: It contains information up to the mid-1980s and it emphasizes European facts and issues.

Grandes biografías. (Great Biographies) Barcelona: Ediciones Océano, 1992. 4 vols. ISBN: 84-7764-593-0. $68.00. Gr. 8-12.

The lives and achievements of 162 noteworthy men and women of all times are described through well-written narratives and well-selected black-and-white photographs and drawings. Beginning with Buddha in volume 1 and ending with John Lennon in volume 4, readers will learn about the times, activities, interests, and personal characteristics of artists, scientists, writers, statesmen, and others from around the world. Each biography is four to six pages long and includes a time chart. These are indeed excellent, concise biographies expressing a most refreshing and objective point of view about truly exceptional individuals from the history of humankind. Readers in the United States will be especially interested in the biographies of Benjamin Franklin, Thomas Jefferson, George Washington, John F. Kennedy, Franklin D. Roosevelt, Elvis Presley, and others.

Grant, Neil. *Atlas visual de los descubrimientos. (Visual Atlas of Discoveries)* Illus: Peter Morter. ISBN: 84-216-1814-8.

Lindsay, William. *Atlas visual de los dinosaurios. (Visual Atlas of Dinosaurs)* Illus: Giuliano Fornari. ISBN: 84-216-1577-7.

Taylor, Barbara. *Atlas visual de los animales. (Visual Atlas of Animals)* Illus: Kenneth Lilly. ISBN: 84-216-1815-6.

Ea. vol.: 64p. Madrid: Editorial Bruño, 1992. $23.95. Gr. 5-10.

These excellent large-format, visual atlases will appeal to readers and viewers of any age. Through spectacular drawings, maps, photographs and charts, and straightforward texts, they provide basic information about discoveries, dinosaurs, and animals in a well-organized, easy-to-understand manner. Thorough indexes add to the informational value of these atlases, originally published in

Great Britain by Dorling Kindersley in 1992. The volumes are definite additions to any collections.

Guinness libro de los récords 1990. (The Guinness Book of Records 1990) Madrid: Producciones Jordan, 1989. 335p. ISBN: 84-87069-01-0. $32.75. Gr. 5-adult.

The Spanish translation of this well-known collection of facts about the natural world, animal kingdom, outer space, science, arts, technology, sports, and other fields—wherever records can be measured and broken.

Historia universal del arte. (Art History of the World) Madrid: Editorial Everest, 1988. 632p. ISBN: 84-241-2700-5. $85.00. Gr. 9-adult.

The art history of the world is presented through thirty-nine essays and 900 excellent illustrations in color. This synthesis of the artistic production of humanity through the centuries is indeed a testament to humankind's creativity and magnificent accomplishments.

Horácková, Jana. *El gran libro de los animales, fauna de todo el mundo. (The Big Book of Animals: Fauna of the World)* Illus: A. Cepická and others. Madrid: Susaeta, 1989. 319p. ISBN: unavailable. $16.95. Gr. 5-10.

This is an attractive large-format publication that introduces readers to the animal kingdom. It includes easy-to-read chapters on evolution, adaptation, habitat, social life, and other aspects of the animal world as well as individual descriptions and illustrations of 535 different animals. Indexes of Spanish and Latin names complement this informative and appealing publication, originally published in Czechoslovakia in 1982.

Imaginario: Diccionario en imágenes para niños. (Imaginary: Picture Dictionary for Children) Illus: Gusti. Madrid: Ediciones SM, 1992. 96p. ISBN: 84-348-3582-7. $16.95. Gr. 2-6.

In an amusing manner, this large-format dictionary in pictures introduces readers/viewers to common words in the Spanish language. Depicting scenes by topics—e.g., in the bedroom, in the bathroom, at school, at play, at the supermarket, at the movies, etc.—followed by words and details from the illustrations, it encourages children to identify nouns, adjectives, and verbs. The witty illustrations and the logical arrangement of activities, scenes, and words make this a most enjoyable review or introduction to the Spanish language. A simple index adds to the value of this fun Spanish dictionary.

Imago: Enciclopedia temática. (Imago: Thematic Encyclopedia)
  Madrid: Santillana, 1992. 15 vols. ISBN: 84-294-3462-3. $319.95.
  Gr. 8-12.

  This well-written, thematic encyclopedia is divided into five
  areas—science, mathematics and computers, literature, history, and
  geography—with three volumes devoted to each field of knowledge.
  Adolescents or others in search of comprehensive overviews to these
  areas will appreciate the straightforward text, clear charts, diagrams,
  and maps as well as easy-to-understand explanations. It is unfortunate, however, that this encyclopedia does not include indexes
  but makes do with a table of contents and a glossary in each
  volume. Despite this serious limitation, many readers will find this
  encyclopedia useful and informative especially if they are searching
  for broad, comprehensive, up-to-date information.   Titles are:
  *1. Estructura y propiedades de la materia. (Structure and
  Properties of Matter); 2. Evolución de la vida. Plantas, Ecología.
  (Evolution, Plants, Ecology); 3. Los animales. El cuerpo humano.
  (Animals, The Human Body); 4. Números, conjuntos y expresiones
  algebraicas. (Numbers, Sets, and Algebraic Expressions);
  5. Matemáticas comerciales y estadística. (Commercial Mathe-
  matics and Statistics); 6. Informática y programación. (Com-
  puters and Programming); 7. ¿Qué es literatura? (What is
  Literature?); 8. Del Renacimiento al Romanticismo. (From the
  Renaissance to Romanticism); 9. Literatura contemporánea.
  (Contemporary Literature); 10. Antigüedad y Edad Media.
  (Antiquity and Middle Ages); 11. De la Edad Moderna al siglo
  XIX. (From the Modern Age to the Nineteenth Century); 12. Siglos
  XIX y XX. (Nineteenth and Twentieth Centuries) 13. El Universo
  y la Tierra. (The Universe and the Earth); 14. América.
  (America); 15. Europa, Africa, Asia y Oceanía. (Europe, Africa,
  Asia and Australia).*

Lamblin, Simone. *Mi diccionario en color. (My Dictionary in Color)*
  Illus: Marianne Gaunt. Mexico: Ediciones Larousse, 1988. 203p.
  ISBN: 968-6147-47-0. $22.95. Gr. 3-6.

  Approximately 1,000 words are included in this attractive, large-
  format Spanish dictionary. Some definitions include watercolor
  illustrations; others use sentences to explain the meaning of each
  word. This is an appealing way to introduce children to Spanish
  dictionaries.

*Larousse diccionario de la lengua española—Esencial. (Larousse's
  Essential Dictionary of the Spanish Language)* Mexico: Larousse
  Planeta, 1994. 727p. ISBN: 84-8016-059-4. pap. $6.95. Gr. 7-
  adult.

More than 54,000 vocabulary entries, including 4,000 from Hispanic America, compose this paperback dictionary. The simple, modern definitions will be welcomed by Spanish speakers from the Americas. Unfortunately, the cheap paper will limit its use.

Larousse diccionario escolar ilustrado júnior. (Larousse Junior's Illustrated Student Dictionary) México: Ediciones Larousse, 1993. 782p. ISBN: 970-607-312-4. pap. $15.95. Gr. 2-6.

The purpose of this readable well-designed dictionary is to include words that are considered indispensable during students' elementary-school years. It includes 15,000 commonly-used Spanish words including synonyms, antonyms, and 2,000 words from Hispanic America. Entries are defined by examples within sentences or phrases. Younger students may find the seventy-six pages of black-and-white and color thematic pictorial illustrations informative. In contrast to other dictionaries for young Spanish speakers, this is indeed a most comprehensive, easy-to-understand, and useful basic dictionary.

Lexipedia. (Lexipedia) Mexico: Encyclopaedia Britannica de México, 1989. Vol. 1: 584p. Vol. 2: 631p. ISBN: 0-85-229-514-6 for the series. $79.50. Gr. 8-adult.

Well-done encyclopedic dictionary that contains useful information about words, countries, and many other topics. Users will appreciate the clear, readable print and good-quality paper and design.

El libro mundial de los inventos. (The World Book of Inventions) Madrid: Maeva Ediciones, 1988. 284p. ISBN: 84-86478-20-0. $27.95. Gr. 6-12.

Divided into general sections on various fields of knowledge such as transportation, games and sports, art, medicine, energy, space, and others, this large-format publication briefly describes the large and small inventions that man has created. The easy-to-read design as well as numerous color photographs make this an appealing introduction to inventions.

Llamazares Álvarez, Ángeles, and José Cruz Rodríguez. *Mi primer diccionario Everest. (My First Everest Dictionary)* Illus: Rocío Martínez. Madrid: Editorial Everest, 1994. 159p. ISBN: 84-241-1205-9. $21.95. Gr. 1-3.

Young children can be introduced to dictionaries through this appealing large-format publication. It includes simple definitions, approximately 1,100 words commonly used by Spanish-speaking children ages six to eight, and at least four charming watercolor illustrations per page that help clarify meaning. Caveat: It is unfortunate that words considered "improper" for young children have been excluded.

López, Claudia, and Liliana Viola. *Tu diccionario ilustrado. (Your Illustrated Dictionary)* Illus: Marcelo Elizalde. Buenos Aires: Editorial Sudamericana, 1995. 65p. ISBN: 950-07-0959-7. $24.95. Gr. 1-3.

Five hundred words common to young Spanish-speaking children are simply defined and colorfully illustrated in this appealing large-format dictionary. This is not a comprehensive reference book, but rather an accessible introduction to dictionaries using definitions from the lexicon of young children. An appendix includes English and French translations.

Mi primer diccionario Andrés Bello. (My First Dictionary Andrés Bello) Chile: Editorial Andrés Bello, 1992. 391p. ISBN: 956-13-1036-8. pap. $20.00. Gr. 2-5.

Readers are introduced to a basic Spanish vocabulary and elements of the Spanish language through amusing illustrations in color and simple definitions and explanations. This is indeed a well-conceived picture dictionary that will assist children (or beginning Spanish speakers) in understanding or reviewing the usage of over 2,000 words including nouns, adjectives, adverbs, pronouns, and verbs. The paperback format, appealing design, and lighthearted cover make this a most pleasant and useful basic Spanish dictionary.

Monreal y Tejada, Luis, and R. G. Haggar. *Diccionario de términos de arte. (Dictionary of Art Terms)* Barcelona: Editorial Juventud, S.A., 1992. 426p. ISBN: 84-261-2701-0. $19.95. Gr. 8-adult.

This excellent dictionary of art terms includes almost 5,000 concise definitions and descriptions from the fields of painting, sculpture, architecture, and the graphic and decorative arts. Students, artists, collectors, and other art devotees will appreciate the brief, clear definitions that will assist them in specifying art terms including foreign words used worldwide.

Muñoz, Elvira. *Diccionario de palabras olvidadas o de uso poco frecuente. (Dictionary of Forgotten or Infrequently Used Words)* Madrid: Editorial Paraninfo, 1993. 409p. ISBN: 84-283-1986-3. $24.95. Gr 9-adult.

The purpose of this dictionary is to contribute to worldwide efforts in support of the Spanish language. Students of the language as well as native speakers will be encouraged to become reacquainted with such infrequently-used words as *bebiente, decidor, comparatista, ascoso, pimpollo,* and many others. The brevity of the definitions and the synonyms provided make this a fun or serious way to explore the richness of the Spanish language.

Nauta diccionario enciclopédico. *(Nauta Encyclopedic Dictionary)* Barcelona: Ediciones Nauta, 1995. 6 vols. ISBN: 84-89140-38-3. $125.00. Gr. 7-adult.

The purpose of this six-volume encyclopedic dictionary is to guide Spanish speakers to vocabulary in the sciences, technology, art, literature, and current topics including colloquial terms and Latin American expressions. Appealing and approachable, it includes more than 90,000 up-to-date entries and at least two color photographs, drawings, or maps per page. This is one of the best current encyclopedic dictionaries in the Spanish language.

Norma diccionario enciclopédico ilustrado. *(Norma Illustrated Encyclopedic Dictionary)* Barcelona: Grupo Editorial Norma, 1994. 7 vols. ISBN: 958-04-1003-8. $135.00. Gr. 5-9.

Students in the middle grades and junior high need easy-to-use, approachable encyclopedic dictionaries such as this one. Of special interest to Spanish speakers from the Americas is the inclusion of neologisms, foreign terms, and Latin American variants as well as colloquial and vulgar terms. Unfortunately, users will note a wide discrepancy in content coverage. For instance, three pages are devoted to the United States, whereas Spain is discussed in six and one-half pages. Other items of concern are the dated census information for many countries and the inferior paper and bindings.

Océano uno color: Diccionario enciclopédico. *(Oceano One Color: Encyclopedic Dictionary)* Barcelona: Océano Grupo Editorial, 1995. 1784p. ISBN: 84-494-0188-7. $37.95. Gr. 8-12.

More than 80,000 entries and 7,500 color illustrations make this up-to-date encyclopedic dictionary a useful addition to most libraries and schools. Especially noteworthy are the inclusion of numerous contemporary scientific and technological entries as well as lexical and encyclopedic entries from Hispanic America. The good-quality paper and comprehensive coverage make up for the tight margins and sometimes cluttered design.

The Oxford-Duden Pictorial Spanish and English Dictionary. Second Edition. New York: Clarendon Press, 1995. 591p. ISBN: 0-19-864514-7. $45.00; pap. ISBN: 0-19-864515-5. $19.95. Gr. 8-adult.

The purpose of this pictorial Spanish-English dictionary is to provide visual clues that can guide the user to the appropriate translation. Assisted by various Spanish and British companies and technical experts, the editors identify more than 28,000 numbered objects and offer their names in both languages. It is divided in broad areas which are further subdivided into highly specialized topics, such as computing, typesetting, communications, and transport. Users should note that this dictionary uses the Spanish and British variants, which in some cases may confuse speakers from Hispanic America (i.e., "Ordenador" instead of "Computadora"). Importantly, however, in many cases it provides Latin American and American terms in parentheses.

Paton, John. *Enciclopedia escolar. (Children's Encyclopedia)* Madrid: Editorial Everest, 1994. 10 vols. ISBN: 84-241-2047-7. $229.00. Gr. 3-6.

Originally published by Grisewood & Dempsey, London in 1989, this well-translated attractive ten-volume encyclopedia is just right for children. It includes more than 1,300 easy-to-understand entries and 2,000 color photographs and drawings. The only caveat in this handsomely designed encyclopedia is that, like other encyclopedias published in Europe, it includes more European content as opposed to Latin American. A comprehensive subject index adds to its usefulness.

Quintanilla González, Ana. *Diccionario inicial Everest. (Everest's Beginning Dictionary)* Madrid: Editorial Everest, 1993. 335p. ISBN: 84-241-1015-3. $12.50. Gr. 2-5.

Attractive format, 2,500 easy-to-understand definitions, illustrative sentences to clarify meanings, synonyms, antonyms, and simple grammatical information make this an appealing dictionary for young Spanish speakers. There are, however, a few caveats: Perhaps it was fastidious censors who decided to exclude such words as *sexo* and others related to "special" parts of the human body. In addition, some readers may be confused by the inclusion of numerous drawings and labels of words that are not defined in any other way.

Raventós, Margaret H., and David L. Gold. *Random House Spanish-English, English-Spanish Dictionary.* New York: Random House, 1995. 622p. ISBN: 0-679-43897-1. $18.00. Gr. 6-adult.

As a basic bilingual dictionary, this well-designed lexicon may serve a purpose. It includes more than 60,000 entries, Western Hemisphere and Spanish usage, and American English spelling and vocabulary. Unfortunately, it incorporates such peninsular

Spanishisms as *Méjico* [sic] and *mejicano* [sic] despite the fact that the official letter in Mexico is "x."

Real Academia Española. *Diccionario de la lengua española.* *(Dictionary of the Spanish Language)* Madrid: Editorial Espasa-Calpe, 1992. 1515p. ISBN: 84-239-4399-2. $225.00. Gr. 9-adult.

The twenty-first edition of the lexicographic bible of the Spanish-speaking world now includes 83,500 entries in one easy-to-use, albeit heavy, volume. More than 12,000 neologisms from the fields of science and technology and from Latin America and the Philippines add to the value and usefulness of this prestigious dictionary. Serious students of the Spanish language must have access to this universally accepted arbiter of the lexical and semantic peculiarities of the language of more than 300 million people worldwide.

Real Academia Española. *Diccionario manual e ilustrado de la lengua española.* Cuarta edición revisada. *(Illustrated Dictionary of the Spanish Language.* Fourth Revised Edition) Madrid: Editorial Espasa-Calpe, S.A., 1989. 1666p. ISBN: 84-239-5978-3. $150.00. Gr. 7-adult.

This is a useful, authoritative, and basic dictionary of the Spanish language. Based on the 1984 edition of the prestigious *Diccionario de la lengua española,* this dictionary also includes words in common use, neologisms as well as words originating in Latin America, and indicates nonstandard words or expressions with an asterisk. The excellent quality of the paper and the appealing cover and illustrations (approximately one per page) add further to the value of this Spanish dictionary.

Rivera González, Melitina. *Mi diccionario 2. 8-12 años. (My Second Dictionary. Ages 8-12)* Madrid: Grupo Anaya, 1993. 479p. pap. ISBN: 84-207-5003-4. $19.95. Gr. 3-6.

The appealing and easy-to-read design of this Spanish paperback dictionary with 9,000 entries will encourage its use by young readers. Each entry includes a clear and simple definition as well as an illustrative example of usage to help clarify meaning. In addition, one pictorial watercolor illustration brightens each page. A few limitations should be noted: New terms such as *SIDA* (AIDS) and *ecosistema* (ecosystem) are not included; it lists each word as used in Spain, disregarding Latin American variants (e.g., *ordenador* (computer); and omits what some adults consider "bad" words for children. Despite these caveats, this is an attractive dictionary for children.

Santamaría, Francisco J. *Diccionario de mejicanismos, 5th ed. (Dictionary of Mexicanisms)* Mexico: Editorial Porrua, 1992. 1207p. ISBN: 968-452-538-9. $63.00. Gr. 10-adult.

This dictionary provides a record of Mexican regionalisms including slang and other nonstandard and popular expressions as used in Mexican Spanish. Serious students of the Spanish language as it is used in Mexico will find historical, cultural, and literary references as well as regional dialects that continue to influence the Spanish language. This is indeed the most complete work devoted exclusively to Mexican regionalisms. The cheap paper, cluttered format, and extensive use of footnotes limit its use to scholars.

Wilkinson, Philip. *Enciclopedia de lugares misteriosos: Costumbres y leyendas de antiguos emplazamientos del mundo entero. (Encyclopedia of Mysterious Places: Customs and Legends from Antique Locations from around the World)* Illus: Robert Ingpen. Translated by María Duarte. Madrid: Grupo Anaya, 1992. 255p. ISBN: 84-207-4508-1. $86.35. Gr. 6-12.

This spectacular large-size encyclopedia, originally published by Dragon's World, will truly captivate readers interested in antique civilizations. More than forty sites worldwide that continue to capture the imagination of all people are included. Forgotten cities, huge temples, and puzzling monuments such as Stonehenge, Tenochtitlán, Machu Picchu, Taj Mahal, the Great Wall of China, and others are described in two or three pages of readable text and excellent full-page color spreads that truly project the mystery and beauty of each site. This encyclopedia is indeed the perfect complement to some of the world's best-known folklore, legends, and history.

NONFICTION

Religion

Ray, Jane. *La historia de navidad.* *(The Story of Christmas)* Illus: Jane Ray. New York: Dutton Children's Books, 1991. 30p. ISBN: 0-525-44830-6. $15.95. Gr. K-6.

Ray's distinctive folk art illustrations depicting the lifestyle of people in the cities of Nazareth and Bethlehem add a special spirit to this Christmas story based on the Gospels of Matthew and Luke in the authorized King James Version of the Bible. The stunning colorful illustrations and exquisite metallic gold highlights are definitely joyous and meaningful; the simple Spanish text is appropriate, albeit unemotional.

Social Sciences

Bennett, Beatriz. *Oficios y más oficios.* *(Occupations and More Occupations)* ISBN: 968-39-0624-9.

Bennett, Manuel. *Deportes olímpicos 1.* *(Olympic Sports 1)* ISBN: 968-39-0693-1.

————. *Deportes olímpicos 2.* *(Olympic Sports 2)* ISBN: 968-39-0334-7.

Ea. vol.: 31p. Illus: Manuel Bennett. (Colección Piñata, Serie: La Vida Social) México: Editorial Patria, 1991-1992. pap. $4.00. Gr. 3-5.

Young readers are introduced to fourteen occupations such as farmer, nurse, teacher, miner, plumber, and others through easy-to-read one-paragraph descriptions and bold, modernistic illustrations in *Oficios y más oficios.* The same format is used in *Deportes olímpicos 1* and *2,* which tell about twenty-four Olympic sports. These are definitely not for readers who are looking for in-depth explanations or descriptions; rather, they are just right for young or reluctant readers who want brief, simple texts with lots of illustrations of high-interest topics. Previous titles in this series are: *El campo y la ciudad (The Country and the City),* *El comercio (Business),* and *El mercado (Markets).*

Guardia Herrero, Carmen de la. *Proceso político y elecciones en Estados Unidos. (Political Process and Elections in the United States)* (Secuencias) Madrid: Ediciones de la Universidad Complutense, 1992. 96p. ISBN: 84-7754-114-0. pap. $8.95. Gr. 9-adult.

Briefly and concisely, the author introduces the reader to the Constitution, political process, electoral college, and presidency of the United States from a historical perspective. In addition, numerous well-selected charts and maps make this an easy-to-understand guide to the presidency of the United States.

Viola, Liliana, editor. *Amores para armar. Colección de cartas de amor. (Love Affairs to Assemble: Collection of Love Letters)* Buenos Aires: Coquena Grupo Editor, 1992. 95p. ISBN: 950-737-108-4. pap. $11.95. Gr. 9-adult.

Love letters from great artists, writers, and politicians to their loved ones are included in this paperback book that will warm the hearts of most readers. Black-and-white illustrations by Chagall, Picasso, Maillol, and postcards from the 1930s add a romantic/erotic touch to the affectionate expressions of Henry Miller, Jean Paul Sartre, Ingrid Bergman, Juan Rulfo, Franz Kafka, Rainer M. Rilke, León Tolstoy, and others.

Folklore

Aliki. *La historia de Johnny Appleseed. (The Story of Johnny Appleseed)* Illus: the author. Translated by Teresa Mlawer. New York: Lectorum Publications, 1992. 32p. ISBN: 0-9625162-6-0. $9.95. Gr. 3-5.

The story of Johnny Appleseed and his efforts to disseminate apple trees across the new colonies is beautifully retold in this easy-flowing Spanish translation. Aliki's cheerful, alternating watercolor and black-and-white illustrations provide just the right zest to this tale of friendship and kindness.

Baden, Robert. *Y domingo, siete. (And Sunday Makes Seven)* Illus: Michelle Edwards. Translated by Alma Flor Ada. Niles, IL: Albert Whitman, 1990. 36p. ISBN: 0-8075-9355-9. $13.95. Gr. 3-6.

Spanish speakers (and those learning Spanish) will definitely enjoy this Spanish translation of Baden's retelling of a Costa Rican tale about two cousins. Carlos, who is poor and kind, is rewarded by the twelve witches for adding to their song about the days of the week while Ricardo, his rich and greedy cousin, receives an unpleasant surprise. The colorful illustrations, which portray scenes of rural Costa Rica, capture the tone and spirit of this lighthearted tale.

Belpré, Pura. *Perez y Martina; un cuento folklórico puertorriqueño. (Perez and Martina: A Puerto Rican Folktale)* Illus: Carlos Sánchez. New York: Viking, 1991. 62p. ISBN: 0-670-84167-6. $15.95. Gr. 2-4.

The popular Hispanic folktale about a beautiful cockroach and an elegant mouse has been a longtime favorite of English- and Spanish-speaking children. This well-known version was originally published in the United States in 1932. The numerous marriage proposals, surprising ending, colorful illustrations, and simple directness of the Spanish language will continue to make this tale a special joy to listen to or to read.

Bennett, Beatriz. *¡A bailar! (Let's Dance!)* (Colección Piñata, Serie: Las Artes) Illus: Manuel Bennett. México: Editorial Patria, 1991. 32p. ISBN: 968-39-0597-8. pap. $4.00. Gr. 3-6.

Readers are introduced to thirteen of the most popular Mexican folkdances, such as *Danza de los viejitos, El jarabe tapatío, La danza de los voladores, La zandunga,* and others. Simple, one-paragraph descriptions tell about the origin and special characteristics of each dance. Bright, modernistic watercolor illustrations convey the mood and essence of each dance. Unfortunately, this book does not contain an index, table of contents, or an introduction. Even so, this is a joyous introduction to the folkdances of Mexico. Previous titles in this series: *Sonidos y ritmos (Sounds and Rhythms)* and *Los títeres (Puppets).*

Los cazadores de miel: un cuento tradicional de Africa. (The Honey Hunters: A Traditional African Tale) Illus: Francesca Martin. Translated by Elena Iribarren. Caracas: Ediciones Ekaré, 1992. 26p. ISBN: 980-257-103-22. $11.50. Gr. 1-3.

This is a beautiful retelling of the traditional African tale that explains why animals became enemies and why they can never live peacefully together. The stunningly detailed, brightly colored, full-page illustrations of animals in the African jungle are especially pleasing. And the fluid Spanish translation is a delight to read or listen to. It is important to note, however, that the word *picamiel* is a poetic license for *gran indicador* or honey guide, a tropical bird of the family *Indicatoridae,* some species of which lead animals or people to the nests of wild honeybees. Unfortunately, this is not explained anywhere in the book and may confuse young Spanish speakers. Despite this caveat, this is truly an outstanding book.

Cerezales, Agustín, Silvia and Manuel.   *La cólera de Aquiles.*
(Achilles' Wrath) ISBN: 84-207-4935-4.
————. *El regreso de Ulises. (Odysseus's Return)* ISBN: 84-207-
4936-2.
————. *Los trabajos de Hércules. (Hercules' Labors)* ISBN: 84-
207-4934-6.
Ea. vol.: 31p. *(El Sendero de los Mitos)* Madrid: Grupo Anaya,
1993. pap. $7.15. Gr. 6-10.
    Adolescents are introduced to Greek mythology through these
fast-paced retellings of popular myths. Black-and-white and color
illustrations on every page re-create well-known episodes and definitely convey the spirit of the times. Achilles' numerous quarrels
and battles are retold in *La cólera de Aquiles.* Odysseus's return to
his sweet Penelope after ten years of wandering is re-created in *El
regreso de Ulises.* Hercules' extraordinary strength, which won
immortality by performing twelve labors demanded by Hera, is
depicted in *Los trabajos de Hércules.*

*Cien cuentos populares españoles. (One Hundred Popular Spanish
Tales)* Selected by José A. Sánchez Pérez. Palma de Mallorca:
José J. de Olañeta, Editor, 1992. 219p. ISBN: 84-7651-061-6.
pap. $20.75. Gr. 6-adult.
    A delightful selection of 100 Spanish tales about kings and
queens, shepherds, animals, thieves, priests, fairies, the devil, dead
people, and other popular topics. They vary in length—from a few
paragraphs to three pages—and come from all regions of Spain.
The traditional appeal of these stories is still evident today in Latin
America and the Spanish-speaking world. The lack of illustrations
limits its use, but all listeners and readers will enjoy the stories.

Cohen, Caron Lee. *El poni de barro: un cuento tradicional Skidi
Pawnee. (The Mud Pony: A Traditional Skidi Pawnee Tale)*
Illus: Shonto Begay. Translated by Teresa Mlawer. New York:
Scholastic, Inc., 1992. 32p. ISBN:0-590-46341-1. pap. $4.95.
Gr. 1-3.
    The moving tale of a boy who is too poor to have a pony of his
own, but gentle enough in spirit for Mother Earth to guard him and
eventually help him to become a chief of his people. The text has
been beautifully translated into Spanish. This adaptation together
with the dreamy and dramatic illustrations definitely convey the
tale's supernatural motif.

Coll, Pep. *Las brujas de Negua.   (The Witches of Negua)* Illus:
Joma. ISBN: 84-246-4707-6.

Desclot, Miguel. *Amores y desamores de Oberón y Titania.*
(Oberón's and Titania's Love Affairs and Disaffections)   Illus:
Pep Montserrat. ISBN: 84-246-4712-2.

————. *Luna de miel en el palacio de cristal.* *(Honeymoon in the
Crystal Palace)* Illus: Miguel Calatayud. ISBN: 84-246-4708-4.

Duran, Teresa. *El primer gigante.* *(The First Giant)* Illus: Asun
Balzola. ISBN: 84-246-4711-4.

Janer Manila, Gabriel. *La Móprea.* *(The Móprea)* Illus: Arnal
Ballester. ISBN: 84-246-4709-2.

Valriu, Caterina. *Las tres hilanderas.* *(The Three Spinners)* Illus:
Jesús Gabán. ISBN: 84-246-4710-6.
Ea. vol.: 32p. (El Saco de la Galera) Barcelona: La Galera, 1995.
$8.95. Gr. 3-5.

Like the previous six traditional tales from around the world,
these six well-done adaptations include easy-to-read, lighthearted
texts and simple, modernistic black-and-white and color illustrations. *Las brujas de Negua* shows the power of witches
according to Catalán folklore. The magic power of Anglo-Saxon
fairies is depicted in *Amores y desamores de Oberón y Titania.*
The seductive power of the devil comes alive in *Luna de miel en el
palacio de cristal.* *El primer gigante* explains the Viking myth
about the origins of the world. New Zealand's fierce monsters are
depicted in *La Móprea.* *Las tres hilanderas* is an ingenious
adaptation of Grimm's popular *The Three Spinners.*

Corona, Pascuala. *El pozo de los ratones y otros cuentos al calor del
fogón.* *(The Mice's Well and Other Stories by the Kitchen Stove)*
Illus: Blanca Dorantes. México: Fondo de Cultura Económica,
1991. 97p. ISBN: 968-16-3664-3. pap. $6.95. Gr. 6-10.

The collection of seven tales from old Mexico is told by the
author's nursemaid. They tell of beautiful maidens, adventurous
thieves, magic mice, and others. The sights, sounds, and smells of
rural Mexico are experienced through these ingenious tales full of
charm and wit. Unfortunately, the black-and-white line illustrations
are mere decorations.

Cuentos de la Mujer Araña: Leyendas de los indios hopis. *(Stories
of Spiderwoman: Legends of the Hopi Indians)* Selected by G.M.
Mullett. Translated by Angela Pérez. (Érase una vez . . .) Palma
de Mallorca: José J. de Olañeta, 1994. 110p. ISBN: 84-7651-
213-9. pap. $13.95. Gr. 8-12.

Eleven Hopi legends tell about the origins of their ancestors and
the snake ceremonies. Others explain the future of the soul, life after
death, and the meanings of courage and kindness. Students of the
Hopis will delight in this fluid Spanish rendition that is a joy to

read.   In addition, the excellent quality of the paper and the appealing design illustrated with colorful Hopi kachinas—dolls that represent one of the rain-bringing ancestral spirits of the Hopi— make this collection a perfect complement to the study of the Hopi culture. (The only unappealing aspect is the childish cover, which doesn't do justice to the content or the inside illustrations.)

de Paola, Tomie. *La leyenda de la flor de Nochebuena. (The Legend of the Poinsettia)* Illus: the author. New York: G. P. Putnam's Sons, 1994. 30p. ISBN: 0-399-22789-X. $15.95. Gr. K-3.

Tomie de Paola's magnificently staged and colored artwork featuring the Mexican legend about the origin of the poinsettia (in Mexico known as the Christmas Flower) is the best part of this story. Spanish-speaking children will empathize with Lucinda who grabs an armful of weeds to bring into church and, later, as she prays, she sees the weeds open into dazzling red flowers decorating the altar. It is important to note that Mexican (and Central American) children will be bothered by a mistake in the translation: ". . . *estirar las tortillas.*" Tortillas are *never* "stretched"!

de Paola, Tomie. *La leyenda de la flor "El Conejo" (The Legend of the Bluebonnet)* Translated by Clarita Kohen. New York: G. P. Putnam's Sons, 1993. 30p. ISBN: 0-399-20937-9. $14.95; ISBN: 0-399-22411-4. pap. $5.95. Gr. 1-3.

The solemn Comanche Indian tale that explains the origin of the Texas bluebonnet flower is now available for young Spanish speakers, who will appreciate La-muy-sola's (She-who-is-alone) sacrifice of her prized possession to save her people from more suffering. DePaola's meticulously staged settings and exquisite sense of color and design are the best part of this well-known retelling.

de Paola, Tomie. *La leyenda del pincel indio. (The Legend of the Indian Paintbrush)* Illus: the author. Translated by Clarita Kohen. New York: G. P. Putnam's Sons, 1993. 38p. ISBN: 0-399-21534-4. $14.95; ISBN: 0-399-22604-4. pap. $5.95. Gr. K-3.

In de Paola's distinctive style, young Spanish speakers are exposed to the Texas legend about a Plains Indian boy who discovers he has a special gift that sets him apart from others in his tribe. Similar in look and tone to *La leyenda de la flor "El Conejo" (The Legend of the Bluebonnet),* this is an artistic rendition of how brilliant flowers now embellish the Earth's landscape.

de Paola, Tomie. *Strega Nona.* *(Strega Nona)* León: Editorial Everest, 1994. 32p. ISBN: 84-241-3349-8. $12.95. Gr. K-3.

Tomie de Paola's engaging version of the traditional tale about Strega Nona, a delightful grandmother-sorcerer and Antonio, her hapless assistant, will delight young Spanish speakers as they relish the magic pot's endless spaghetti production. Fortunately, the watercolor illustrations are as comical as the original. Though perfectly understandable, this translation done in Spain uses repeatedly the Peninsular Spanish pronoun for the second person plural (*vosotros*) and its corresponding verb endings, which are not used by Spanish speakers in Hispanic America.

Dorros, Arthur. *Por fin es carnaval.* *(Tonight Is Carnaval)* Illus: Members of the Club de Madres Virgen del Carmen of Lima, Peru. Translated by Sandra Marulanda Dorros. New York: Puffin Warne/Penguin, 1995. 32p. ISBN: 0-14-055471-8. pap. $4.99. Gr. 2-4.

Life in the Andes Mountains is presented from the point of view of a boy eagerly awaiting Carnaval. Dorros's appealing and informative text, which emphasizes the strong communal life of Andean villages and the numerous tasks performed by all family members, is aptly rendered into Spanish. The most distinctive aspect of this paperback book are the illustrations: Photographs of *arpilleras*— cheerful South American wall hangings made from cut-and-sewn pieces of cloth in bright primary colors.

Dupré, Judith. *La boda de la ratoncita: Una leyenda maya.* *(The Mouse Bridge: A Mayan Legend)* Illus: Fabricio Vanden Broeck. Translated by Carlos Ruvalcaba. Miami: Santillana, 1995. 32p. ISBN: 1-56014-583-8. pap. $12.95. Gr. 2-5.

Set in Mexico, this Mayan folktale, beautifully rendered into Spanish, tells how mouse parents search for the most powerful husband to love and protect their perfect daughter. Detailed, muted blue, green, and brown drawings match a gentle prose in which the Moon, the Sun, the Cloud, the Wind, and the Wall reject the appeals of the determined parents. Spanish-speaking readers and listeners will rejoice at the happy celebration between a burrowing mouse and the perfect mouse. The endpapers, which contain attractive blue-gray Mayan hieroglyphics and an author's note, make this folktale ideal to complement a unit on Mexican pre-Columbian history.

Estaba el señor don Gato. *(There Was a Mr. Cat)* (Canciones Tradicionales para Cantar y Contar) Illus: Carmen Salvador.

Caracas: Ediciones Ekaré, 1993.   22p.   ISBN: 980-257-134-2. pap. $6.95. Gr. Preschool-3.

The traditional song from the Spanish-speaking world, *Estaba el señor don Gato*, has been reproduced here with charming color illustrations, one stanza per page. The easy-to-read text, which tells about the misadventures and unexpected events in the life of elegant señor don Gato, is a joy to read or listen to. The only caveat in this otherwise wonderful paperback publication is its reduced size— 8 1/2 by 6 inches—which limits its use with groups of young Spanish speakers.

Gómez Benet, Nuria. *Pepenar palabras: Nahuatlismos.   (Searching for Words: Nahuatlisms)* Illus: Fabricio Vanden Broeck. (Colección Piñata Serie: Cuentos, leyendas y tradiciones) México: Editorial Patria, 1992. 31p. ISBN: 968-39-0640-0. pap. $4.00. Gr. 4-10.

In a brief, rhyming and delightful text, readers are reminded of Spanish words of Nahuatl—the Uto-Aztecan language of the Nahuatl people from pre-Columbian Mexico—origin. Like previous titles in this wonderful series on the folklore of Mexico, this one includes most appropriate watercolor illustrations depicting authentic Mexican scenes. This is indeed a charming overview of Mexican culture through its contributions to the Spanish language.

González, Lucía M. *The Bossy Gallito/El gallo de bodas: A Traditional Cuban Folktale.* Illus: Lulu Delacre. New York: Scholastic, Inc., 1994. 28p. ISBN:0-590-46843-X. $14.95. Gr. K-4.

This well-known cumulative tale from the Spanish-speaking world is aptly set in Calle Ocho in Little Havana, the heart of Miami's Cuban community. This bilingual version tells about a bossy little rooster who, on his way to his uncle's wedding, cannot resist picking two kernels of corn from the puddle. He becomes messy in the process and asks a cast of unwilling characters to clean his beak, which they refuse, until his friend, the sun, solves his problem and everyone complies. Spanish-speaking readers and listeners will rejoice in the symmetry, rhythm, and word play so beautifully depicted in the original Spanish-language version. The well-done, fluid English translation reads well, but like any verse translation it lacks the humorous use of words—different words that in Spanish sound alike but have different meanings. The charming, watercolor illustrations, which are bordered by ovals, provide a contemporary yet traditional festive tone to this Cuban (and Hispanic) tale.

Hall, Nancy Abraham, and Jill Syverson-Stork. *Los pollitos dicen/The Baby Chicks Sing: Juegos, rimas y canciones infantiles de países de habla hispana/Traditional Games, Nursery Rhymes, and Songs from Spanish Speaking Countries.* Illus: Kay Chorao. Boston: Little, Brown, and Company, 1994. 32p. ISBN: 0-316-34010-3. $15.95. Gr. Preschool-3.

Seventeen bilingual (Spanish/English) traditional rhymes, songs, and games from the Spanish-speaking world are included in this well-selected collection. Children and their parents will enjoy longtime favorites such as *"Los pollitos dicen," "Un elefante," "A la víbora de la mar,"* and *"De colores."* The full-page watercolor spreads depicting children at play are lively and cheerful; yet they abound in uncalled-for stereotypes of rural Latin American scenes and people. Latin America is more than tourist-type photos and quaint scenes. Nonetheless, these rhymes and their musical arrangements will be welcomed by parents and teachers of young Spanish speakers.

Hernúñez, Pollux. *Monstruos, duendes y seres fantásticos de la mitología cántabra. (Monsters, Goblins, and Fantastic Beings of Cantabrian Mythology)* Illus: José Ramón Sánchez. Madrid: Anaya, 1994. 139p. ISBN: 84-207-5630-X. $23.95. Gr. 6-9.

Like the previous thirteen titles in this splendid series of myths and legends from around the world, this attractive large-format publication includes thirty-four Cantabrian myths and legends about monsters, goblins, and other fantastic beings from ancient up to modern times. Stunning full-page color and black-and-white illustrations, a map, and a well-done prologue complement this fine collection. This is indeed a wonderful introduction to Cantabria, a region in Northern Spain.

Jaramillo, Nelly Palacio, compiler. *Grandmother's Nursery Rhymes: Lullabies, Tongue Twisters, and Riddles from South America/Las nanas de abuelita: Canciones de cuna, trabalenguas y adivinanzas de Suramérica.* Illus: Elivia. New York: Henry Holt, 1994. 30p. ISBN: 0-8050-2555-3. $14.95. Gr. Preschool-3.

Twenty well-known nursery rhymes, tongue twisters, and riddles from the Spanish-speaking world are included in this bilingual (Spanish/English) edition with bold, childlike watercolor illustrations. Spanish-speaking children will enjoy the spontaneous rhyme of their oral tradition; English-speaking children will at least understand the fun through these well-done English translations. Needless to say, like in all translations, the special charm of the original Spanish word play and rhyme is difficult to convey in translation, but the compiler and translator has done a good job here for English-speaking readers and listeners.

Kellogg, Steven. *Paul Bunyan: Un cuento fantástico. (Paul Bunyan: A Tall Tale)* Illus: the author. Translated by Aída E. Marcuse. New York: Mulberry/Morrow, 1994. 40p. ISBN: 0-688-13202-2. pap. $5.95. Gr. K-4.

Steven Kellogg's outrageous and extravagant exaggerations are now available to young Spanish speakers, who will enjoy reading or listening to numerous events about the life of Paul Bunyan, the unusual lumberjack whose remarkable strength and size resulted in many fantastic adventures. Kellogg's original, full-color illustrations are the perfect introduction to the legendary north woodsman.

Kellogg, Steven. *Pecos Bill. (Pecos Bill)* Illus: the author. Translated by Aída E. Marcuse. New York: Mulberry/Morrow, 1995. 38p. ISBN: 0-688-14020-3. pap. $5.95. Gr. K-3.

Just like *Paul Bunyan*, Kellogg's earlier work based on an American folk hero, this one re-creates some of the legends of Pecos Bill, as remembered and researched by the artist. Spanish-speaking children will enjoy the spirit of carefree, deadpan exaggeration evident in Kellogg's lively visual humor and the engaging Spanish rendition of the original, well-paced English text.

Lippert, Margaret H. *La hija de la serpiente: Leyenda brasileña. (The Sea Serpent's Daughter: A Brazilian Legend)* Illus: Felipe Dávalos. ISBN: 0-8167-3053-9; pap. ISBN: 0-8167-3054-7.

Mike, Jan M. *La zarigüeya y el gran creador de* [sic] *fuego: Leyenda mexicana. (Opossum and the Great Firemaker: A Mexican Legend)* Illus: Charles Reasoner. ISBN: 0-8167-3055-5; pap. ISBN: 0-8167-3056-3.

Palacios, Argentina. *El rey colibrí: Leyenda Guatemalteca. (The Hummingbird King: A Guatemalan Legend)* Illus: Felipe Davalos. ISBN: 0-8167-3051-2; pap. ISBN: 0-8167-3052-0.

————. *El secreto de la llama: Leyenda peruana. (The Llama's Secret: A Peruvian Legend)* Illus: Charles Reasoner. ISBN: 0-8167-3049-0; pap. ISBN: 0-8167-3050-4.

Ea. vol.: 32p. (Leyendas del Mundo) Translated by Argentina Palacios. Mahwah, NJ: Troll, 1993. $11.89; pap. $3.95. Gr. 3-6.

Fortunately, this beautifully illustrated series, Legends of the World, has been retranslated into Spanish. In contrast to the previous edition—also 1993—these titles will now allow Spanish speakers to enjoy these traditional tales from Brazil, Mexico, Guatemala, and Peru. *La hija de la serpiente* relates how the Sea

Serpent's gift of darkness to his daughter brings night to the people of the rain forest. *La zarigüeya y el gran creador de fuego* shows how Opossum outwits the larger and more powerful Iguana. How a young chief is transformed into a quetzal, a symbol of freedom, is depicted in *El rey colibrí*. And the Peruvian rendition of the Great Flood is shown in *El secreto de la llama*.

McDermott, Gerald. *Coyote: Un cuento folclórico del sudoeste de Estados Unidos. (Coyote: A Trickster Tale from the American Southwest)* Illus: the author. Translated by Aída E. Marcuse. San Diego: Harcourt Brace, 1995. 32p. ISBN: 0-15-200032-1. pap. $5.00. Ages 2-5.

Coyote, the trickster-fool character so common in Native American folklore, is a big, bumbling, interfering copycat: he's rude, boastful, vain, and always in trouble. Like the original English version, this Spanish rendition is simple, with the casual, direct tone and satisfying repetition of the oral tradition and exaggerated, traditional geometric designs in brilliant blues and warm rust browns. Coyote is great for storytelling—children will love the slapstick action and the bright, comic art about this gawky fool.

Mohr, Nicholasa, and Antonio Martorell. *La canción del coquí y otros cuentos de Puerto Rico. (The Song of El Coquí and Other Tales of Puerto Rico)* New York: Viking Press, 1995. 42p. ISBN: 0-670-862-96-7. $15.99. Gr. 3-5.

Maintaining the lyrical and dramatic storytelling of the original version, this Spanish rendition depicts the rich, mixed heritage of Puerto Rican folklore. The most compelling is "*La mula cimarrona*," which tells about the mule brought from Spain to labor in a wretched work camp that escapes with a slave to freedom with los cimarrones in the mountains. The others are "*La canción del coquí*," a creation story about the great god of storms, Huracán, and "*La guinea*," a story of the bird that escapes the bullets of the slavetraders in West Africa and comes with the slaves to the island. The bright, double-page spread impressionistic paintings evoke the mythical transformation and the island landscape; however, the abrupt switches in scale and viewpoint may confuse young readers and viewers.

Molina, Silvia. *Los tres corazones: Leyendas totonacas de la creación. (The Three Hearts: Creation Legends of the Totonacas)* Illus: Maribel Suárez. Mexico: Ediciones Corunda, 1992. 32p. ISBN: 968-6044-49-3. $13.95. Gr. 4-7.

The creation of gods, the sun, the moon, Venus, humankind, animals, and how men learned to cultivate corn, according to the Totonacan people of ancient Mexico, are narrated in this well-paced legend. Simple, albeit colorful illustrations definitely capture the mood of this pre-Columbian culture.

¿No será puro cuento...? (Pure Fiction!)   (Fomento Cultural) Mexico: Consejo Nacional de Fomento Educativo, 1991.   82p. ISBN: 968-29-3725-6.   pap. $7.95.   Gr. 5-8.

Despite the homely presentation—cheap paper, prosaic black-and-white illustrations, unappealing cover—of this paperback publication, readers and listeners of all ages will thoroughly enjoy this collection of twenty tales from the oral tradition of Mexico.   The brevity of each tale—from two to six pages—combined with the fast pace, ingenious characters, and amusing situations are truly an irresistible delight. They tell about devils and goblins, peasants and animals, brave men and beautiful women. Pure fun!

Once cuentos maravillosos. (Eleven Wonderful Stories)   Illus: María Fernanda Oliver and others.   Caracas: Ediciones Ekaré-Banco del Libro, 1990.   95p.   ISBN: 980-257-075-3. $15.95.   Gr. 5-9.

An excellent collection of eleven traditional tales about animals, gods, peasants, artists, heroes, and others from around the world and has been enjoyed by several generations of Latin Americans. Readers and listeners will enjoy their brevity and simplicity as well as the universal wishes, dreams, and fears expressed in each tale. Each tale includes at least one full-page illustration in color; however, these vary quite a bit—some illustrations are exciting and fun, others are prosaic and merely decorative.   Students of folklore will be interested in a Latin American version of "Cinderella" ("María Tolete"), the Venezuelan version of Hansel and Gretel ("Onza, Tigre y León"), and other Latin American adaptations of well-known tales.

Orozco, José-Luis.   *De Colores and Other Latin-American Folk Songs.* Illus: Elisa Kleven.   New York: Dutton, 1994.   56p.   ISBN: 0-525-45260-5. $16.99.   Ages 3-8.

Joyous children's folksongs from the Spanish-speaking world are presented here with lyrics in both Spanish and English, simple arrangements for the voice, piano and guitar, and easy-to-follow suggestions for musical games and group sing-alongs.   It includes long-time favorites such as *"Los elefantes," "Las mañanitas," "Los pollitos," "La piñata," "Naranja dulce,"* as well as two of Orozco's own songs.   Exuberant full-page illustrations brimming with the excitement of Latin American color and traditions make this a truly festive collection of singing games, lullabies, finger rhymes, and songs.

Ramírez, Arnulfo G., and others. *Adivinanzas Nahuas de ayer y hoy. (Nahuatl Riddles of Yesterday and Today)* Illus: Cleofas Ramírez Celestino. México: Instituto Nacional Indigenista, 1992. 89p. ISBN: 968-496-223-1. pap. $19.95. Gr. 5-12.

Bilingual (Spanish-Nahuatl) collection of Nahuatl riddles from central Mexico that includes some from pre-Colonial times and others that are still in use today. Stunning, detailed watercolor illustrations accompany each riddle. This large-format publication is indeed a fun and enjoyable manner to expose readers to the utensils, instruments, clothes, customs, food, and other aspects of Nahuatl culture.

Ruiz, Ernesto. *Encuéntrame: Fiestas populares venezolanas. (Find Me: Traditional Venezuelan Holidays)* Illus: Kees Verkaik. Caracas: Ediciones Ekaré, 1993. 24p. ISBN: 980-257-115-6. pap. $8.95. Gr. 3-6.

Through games, a simple text, and lively, full-page watercolor illustrations, nine traditional holidays from Venezuela including San Juan Evangelista (January 3), Carnaval (40 days before Easter), Quema de Judas (Easter Sunday), Diablos de Chuao (Thursday after Trinity Sunday), Velorio de Cruz de Mayo (May 3), Baile de Negros o Tamunanque (June 13), Tambores de San Juan (June 24), Las Turas (September 23), Paradura del Niño (between December 25 and February 2). A well-written appendix provides further information about the origin and meaning of each holiday.

Schon, Isabel. *Tito Tito: Rimas, adivinanzas y juegos infantiles. (Tito, Tito: Rhymes, Riddles, and Children's Games)* Madrid: Editorial Everest, 1994. 48p. ISBN: 84-241-3351-X. $11.95; ISBN: 84-241-3336-6. pap. $6.95. Gr. Preschool-3.

Well-known Hispanic rhymes, riddles, and children's games selected from the popular Hispanic tradition that young Spanish-speaking readers and listeners have enjoyed for generations are included. Colorful, watercolor illustrations add to the whimsical feeling of the book.

Urteaga, Luis. *Fábulas del otorongo, el oso hormiguero y otros animales de la Amazonía. (Fables of the Leopard, Ant Eater and Other Animals of the Amazon)* Illus: Gredna Landolt. Lima: Ediciones Peisa, 1992. 36p. ISBN: Unavailable. pap. $7.95. Gr. 4-6.

Five tales from the Shipibo-Coniba oral tradition from the Amazon region of Peru that tell about clever leopards, fast turtles, wise deer, and other animals. These fast-moving tales are an excellent introduction to this culture; the lively four-tone illustrations definitely capture the mood and tone of the tales.

Valeri, M. Eulàlia. *El pez de oro. (The Golden Fish)* Illus: Francesc Infante. Translated by José A. Pastor Cañada. Barcelona: La Galera, 1994. 24p. ISBN: 84-246-1938-2. $13.00. Gr. 3-5.

This delightful contemporary version of the popular Russian tale about a poor, old fisherman, his avaricious wife, and a golden fish. Bold watercolor illustrations with a Russian flavor and a fluid narrative make this well-known tale just right for individual reading or story time. Some adults will chuckle at this story's new ending that commands the fisherman to make joint decisions with his wife as opposed to always following her orders.

Veray, Amaury. *Villancico Yaucano. (Christmas Carol from Yauco)* Illus: Iván Camilli. Río Piedras: Editorial de la Universidad de Puerto Rico, 1992. 26p. ISBN: 0-8477-2506-5. $13.95. Gr. Preschool-3.

This illustrated version of the Puerto Rican Christmas Carol combines the simplicity of Puerto Rican folklore with the illustrator's obvious interest and experience in animated cartoons. Perhaps some adults will object to this lighthearted depiction of the Nativity, but all readers and viewers will enjoy this unaffected depiction of Puerto Rican scenes, especially the flowers, fruits, and colors.

Zemach, Margot. *Los tres deseos: un cuento viejo. (The Three Wishes: An Old Story)* Illus: the author. Translated by Aída E. Marcuse. New York: Farrar, Straus, and Giroux, 1993. 30p. ISBN: 0-374-34662-3. $16.00. Ages 4-8.

Zemach's warm retelling of the traditional tale about a poor woodcutter and his wife who rescue a devil's imp and are granted three wishes, which they first misuse and later contentedly share with their dog, is now available to Spanish speakers. The humble characters, simple homes, and the surrounding forest depicted in subtle autumnal colors tinged with grays and blues will remind Spanish speakers of approaching winter.

Zubizarreta, Rosalma, and others. *The Woman Who Outshone the Sun: The Legend of Lucia Zenteno. (La mujer que brillaba aún más que el sol: La leyenda de Lucía Zenteno)* Illus: Fernando Olivera.

San Francisco: Children's Book Press, 1991. 32p. ISBN: 0-89239-101-4. $13.95. Gr. 3-6.

Based on a poem by Alejandro Cruz, this is a bilingual (English/Spanish) retelling of the Zapotec legend from Oaxaca, Mexico, where Lucía Zenteno, a beautiful woman with magical powers, is exiled from a mountain village and punishes the villagers by taking away their water. Bright, colorful watercolor illustrations definitely capture the mood of the people of Oaxaca, Mexico. For those adults who insist on bilingual books, they will not be disappointed. But the Spanish translation, although understandable and correct, does suffer like all literal translations. At times, it is awkward and clumsy to read. Nonetheless, this is an appealing version of a Zapotec legend with an added moral: people must show that they are truly sorry and learn to live with love and understanding in their hearts.

Language

Martínez de Sousa, J. *Dudas y errores de lenguaje.* *(Language Doubts and Errors)* Madrid: Editorial Paraninfo, 1992. 366p. ISBN: 84-283-1287-7. pap. $20.50. Gr. 8-adult.

The purpose of this guide is to assist in the correct spelling and editing of the Spanish language. Brief chapters, simple rules, and numerous examples demonstrate the usage of abbreviations, accents, last names, barbarisms, punctuation marks, irregular verbs, idioms, and others. This is not a comprehensive work, but rather it is an easy-to-use basic guide of the Spanish language.

Mendieta, Salvador. *Manual de estilo de TVE.* *(TVE Style Manuel)* Barcelona: Editorial Labor, S.A., 1993. 191p. ISBN: 84-335-3529-3. pap. $9.95. Gr. 9-adult.

The purpose of this style manual of the Spanish language is to present a balance between literary language and the vernacular. In a concise, direct, and easy-to-understand manner, it gives rules and examples of usage, punctuation, and pronunciation utilized in the preparation of texts for television. This is an excellent guide for writers in Spain and Hispanic America, who are interested in an up-to-date guide that takes into account recent changes and developments in the Spanish language.

Miranda, José Alberto. *Usos coloquiales del español.* *(Colloquial Spanish)* Salamanca: Publicaciones del Colegio de España, 1992. 166p. ISBN: 84-86408-26-1. pap. $16.95. Gr. 9-adult.

In a simple manner, the author has selected several usage levels of the Spanish language characteristic of conversational and informal language as well as terms that are generally regarded as vulgar, substandard, or derogatory. Students of Spanish as a second language will appreciate numerous examples of idioms that are generally used with ironic, familiar, or hyperbolic connotations. Unfortunately, this slim volume does not include an index nor a useful table of contents.

Sol, Ramón. *Manual práctico de estilo.* *(Practical Style Manual)* Barcelona: Ediciones Urano, 1992. 253p. ISBN: 84-7953-020-0. pap. $32.95. Gr. 9-adult.

This style manual is an easy-to-use guide for editors, translators, writers, typesetters, students, and others for the preparation of Spanish-language manuscripts. It includes such topics as punctuation marks, bibliographies, tables of contents, language and style issues in fiction, and a special chapter on typographical concerns as they relate to the United States.

Vivaldi, Gonzalo Martin. *Curso de redacción: Teoría y práctica de la composición y del estilo.* *(Writing: Theory and Practice)* Madrid: Editorial Paraninfo, 1993. 491p. ISBN: 84-283-0382-7. pap. $22.95. Gr. 9-adult.

This twenty-third edition of the popular writing and style handbook for writers of the Spanish language includes such contemporary issues as "syntactical barbarisms," "the psychological style," and "deadly boredom." Students also will appreciate numerous examples of acceptable and unacceptable usage as well as practical exercises and useful suggestions.

Science and Technology

El agua. *(Water)* ISBN: 84-348-4713-2.
El árbol y el bosque. *(The Tree and the Forest)* ISBN: 84-348-4208-4.
El tiempo y sus secretos. *(Weather and Its Secrets)* ISBN: 84-348-4507-5.
Viaja por el universo. *(Travel through the Universe)* ISBN: 84-348-4108-8.
Ea. vol.: 48p. Translated from the French by Fernando Bort. (Biblioteca Interactiva/Mundo Maravilloso/Naturaleza) Madrid: Ediciones SM, 1993-1995. $12.95. Gr. 4-8.

These "interactive" titles, originally published by Gallimard Jeunesse France in 1993-1994, include numerous fold-outs, flaps, and transparent plastic overlays. Detailed, glossy color illustrations and simple, easy-to-understand explanations introduce young readers and viewers to the water cycle, the importance of forests and trees, the secrets of the atmosphere and weather and their effects on our planet, and the wonders of the universe. Youngsters will surely enjoy viewing and manipulating these well-done models of these marvels of nature and science. Each title includes a glossary and an index.

Aliki. *Mis cinco sentidos. (My Five Senses)* Translated by Daniel Santacruz. (Aprende y Descubre la Ciencia) New York: Harper Arco Iris/HarperCollins, 1995. 32p. ISBN: 0-06-025358-4. $14.95; ISBN: 0-06-445138-0. pap. $4.95. Ages 4-6.

Readers and viewers are introduced to the five senses. Spanish-speaking young readers and listeners will appreciate this simple, easy-flowing Spanish rendition with appealing full-page color illustrations that do an excellent job of demonstrating the use of the senses.

Los animales. (Animals) ISBN: 84-8016-117-5.
Los dinosaurios. (Dinosaurs) ISBN: 84-8016-121-3.
La tierra. (Earth) ISBN: 84-8016-116-7.

Ea. vol.: 125p. (Mi Primera Enciclopedia) Barcelona: Larousse Planeta, 1994. $9.95. Gr. 3-5.

Simply and succinctly, this small-size (5 by 7 inches) series introduces readers to various concepts in the sciences and social sciences. The bright watercolor drawings and charts, the brief, easy-to-understand texts, and the uncluttered indexes make this series just right for reluctant readers. *Los animales* describes animals' anatomy, food, behavior, and adaptation to their habitat. *Los dinosaurios* tells about the life, evolution, and special characteristics of dinosaurs. *La tierra* introduces the continents, oceans, mountains, weather, and seasons. Other titles in this series are: *El espacio (Space), El cuerpo (The Human Body), Las plantas (Plants), El mar (The Ocean), La historia (History), Los transportes (Transportation), Fabricar (Manufacturing), Los pueblos (People), Las ciencias (Science).*

Animales de granja. (Farm Animals) ISBN: 84-01-31298-1.
Animales del zoo. (Zoo Animals) ISBN: 84-01-31300-7.
Animales domésticos. (Pets) ISBN: 84-01-31304-X.
Camiones. (Trucks) ISBN: 84-01-31302-3.
Coches. (Cars) ISBN: 84-01-31330-9.
Dinosaurios. (Dinosaurs) ISBN: 84-01-31332-5.
Excavadores y volquetes. (Diggers and Dumpers) ISBN: 84-01-31336-8.

Ea. vol.: 21p. (Descúbrelos) Madrid: Plaza & Janés, 1991. $9.95. Gr. 1-3.

Through full-page photographs and drawings in color and easy-to-read and easy-to-understand descriptions, young readers are introduced to farm and zoo animals, pets, trucks, cars, dinosaurs, and diggers and dumpers. These are indeed simple, attractive introductions to high-interest topics.

Ardley, Neil. *101 grandes experimentos: La ciencia paso a paso. (101 Great Science Experiments)* Translated by Genís Pascual. Barcelona Ediciones B, 1994. 120p. ISBN: 84-406-4480-9. $22.95. Gr. 4-7.

Using everyday objects, children are encouraged to do simple experiments to discover basic scientific principles and to understand how these principles control the world around us. The book includes one-page experiments about air, liquids, heat, light, color, growth, magnets, sound, electricity, and simple machines. Like other science books originally published by Dorling Kindersley, London, these include sharp, clear, color photographs, and easy-to-follow directions.

Ardley, Neil. *Mis libros de ciencia: el aire. (My Science Book of Air)* ISBN: 84-7368-106-1.
————. *Mis libros de ciencia: el color. (My Science Book of Colour)* ISBN: 84-7368-105-3.
————. *Mis libros de ciencia: el sonido. (My Science Book of Sound)* ISBN: 84-7368-122-3.
————. *Mis libros de ciencia: la electricidad. (My Science Book of Electricity)* ISBN: 84-7368-123-1.
————. *Mis libros de ciencia: la luz. (My Science Book of Light)* ISBN: 84-7368-104-5.
————. *Mis libros de ciencia: las plantas. (My Science Book of Growth)* ISBN: 84-7368-120-7.
————. *Mis libros de ciencia: los imanes. (My Science Book of Magnets)* ISBN: 84-7368-121-5.
Ea. vol.: 29p. (Mis Libros de Ciencia) Translated by José Antonio Bravo. Barcelona: Emeká Editores, 1991. $11.50. Gr. 3-6.

The purpose of this attractive series is to expose children to various scientific facts through simple experiments with things easily found at home. Clear photographs and easy-to-follow instructions provide step-by-step explanations of each project/experiment. Children will enjoy learning about air, color, electricity, magnets, light, plants and sound through these fun activities. (One minor note: Spanish-speaking children in the United States should be told that *judías* is the Spanish word used in Spain for kidney beans. See *Las plantas*, p. 8.)

Baker, Wendy, and Andrew Haslam. *Los insectos. (Insects)* Barnes. ISBN: 84-348-3996-2.
Glover, David. *Las máquinas. (Machines)* ISBN: 84-348-3997-0.
Watts, Claire, and Alexandra Parsons. *Las plantas. (Plants)* ISBN: 84-348-3998-7.
Ea vol.: 48p. (Experimenta Con) Photos by Jon Barnes. Madrid: Ediciones SM, 1993. $19.95. Gr. 3-7.
The purpose of this series is to make science a fun activity by describing numerous experiments that young readers can do to observe the special characteristics of insects, machines, and plants. The simple explanations, clear photographs, and drawings are just right for those scientists-to-be who are eager to do simple experiments. The brevity of each chapter, appealing design, and easy-to-follow instructions make this series, originally published by Two-Can Publishing in London, useful, fun, and informative. Previous titles in this series are: *La electricidad (Electricity), El sonido (Sound), La Tierra (Earth)*.

Balestrino, Philip. *El esqueleto dentro de ti. (The Skeleton Inside You)* Illus: True Kelley. Translated by Daniel Santacruz. New York: HarperCollins, 1995. 32p. ISBN: 0-06-025467-X. $12.95. ISBN: 0-06-445144-5. pap. $4.95. Gr. 3-5.
Amusing, cartoon-like color illustrations and an easy-to-understand text describe the structure and characteristics of the human skeleton. This wonderful Spanish translation conveys, in a lighthearted manner, the importance of bones, ligaments, and joints as the framework of the human body.

Balzano, Bruno, and Annie Bonhomme. *La naturaleza y yo. (Nature and I)* Translated from the Italian by María Cristina Romanini. Barcelona: Ediciones B, 1994. 46p. ISBN: 84-406-4472-8. $11.95. Gr. 3-5.
Children are introduced to nature during a camping trip with papa and mama Rabbit and their four eager bunnies and papa and mama Fox and their three little foxes. While camping, they ask such questions as: Why do birds make their nests in the trees? Why does the wind blow? Why is land cultivated? Why do stars shine at night? This is not a basic science book, rather it is a fun way to encourage children to enjoy and observe nature through bright watercolor illustrations and appealing situations.

Beautier, Francois. *Descubrir la tierra.* *(Discovering the Earth)* Illus: Francois Davot. ISBN: 1-56294-175-5.
Chiesa, Pierre. *Volcanes y terremotos.* *(Volcanoes and Earthquakes)* Illus: Jean-Louis Henriot. ISBN: 1-56294-176-3.
Le Loeuff, Jean. *La aventura de la vida.* *(The Adventure of Life)* Illus: Véronique Ageorges. ISBN: 1-56294-177-1.
Pouts-Lajus, Serge. *Robots y ordenadores.* *(Robots and Computers)* ISBN: 1-56294-178-X.
> Ea. vol.: 96p. (Explorer) Madrid: Ediciones Larousse, 1991. Distributed by Brookfield, CT: The Millbrook Press, 1992. $15.90. Gr. 7-12.
> Originally published by Editions Nathan, France, in 1989-1990, this outstanding series introduces readers to the diversity of shapes and forms found on the Earth, to ancient and contemporary volcanoes and earthquakes, to the principles of evolution, and to the world of computers and robots. A combination of high-quality photographs, illustrations and diagrams in color, a fluid and informative narrative in Spanish, as well as appealing design and layout of every page definitely contribute to adolescents's understanding of these scientific concepts.

Benton, Michael, Dr. *Dinosaurios y otros animales prehistóricos de la A a la Z.* *(Dinosaurs and Other Prehistoric Animal Factfinder)* Translated by Luis Ignacio de la Peña. New York: Larousse/ Kingfisher, 1995. 255p. ISBN:1-85697-542-8. pap. $12.95. Gr. 3-6.
> Spanish-speaking children worldwide are just as interested in dinosaurs as English-speaking children are. Hence, this nicely designed and well-translated quick-reference source about prehistoric life is just what Spanish-speaking children need. More than 200 entries, one per page, profile dinosaurs and other animals alphabetically by scientific name. Each entry includes a small but excellent color painting or black-and-white sketch, a paragraph or two of text that highlights distinguishing features, and, located in a box atop each page, at-a-glance information such as a time line, a chart establishing the creature's size relative to human beings and a pronunciation guide.

Berman, Ruth. *El bisonte americano.* *(American Bison)* ISBN: 0-87614-976-X.
Stuart, Dee. *El asombroso armadillo.* *(Astonishing Armadillo)* ISBN: 0-87614-975-1.
> Ea. vol.: 48p. (A Carolrhoda Nature Watch Book) Translated by Carmen Gómez. Minneapolis: Carolrhoda Books, 1994. $19.95. Gr. 4-7.

The life cycles, physical characteristics, and habitat of the bison and the armadillo are discussed in these well-translated books, originally published in English in 1992 and 1993. Numerous photographs in color of bisons and armadillos in their natural habitats are included on every page.

Brown, David O., and others. *El elefante marino. (The Elephant Seal)* ISBN: 84-348-3722-6.
Stacey, Pamela. *El pez alga. (Sea Horse)* ISBN: 84-348-3721-8.
Ea. vol.: 24p. Translated from the French by Cristina M. Aceña. (Cousteau y el Mar) Madrid: Ediciones SM, 1992. $14.95. Gr. 2-5.

Stunning, double-spread photographs in color, many underwater and close-up pictures of animals in their natural habitats, and easy-to-understand texts tell about life beneath the surface of the water. They describe the customs, mating habits, and special characteristics of elephants, seals and sea horses. Previous titles in this truly spectacular series, originally published by Hachette and The Cousteau Society in France in 1991, are: *El coral vivo (Live Coral), El garibaldi, pez de Pacífico ("Garibaldi" Fish of the Pacific).*

Bryan, Jenny. *El milagro de la vida. (The Miracle of Life)* Illus: Graeme Chambers and Keith Fowles. Translated by Reis Camilleri Abelló. Madrid: Ediciones Beascoa, 1994. 17p. ISBN: 84-488-0194-6. $26.95. Gr. 4-8.

Like its predecessor *El cuerpo humano (The Human Body),* originally published by Victoria House Publishing, this large-format publication provides a unique view of the development of a baby during pregnancy. Through computer-designed plastic overlays and color drawings and an easy-to-understand text, readers and viewers are introduced to the female anatomy, pregnancy, and the process of birth.

Burgos, Estrella. *El naturalista de los cielos: William Herschel. (The Naturalist of the Skies: William Herschel)* 100p. ISBN: 968-6177-52-3.
Fresán, Magdalena. *El sabio apasionado: Robert Koch. (The Passionate Scholar: Robert Koch)* 109p. ISBN: 968-6177-54-X.
García, Marie. *La cacería de lo inestable: Marie Curie. (The Hunt of the Unstable: Marie Curie)* 124p. ISBN: 968-6177-55-8.
Ea. vol.: Mexico: Consejo Nacional para la Cultura y las Artes/ Pangea Editores, 1992-1993. pap. $8.95. Gr. 8-12.

Like the previous thirty titles in this series whose purpose is to introduce young readers to the world of science through the life and work of some of the world's most renowned scientists, each title includes a brief biographical sketch that highlights significant aspects in the lives of these scientists as well as selected fragments of their writings in a clear and comprehensible language. In addition, each title contains a subject index, a glossary, and simple but informative black-and-white photographs. This unassuming paperback series is a wonderful introduction to scientists and their work.

Burnie, David. *Luz.* *(Light)* Sara Román Navarro. ISBN: 84-372-4533-8.

Cooper, Christopher. *Materia.* *(Matter)* Translated by Sara Román Navarro. ISBN: 84-372-4537-0.

Lafferty, Peter. *Fuerza y movimiento.* *(Force and Motion)* Translated by Mónica Isabel Luna Estévez. ISBN: 84-372-4534-6.

Parker, Steve. *Electricidad.* *(Electricity)* Translated by Alejandro de Hoz García-Bellido. ISBN: 84-372-4535-4.

Ea. vol.: 64p. (Ciencia Visual Altea) Madrid: Santillana, 1993. $15.98. Gr. 4-9.

Light, matter, force, motion, and electricity are described in the excellent quality of other Eyewitness's series. Originally published in 1992 by Dorling Kindersley, London, these titles include numerous attractive color photographs, drawings, and charts and brief, easy-to-understand texts explaining the history of science up to recent discoveries. Each volume includes an index. *Luz* describes the history of light from the earliest solar myths up to recent optical discoveries. *Materia* explains the early concepts of four elements up to current findings about the atom. *Fuerza y movimiento* tells about the forces that move the Earth. And the earliest discoveries about electricity up to the most modern technology are depicted in *Electricidad*. All Spanish-speaking readers will be enticed into the world of science by this outstanding series.

Burton, Jane. *Los animales aprenden.* *(How Animals Learn)* ISBN: 84-263-2066-X.

————. *Los animales comen.* *(How Animals Eat)* ISBN: 84-263-2069-4.

————. *Los animales hablan* *(How Animals Talk)* ISBN: 84-263-2068-6.

————. *Los animales luchan.* *(How Animals Fight)* ISBN: 84-263-2067-8.

————. *Mantenerse a salvo.* *(Staying Safe)* ISBN: 84-263-2065-1.

————. *Mantenerse frescos.* *(Staying Cool)* ISBN: 84-263-2063-5.

————. *Mantenerse limpios.* *(Staying Clean)* ISBN: 84-263-2062-7.

————. *Mantenerse templados.* *(Maintaining Body Temperature)*
ISBN: 84-263-2064-3.

Ea. vol.: 24p. (Actividades de los Animales) Translated by
Miguel A. Lafuente Rosales, Zaragoza: Editorial Luis Vives, 1991.
$6.30. Gr. 3-6.

Through various activities performed by animals, children will
see how animals learn, eat, talk, fight; stay safe, cool, clean; and
maintain their bodies' temperatures. Excellent close-up photographs in color and clear, interesting descriptions make this series,
originally published in Great Britain in 1970, a fascinating way to
learn about animals. Simple subject indexes and glossaries add
further to each title.

Butterfield, Moira. *Descubre todos los secretos de un barco.* *(Look
Inside Cross-Sections of Ships)* Illus: Jonothan Potter. ISBN: 84-
406-5237-2.

Johnstone, Michael. *Descubre todos los secretos de un avión.* *(Look
Inside Cross-Sections of Planes)* Illus: Hans Jenssen. ISBN: 84-
406-5236-4.

Ea. vol.: 32p. (A Través de la Imagen) Translated by Genís
Pascual. Barcelona: Ediciones B, 1995. $22.95. Gr. 4-8.

Sharp, detailed, cross-section color drawings show inside and
outside views of ships and airplanes. *Descubre todos los secretos
de un barco* describes eleven popular types of ships such as a
trireme, an ancient Greek warship; Henry VIII's "Mary Rose"; the
Mayflower; an aircraft carrier; and a transatlantic. *Descubre todos
los secretos de un avión* describes eleven airplanes from the German
Fokker used in World War I to the Concorde. Each volume
includes brief texts and simple, technical facts about each ship and
airplane, a glossary, and an index. Like other large-format cross-
section books originally published by Dorling Kindersley, these
titles are just right to expose young readers and viewers to the
technology of ships and airplanes.

Butterfield, Moira. *1001 secretos de la tierra.* *(1001 Secrets of the
Earth)* ISBN: 84-8016-052-7.

————. *1001 secretos de los animales.* *(1001 Animal Secrets)*
ISBN: 84-8016-051-9.

Ea. vol.: 48p. Barcelona: Larousse Planeta, 1993. $16.95. Gr.
3-7.

Numerous facts about the animal kingdom and about planet
Earth are included in these large-format books, originally published
by Times Four Publishing in Great Britain in 1992. The well-
organized and easy-to-understand design of these books are sure to
increase readers's and viewers's interests in these topics. In

addition, many color drawings, "Incredible but true" sections under each topic, and a very complete index add to the appeal of this series.

Carwardine, Mark. *Ballenas, delfines y marsopas. (Whales, Dolphins and Porpoises)* Illus: Martin Camm. ISBN: 84-01-31472-0.
Cruickshank, Gordon. *Cómo funcionan los coches. (Cars and How They Work)* Illus: Alan Austin. ISBN: 84-01-31471-2.
    Ea. vol.: 64p. (Ventana al Mundo) Barcelona: Plaza & Janés, 1993. $13.75. Gr. 5-8.

    Two more titles of this attractive series, originally published by Dorling Kindersley, London, in 1992, whose purpose is to introduce young readers to the world in which they live. Like the previous fourteen titles, these include numerous clear drawings, diagrams, and charts in color and brief, easy-to-understand descriptions. *Ballenas, delfines y marsopas* tells about the life, migration habits, favorite foods, and other important aspects about these surprising mammals. *Cómo funcionan los coches* relates the special appeal and technical innovations that cars have experienced from the earliest ones in the nineteenth century to cars of the future. Car lovers will have a feast.

Causse, Christine. *Albatros. (Albatross)* ISBN: 84-348-3720-X.
————. *Ballenas jorobadas. (Whales)* ISBN: 84-348-3757-9.
————. *Manatíes (Manatees)* ISBN: 84-348-3758-7.
————. *Nutrias marinas. (Sea Otters)* ISBN: 84-348-3719-6.
    Ea. vol.: 28p. Translated from the French by Cristina M. Aceña. (Cousteau y Los Animales) Madrid: Ediciones SM, 1992. $9.75. Gr. K-2.

    Through full-page photographs in color in natural settings and a very brief text, young readers are introduced to the albatross, whales, manatees, and sea otters. The last ten pages provide further information such as habitat, migration patterns, and food as well as a glossary and games. Previous titles in this series, originally published by Hachette and The Cousteau Society in France in 1991, are *Delfines (Dolphins), Tortugas (Turtles), Focas (Seals), and Pingüinos (Penguins)*.

Cawthorne, Nigel. *Avión. (Airliner)* ISBN: 84-406-2746-7.
Furniss, Tim. *Cohete espacial. (Space Rocket)* ISBN: 84-406-2747-5.
Trier, Mike. *Supercoche. (Supercar)* ISBN: 84-406-2745-9.
    Ea. vol.: 32p. (Ingenieros en Acción) Translated by: Genís Pascual. Barcelona: Ediciones B, 1992. $12.50. Gr. 5-8.

Through diagrams, drawings, photographs in color, and clear explanations, this series, originally published in Great Britain in 1988, shows how designers, engineers, and technicians work together to produce airplanes, space rockets, and supercars. Each title discusses special problems that different production teams must solve such as how to make faster airplanes or more powerful car engines. A glossary and subject index add to the value of these technical books.

Chamizo, José Antonio. *El maestro de lo infinitamente pequeño: John Dalton.* *(The Master of the Infinitesimally Small: John Dalton)* ISBN: 968-6177-46-9.

Fresán, Magdalena. *El perdedor iluminado: Ignaz Philipp Semmelweis.* *(The Enlightened Loser: Ignaz Philipp Semmelweis)* ISBN: 968-6177-38-8.

Gallardo-Cabello, Manuel. *Atrapados en la doble hélice: Watson y Crick.* *(Trapped in the Double Propeller: Watson and Crick)* ISBN: 968-6177-45-0.

García, Horacio. *El alquimista errante: Paracelso.* *(The Errant Alchemist: Paracelsus)* ISBN: 968-6177-43-4.

Lozoya, Xavier. *El preguntador del rey: Francisco Hernández.* *(The King's Inquirer: Francisco Hernández)* ISBN: 968-6177-42-6.

Rojas, José Antonio. *El visionario de la anatomía: Andreas Vesalius.* *(Anatomy's Visionary: Andreas Vesalius)* ISBN: 968-6177-42-2.

Rojo, Ariel. *El príncipe del conocimiento: Georges Louis de Buffon.* *(The Prince of Knowledge: Georges Louis de Buffon)* ISBN: 968-6177-48-5.

Stanislawski, Estanislao C., and Silvia M. Stanislawski. *El descubridor del oro de Troya: Heinrich Schliemann.* *(The Gold Discoverer of Troy: Heinrich Schliemann)* ISBN: 968-6177-37-X.

Swaan, Bram de. *El malabarista de los números: Blaise Pascal.* *(The Number Juggler: Blaise Pascal)* ISBN: 968-6177-36-1.

Ea. vol.: 110p. Mexico: Pangea Editores, 1991-1992. pap. $8.95. Gr. 8-12.

Like previous titles in this series whose purpose is to introduce young readers into the world of science through the life and work of some of the world's most renowned scientists, each title includes a brief biographical sketch that highlights significant aspects in the lives of these scientists as well as selected fragments of their writings in a clear and comprehensible language. In addition, each title contains a subject index, a glossary, and simple but informative black-and-white photographs. This unassuming paperback series is a wonderful introduction to scientists and their work.

Chinery, Michael. *Las costas. (Seashores)* Illus: Wayne Ford and others. Translated by Alejandro Fernández Susial. (Enciclopedia de los Animales Salvajes) Madrid: Editorial Everest, 1995. 40p. ISBN: 84-241-2053-1. $12.95. Gr. 4-8.

Originally published in 1991 by Grisewood Dempey, London, this attractive series, Wild World of Animals, is now available to Spanish speakers. Exquisite, full-page watercolor illustrations and brief, informative texts depict the fauna along the seashores. With just enough facts and "Do you know" insets as well as a useful glossary, this volume is a wonderful introduction to seashores. Other titles in this series are: *Los desiertos (Deserts), Las selvas (Jungles), Las sabanas y las praderas (Prairies), Los océanos (Oceans), Los Polos (The Poles), Los bosques (Forests), Los lagos y los ríos (Lakes and Rivers)*.

La ciencia. (Science) ISBN: 84-01-31509-3.
Insectos y arañas. (Insects and Spiders) ISBN: 84-01-31545-X.
Mamíferos. (Mammals) ISBN: 84-01-31544-1.

Ea. vol.: 49p. (Enciclopedia Ilustrada) Translated by Josep Sala Barbany. Barcelona: Plaza & Janés, 1994. $15.95. Gr. 4-7.

These appealing, large-format books are just right to introduce children to the world of science, insects and spiders, and mammals. Like other titles originally published by Dorling Kindersley, London, these include sharp, color photographs and drawings and simple, clear explanations of basic scientific principles, and the special characteristics of insects, spiders, and mammals. Previous titles in this hard-to-resist series are: *Animales de la jungla (Jungle Animals), Aves (Birds), Tu comida (Your Food), Tu cuerpo (Your Body), Dinosaurios (Dinosaurs), El espacio (Space), La tierra (The Earth), Vida Marina (Marine Life), Vivir en el pasado (Life in the Past)*.

Clemson, David and Wendy Clemson. *Mi primer libro de mates. (My First Math Book)* Translated by María Millán. Barcelona: Editorial Molino, 1994. 45p. ISBN: 84-272-1926-1. $23.95. Gr. K-2.

Originally published by Dorling Kindersley, London, in 1991, this attractive large-format publication introduces children to the world of numbers, symbols, shapes, and mathematical concepts. Through simple games and puzzles, children will discover numbers, weights and measures, and fractions. The sharp color photographs, simple text, and easy-to-understand glossary make this the ideal first book of math.

Cole, Joanna. *El autobús mágico en el interior de la tierra. (The Magic School Bus Inside the Earth)* Illus: Bruce Degen. Translated by Paz Barroso. New York: Scholastic, Inc., 1993. 40p. ISBN: 0-590-46342-X. pap. $5.95. Gr. 2-4.

The wonderful appeal of the magic school bus is now available to Spanish speakers as they travel to the center of the Earth and in the process learn about fossils, rocks, and volcanoes in Señorita Carola's geology class. Degen's bright, colorful artwork alongside the children's witty thoughts and banter are just right for Spanish-speaking geologists-to-be.

Computadoras al instante. *(Computers Simplified)* ISBN: 0-13-178872-8.
MS-DOS 6.2 al instante. *(MS-DOS 6.2 Simplified)* ISBN: 0-13-123282-7.
Ea. vol.: 122p. (Aprender a Simple Vista) Englewood Cliffs, NJ: Prentice Hall Career & Technology, 1993. pap. $14.95. Gr. 8-adult.

Even the most avid skeptics will be attracted to computers through these well-produced, user-friendly manuals to computers and MS-DOS. Simple explanations, clever cartoon characters, and clear, color illustrations will encourage all beginners to learn about the basic parts and functions of computers and the MS-DOS operating system. Spanish speakers will definitely applaud these well-conceived Spanish renditions that should serve as models of technical translations at their best.

Cooper, Jason. *Arboles.* *(Trees)* ISBN: 0-86592-498-8.
————. *Cactos.* *(Cactus)* ISBN: 0-86592-546-1.
————. *Flores.* *(Flowers)* ISBN: 0-86592-497-X.
————. *Plantas insectívoras.* *(Insect-Eating Plants)* ISBN: 0-86592-548-8.
————. *Plantas singulares. (Strange Plants)* ISBN: 0-86592-547-X.
————. *Setas y hongos. (Mushrooms)* ISBN: 0-86592-499-6.
Ea. vol.: 24p. (Los Jardines de la Tierra) Translated by Argentina Palacios. Vero Beach, FL: Rourke Enterprises, 1991. $8.95. Gr. 3-5.

Readers are introduced to the Earth's garden—trees, cacti, flowers, plants, and mushrooms—through brief, easy-to-understand texts and attractive photographs in color. Simple glossaries and subject indexes add to the value of this series for scientists-to-be.

Cooper, Jason. *Automóviles.* *(Automobiles)* ISBN: 0-86592-510-0.
————. *Aviones.* *(Airplanes)* ISBN: 0-86592-507-0.
————. *Botes y barcos. (Boats and Ships)* ISBN: 0-86592-474-0.
————. *Camiones. (Trucks)* ISBN: 0-86592-509-7.

————. *Motocicletas. (Motorcycles)* ISBN: 0-86592-508-9.

————. *Trenes. (Trains)* ISBN: 0-86592-515-1.

Ea. vol.: 24p. (Máquinas de Viaje) Translated by Argentina Palacios. Vero Beach, FL: Rourke Enterprises, 1991. $8.95. Gr. 3-5.

A brief and easy-to-understand text and clear photographs in color provide an overview of the history and characteristics of various types of traveling machines.

Cooper, Jason. *Canales. (Canals)* ISBN: 0-86592-923-8.

————. *Castillos. (Castles)* ISBN: 0-86592-937-8.

————. *Faros. (Lighthouses)* ISBN: 0-86592-936-X.

————. *Puentes. (Bridges)* ISBN: 0-86592-934-3.

————. *Rascacielos. (Skyscrapers)* ISBN: 0-86592-935-1.

————. *Represas. (Dams)* ISBN: 0-86592-924-6.

Ea. vol.: 24p. (Maravillas de la Humanidad) Translated by Aída E. Marcuse. Vero Beach, FL: Rourke Enterprises, 1991. $8.95. Gr. 3-5.

Brief, easy-to-understand texts and clear photographs in color introduce readers to six man-made wonders—canals, castles, lighthouses, bridges, skyscrapers, and dams. Only one unfortunate grammatical mistake on one of the titles, *Represas*, detracts from this otherwise excellent translation: *"A veces, el beneficio que se obtiene - como ser [sic], la energía . . . "* (p. 19).

Cosgrove, Brian. *La atmósfera y el tiempo. (Weather)* ISBN: 84-372-3759-9.

McCarthy, Colin. *Reptiles. (Reptiles)* ISBN: 84-372-3761-0.

Ea. vol.: 64p. (Biblioteca Visual Altea) Madrid: Altea, 1991. $16.50. Gr. 4-9.

Like previous titles in this outstanding large-format series, originally published in Great Britain as Eyewitness Encyclopedia, these contain numerous excellent close-up photographs, charts, and drawings in color and concise, clear explanations about the weather and reptiles. As attractive, easy-to-understand introductions to numerous topics, these titles are difficult to surpass.

de Paola, Tomie. *El libro de las arenas movedizas. (The Quicksand Book)* Translated by Teresa Mlawer. New York: Holiday House, 1993. 32p. ISBN: 0-8234-1056-0. $14.95; pap. ISBN: 0-8234-1057-9. $5.95. Gr. 1-3.

Humor and information abound in this easy-to-understand translation of de Paola's explanation of quicksand including what it is, how it works, where it is found, and which survival strategies work best. The proscenium arch effect of tropical leaves in jungle greens, yellows, and browns effectively highlight the vicissitudes of life and quicksand.

de Paola, Tomie. *El libro de las nubes.* *(The Cloud Book).* Translated by Teresa Mlawer. New York: Holiday House, 1993. 32p. ISBN: 0-8234-1054-4. $14.95; ISBN: 0-8234-1055-2. pap. $5.95. Gr. 2-4.

In this well-done translation, Spanish speakers are introduced to the ten most common types of clouds including the myths they've inspired and what they can tell about coming weather changes. Perhaps there is more information about clouds here than young readers care to know, yet de Paola always manages to add a delightful sense of humor to his well-conceived illustrations.

Del 'big bang' a la electricidad. (From the "Big Bang" to Electricity) ISBN: 84-348-4209-2.
El fuego, ¿amigo o enemigo? (Fire: Friend or Enemy?) ISBN: 84-348-4109-6.
Volar, el sueño del hombre. (To Fly: Man's Dream) ISBN: 84-348-4506-7.

Ea. vol.: 48p. Translated from the French by Fernando Bort. (Biblioteca Interactiva/Mundo Maravilloso/Ciencias) Madrid: Ediciones SM, 1994-1995. $12.95. Gr. 4-8.

Originally published by Gallimard Jeunesse France, in 1993-1994, these "interactive" titles include numerous fold-outs, flaps, and transparent plastic overlays intermingled between detailed, glossy color illustrations, and simple, easy-to-understand explanations that introduce young readers and viewers to the importance of energy and fire, and to the wonders of flying. These well-constructed, attractive publications are sturdy enough to withstand eager hands as they consider before/after views of various scientific concepts and applications. Each title includes a glossary and an index.

Diccionario visual Altea de arquitectura. (The Visual Dictionary of Buildings) ISBN: 84-372-4531-1.
Diccionario visual Altea de las cosas de cada día. (The Visual Dictionary of Everyday Things) ISBN: 84-372-4527-3.
Diccionario visual Altea de las plantas. (The Visual Dictionary of Plants) ISBN: 84-372-4529-X.
Diccionario visual Altea de los animales. (The Visual Dictionary of Animals) ISBN: 84-372- 4525-7.
Diccionario visual Altea de los automóviles. (The Visual Dictionary of Cars) ISBN:84-372-4530-3.

Diccionario visual Altea de naves y navegación. (The Visual Dictionary of Ships and Sailing) ISBN: 84-372-4526-5.

Diccionario visual Altea del cuerpo humano. (The Visual Dictionary of the Human Body) ISBN: 84-372-4528-1.
Ea. vol.: 64p. (Diccionarios Visuales Altea) Madrid: Santillana, 1992-1993. $24.95. Gr. 5-12.

The excellent quality of these large-format visual dictionaries, originally published by Dorling Kindersley in London, is now available to Spanish speakers. Each volume includes more than 200 detailed and eye-catching photographs and drawings in color and brief texts that explain the interior and exterior of everyday things, cars, ships; the functions, organs and characteristics of animals; and the systems and organs of the human body. Complete indexes add to the value of each dictionary.

Dillner, Luisa. *El cuerpo humano. (The Human Body)* Translated by Miguel Roldán. Madrid: Ediciones Beascoa, 1993. 16p. ISBN: 84-7546-842-X. $25.00. Gr. 4-8.

Originally published by Victoria House Publishing, London, in 1993, this large-format publication provides a unique view of the human body and its functions. Through computer-designed plastic overlays and color drawings and a straightforward text, readers are introduced to various systems and organs of the human body. (This book also is available from Editorial Sigmar in Argentina.)

Dillner, Luisa. *El cuerpo humano. (The Human Body)* Translated by Graciela Jáurequi Lorda de Castro. Buenos Aires: Editorial Sigmar, 1993. 17p. ISBN: 950-11-0926-7. $29.95. Gr. 4-8.

Originally published in Great Britain by Victoria House Publishing, this large-format publication provides a unique view of the human body and its functions. Through carefully designed plastic overlays and color illustrations, and a straightforward text, readers are introduced to various systems and organs of the body. (This book is also available from Ediciones Beascoa.)

Dinnen, Jacqueline. *Huracanes y tifones. (Hurricanes and Typhoons)* ISBN: 84-7894-176-2.

————. *Volcanes. (Volcanoes)* ISBN: 84-7894-180-0.

Walker, Jane. *Avalanchas y corrimientos. (Avalanches and Land-slides)* ISBN: 84-7894-179-7.

————. *Hambre, sequía, y plagas. (Famine, Drought, and Plagues)* ISBN: 84-7894-181-9.

————. *Maremontos e inundaciones. (Tidal Waves and Floods)* ISBN: 84-7894-178-9.

—————. *Terremotos.* *(Earthquakes)* ISBN: 84-7894-177-0.
Ea. vol.: 32p. (Desastres Naturales) Madrid: Aglo Ediciones,
1995. $15.95. Gr. 5-9.

Features of this series include excellent color photographs,
drawings, maps, and charts. The brief, easy-to-understand texts
introduce readers to natural disasters: hurricanes and typhoons;
volcanoes; avalanches and landslides; famine, drought and plagues;
tidal waves and floods; and earthquakes.

Each title describes their history, actions, and effects on the
environment and human beings and includes a glossary, an index,
and a section on facts and figures. Originally published by Aladdin
Books, London, this well-designed, approachable series will
contribute to readers's understanding of these natural disasters.

Dorros, Arthur. *Ciudades de hormigas.* *(Ant Cities)* Illus: the
author. Translated by Daniel Santacruz. (Aprende y Descubre la
Ciencia) New York: Harper Arco Iris/HarperCollins, 1995. 32p.
ISBN: 0-06-025360-6. $14.95; ISBN: 0-06-445137-2. pap.
$4.95. Ages 5-7.

This well-translated book is a useful, simplified explanation
about ants and how they live and work together to build and
maintain their cities. Like the original English version, some
aspects of ant species are not clearly explained and, most
importantly, if children followed Dorros's guidance to observe ants
close-up by using a homemade ant farm with holes punched in a jar
lid, the tiny critters would escape. Despite these caveats, young
Spanish-speaking children will find the information on ants well
within their grasp.

Endacott, Geoff. *Inventos y descubrimientos.* *(Discovery and Inven-
tions)* ISBN: 84-7553-28-1.
Whitfield, Philip. *Océanos.* *(Oceans)* ISBN: 84-87553-27-3.
Ea. vol.: 72p. (Curiosidades de la Ciencia) Madrid: Celeste
Ediciones, 1992. $16.50. Gr. 4-7.

This excellent series, "Strange and Amazing Worlds," originally published in the United Kingdom in 1991, introduces readers
to numerous discoveries and inventions beginning with the world
of printing to space travel and to the surprising life of the oceans.
The superior presentation of this series: spectacular photographs in
color, clear charts and diagrams, well-designed graphics alongside
most interesting texts and note sections makes it hard to resist.
Easy-to-use indexes make this series even more useful.

El espacio. *(Space).* ISBN: 84-01-31483-6.
La tierra. *(Earth).* ISBN: 84-01-31482-8.

52   *Recommended Books in Spanish for Children and Young Adults*

Vida marina (Sea Life) ISBN: 84-01-31481-X.
Ea. vol.: 49p. (Enciclopedia Ilustrada) Barcelona: Plaza y Janés Editores, 1993. $15.95. Gr. 3-6.

Originally published by Dorling Kindersley, London in 1992, these outstanding large-format nature books with double-page spreads of color photographs and drawings and simple explanations are sure to appeal to all readers and viewers. A glossary and an index add to the value of each title. Also in this series, *Animales de la jungla (Jungle Animals)*.

Evans, Mark. *Conejo. (Rabbit)* ISBN: 84-305-7395-X.
————. *Gato. (Kitten)* ISBN: 84-305-7394-1.
————. *Perro. (Puppy)* ISBN: 84-305-7393-3.
Ea. vol.: 45p. (Animales de Compañía) Madrid: Susaeta, 1993. $9.95. Gr. 3-6.

The purpose of this series is to help children appreciate and understand pets—rabbits, kittens, and puppies. Clear photographs in color and easy-to-understand texts explain to children how to care and play with their pets. These are indeed excellent guides, originally published by Dorling Kindersley, London, in 1992, for children (and their parents) to encourage good and conscientious habits towards the care of pets.

Fowler, Allan. *El animal más grande del mundo. (The Biggest Animal Ever)* ISBN: 0-516-36001-9.
————. *¿Cuál es tu flor favorita? (What's Your Favorite Flower?)* ISBN: 0-516-36007-8.
————. *¡Nos gusta la fruta! (We Love Fruit)* ISBN: 0-516-36006-X.
————. *Los planetas del sol. (The Sun's Family of Planets)* ISBN: 0-516-36004-3.
————. *Las tortugas no tienen apuro. (Turtles Take Their Time)* ISBN: 0-516-36005-1.
————. *Y aún podría ser agua. (It Could Still Be Water)* ISBN: 0-516-36003-5.
Ea. vol.: 32p. Translated by Aída E. Marcuse. (Mis Primeros Libros de Ciencia) Chicago: Children's Press, 1993. $9.45. Gr. 1-2.

Through full-color photos and a minimal text, young readers are introduced to basic facts about whales, flowers, fruits, plants, turtles, and water. Despite two errors, this is an easy-to-read Spanish translation that Spanish-speaking scientists-to-be will welcome.

Fowler, Allan. *¿Cómo sabes que es invierno? (How Do You Know It's Winter?)* Translated by Aída E. Marcuse. (Mis Primeros Libros de Ciencia) Chicago: Children's Press, 1994. 32p. ISBN: 0-516-34915-5. $13.93. Gr. K-3.

A brief, simple text and clear, color photographs describe the special characteristics of the winter season. Previous titles in this series are *¿Cómo sabes que es otoño? (How Do You Know It's Autumn?), ¿Cómo sabes que es primavera? (How Do You Know It's Spring?), ¿Cómo sabes que es verano? (How Do You Know It's Summer?)*

Fowler, Allan. *El gusto de las cosas. (Tasting Things)* ISBN: 0-516-34911-2.

————. *Lo que escuchas. (Hearing Things)* ISBN: 0-516-34909-0.

————. *Lo que sientes al tocar. (Feeling Things)* ISBN: 0-516-34908-2.

————. *Lo que ves. (Seeing Things)* ISBN: 0-516-34910-4.

————. *El olor de las cosas. (Smelling Things)* ISBN: 0-516-34912-0.

————. *El sol siempre brilla en alguna parte. (The Sun Is Always Shining Somewhere)* ISBN: 0-516-34906-6.

Ea. vol.: 32p. (Mis Primeros Libros de Ciencia) Photos by Fotos VALAN. Translated by Aída E. Marcuse. Chicago: Children's Press. 1992. $9.45. Gr. 1-2.

Like previous titles in this series, these books include full-color photographs and a simple text that introduces readers to the senses of taste, hearing, touch, sight, and smell as well as the importance of the sun. Despite their small size—6 1/4 by 7 1/4 inches—and generally monotonous tone, these science books for the very young will be welcomed by Spanish speakers.

Ganeri, Anita, and Jane Parker. *Arboles, aves, insectos. (Trees, Birds, Insects)* ISBN: 84-207-6711-5.

Taylor, Barbara. *Luz, sonido, electricidad y magnetismo. (Light, Sound, Electricity, and Magnetism)* ISBN: 84-207-6712-3.

Ea. vol.: 96p. (Aula Abierta) Illus: David Burroughs and others. Translated by Carlos Laguna and others. Madrid: Grupo Anaya, 1995. $16.95. Gr. 5-8.

The purpose of this series is to introduce readers to trees, birds, insects, light, sound, electricity, and magnetism by providing basic scientific facts about each topic and relating each to other fields such as geography, literature, mathematics, the environment, history, music and art. Originally published by Aladdin, London, these attractive, large-format publications include sharp, clear photographs and drawings and brief, easy-to-understand texts as well as well-done glossaries and indexes.

Glover, David. *Las construcciones. (Buildings)* ISBN: 84-348-4443-5.
Wyse, Liz. *El cuerpo humano. (The Human Body)* ISBN: 84-348-4442-7.
Ea. vol.:   48p.   (Experimenta Con)   Photos by Jon Barnes. Translated by Fernando Bort Misol.   Madrid: Ediciones SM, 1994. $19.95. Gr. 3-7.
Like previous titles in this excellent series whose purpose is to make science a fun activity, these titles describe numerous experiments that young readers can do.   Through simple explanations, clear drawings, and photographs (many of children of various ethnic groups), scientists-to-be are encouraged to construct models of aqueducts, towers, bridges, and roofs as well as various systems and parts of the human body.   The brevity of each chapter, appealing design, and easy-to-follow instructions make this series, originally published in 1994 by Two-Can Publishing in London, useful, fun, and informative.

Goodall, Jane. *La familia del chimpancé. (The Chimpanzee Family Book)*   Photos by Michael Neugebauer.   Mexico: Sitesa, 1991. 68p.   ISBN: 0-88708-090-1.   pap. $10.00.   Gr. 5-8.
Originally published in 1989 by the Jane Goodall Institute for Wildlife Research, Education and Conservation, Neugebauer Press, London, this attractive paperback publication introduces readers to a family of wild chimpanzees from Gombe National Park, Tanzania, in East Africa. Candid photographs in color and a fluid narrative describe their habitat and special characteristics.   It ends with the author's plea to protect chimpanzees in other parts of the world.   As a deeply-felt introduction to chimpanzees, this one is hard to beat.

Greenaway, Theresa. *El pantano. (Swamp Life)* Photos by Jane Burton and Kim Taylor. ISBN: 84-207-4925-7.
Gunzi, Christiane. *Una cueva. (Cave Life)* Photos by Frank Greenaway. ISBN: 84-207-4926-5.
Taylor, Barbara. *El bosque. (Woodland)* Photos by: Kim Taylor and Jane Burton. ISBN: 84-207-4927-3.
————. *El litoral. (Shoreline)* Photos by Frank Greenaway. ISBN: 84-207-4928-1.
Ea. vol.: 29p. Translated by Juan Manuel Ibeas. (Mira de Cerca) Madrid: Grupo Anaya, 1993. $17.95. Gr. 4-8.
Like the previous eight titles in this stunning series, originally published by Dorling Kindersley, London, in 1993, these include spectacular, detailed, close-up views of animals and plants in their

natural habitats. The easy-to-understand texts, index, and glossary combined with sharp, full-page color photographs on every page make these introductions to swamp life, cave life, the woodlands, and shorelines an engrossing experience for readers and viewers of any age.

Grindley, Sally. *El libro de los animales.* *(The Animal Book)* Illus: Stuart Trotter. Translated by Esteban Riambau. Barcelona: Editorial Molino, 1993. 47p. ISBN: 84-272-3337-X. $19.95. Gr. 2-5.

Children will learn numerous facts about animals in this attractive, large-format book, originally published in Great Britain in 1992. Full-page illustrations in color and brief texts describe such concepts as farm animals, night animals, strange birds, dangerous animals, how animals care for their young, and other interesting aspects about the animal world in this well-conceived book.

Gunzi, Christiane. *Una charca marina,* *(Rock Pool).* Photos by Frank Greenaway. Translated by Juan Manuel Ibeas. ISBN: 84-207-4857-9.

Taylor, Barbara. *La charca. (Pond Life)* Photos by Frank Greenaway. Translated by Nuria Hernández de Lorenzo. ISBN: 84-207-4751-3.

————. *La pradera.* *(Meadow)* Photos by Kim Taylor and Jane Burton. Translated by Juan Manuel Ibeas. ISBN: 84-207-4856-0.

————. *El río.* *(River Life)* Photos by Frank Greenaway. Translated by Juan Manuel Ibeas. ISBN: 84-207-4855-2.

————. *La selva tropical. (Rainforest)* Photos by Frank Greenaway. Translated by Nuria Hernández de Lorenzo. ISBN: 84-207-4750-5. Ea. vol.: 29p. (Mira de Cerca) Madrid: Grupo Anaya, 1992-1993. $15.95. Gr. 4-8.

Spectacular photographs in color including detailed, close-up views of animals and plants in their natural habitats will surely spark young readers' interest in rock pools, ponds, rivers, rainforests, and meadows. The straightforward text with easy-to-understand explanations as well as indexes and glossaries add to the value of this series for scientists-to-be. Other titles in this series, originally published by Dorling Kindersley, are *El desierto (Desert), El arrecife de coral (Coral Reef).*

Heller, Ruth. *Las gallinas no son las únicas. (Chickens Aren't the Only Ones)* Illus: the author. Translated by Alma Flor Ada. New York: Grosset & Dunlap, 1992. 42p. ISBN: 0-448-40586-5. $10.95. Gr. K-2.

Like the original English version first published in 1981, this festive science lesson for young Spanish-speaking readers with buoyant but realistic full-color drawings explains that not only chickens lay eggs. The well-done Spanish translation is just right for scientists-to-be as well as young audiences eager to read or hear about other animals and their eggs.

Ingpen, Robert, and Margaret Dunkle. *Conservación: Una forma inteligente de explicar a los niños qué es la conservación. (Conservation: An Intelligent Way to Explain Conservation to Children)* Translated by Hilda Becerril. ISBN: 968-847-210-7. Mexico: Editorial Origen, 1991. 38p. $13.95. Gr. 3-5.

In a direct and easy-to-understand manner, the authors explain the purposes and benefits of conservation. Exquisite, full-page color illustrations on every other page add impact to this well-translated book, originally published in 1987 by Hill of Content, Melbourne, Australia.

Jeunesse, Gallimard. *La abeja. (The Bee)* Illus: Ute Fuhr and Raoul Sautai. ISBN: 84-348-4036-7.

————. *El barco. (The Ship)* Illus: Christian Broutin. ISBN: 84-348-3810-9.

————. *La casa. (The House)* Illus: Donald Grant. ISBN: 84-348-3728-5.

————. *El dinosaurio. (The Dinosaur)* Illus: Jame's Prunier and Henri Galeron. ISBN: 84-348-3725-0.

————. *¿Dónde está? (Where Is It?)* Illus: Henri Galeron. ISBN: 84-348-4037-5.

————. *La granja. (The Farm)* Illus: Sylvaine Pérols. ISBN: 84-348-3809-5.

————. *El pájaro. (The Bird)* ISBN: 84-348-3726-9. Illus: René Mettler.

————. *El ratón. (The Mouse)* ISBN: 84-348-3727-7. Illus: Sylvaine Pérols.

————. *El río. (The River)* Illus: Laura Bour. ISBN: 84-348-3811-7.

Ea. vol.: 34p. Translated by Paz Barroso. (Mundo Maravilloso) Madrid: Ediciones SM, 1992-1993. $9.95. Gr. 2-4.

Like previous titles in this attractive series, originally published in France, these include transparent plastic overlays intermingled between glossy pages with color illustrations which show inside/outside and before/after views of houses, ships, farms, bird nests, dinosaurs, and habitats of various rodents. These well-conceived books will certainly appeal to readers as they learn about various types of bees, ships, houses, dinosaurs, farms, birds, rivers, mice, and other rodents. Younger readers may be disappointed because of the small size of the text and some of the illustrations.

Jeunesse, Gallimard, and Pascale de Bourgoing. *El árbol.* *(The Tree)* Illus: Christian Broutin. ISBN: 84-348-4056-1.

————. *La manzana.* *(The Apple)* Illus: Pierre-Marie Valat. ISBN: 84-348-4057-X.

Ea. vol.: 42p. Translated by Paz Barroso. (Mundo Maravilloso) Madrid: Ediciones SM, 1993. $9.95. Gr. 2-4.

Like the previous twenty titles in this well-conceived series, originally published in France in 1989, these introduce young readers to trees, apples, and other fruits. Appealing color illustrations and transparent plastic overlays intermingled between glossy pages provide various views of trees during different seasons as well as inside/outside views of flowers and fruits. The simple texts are easy-to-understand even by the very young.

Jeunesse, Gallimard. *El avión.* *(The Airplane)* Illus: Donald Grant. ISBN: 84-348-3536-3.

————. *Bajo la tierra.* *(Under the Earth)* Illus: Daniéle Bour. ISBN: 84-348-3469-3.

————. *El coche, el camión, la bicicleta, la moto.* *(The Car, the Bus, the Bicycle, the Motorcycle)* Illus: Sophie Kniffke. ISBN: 84-348-3472-3.

————. *La flor.* *(The Flower)* Illus: René Mettler. ISBN: 84-348-3537-1.

————. *El huevo.* *(The Egg)* Illus: René Mettler. ISBN: 84-348-3468-5.

————. *La mariquita.* *(The Ladybird)* Illus: Sylvaine Pérols. ISBN: 84-348-3467-7.

————. *El tiempo.* *(The Weather)* Illus: Sophie Kniffke. ISBN: 84-348-3470-7.

Ea. vol.: 42p. Translated by Paz Barroso. (Mundo Maravilloso) Madrid: Ediciones SM, 1991-1992. $9.95. Gr. 2-4.

These well-written books, originally published in France, introduce young readers to airplanes, life under the Earth, various means of transportation, flowers, eggs, ladybirds, and the weather. Of interest to the scientist-to-be are transparent acetate pages intermingled between glossy pages which provide various views of the same illustration, such as the outside and inside of a car, airplane, flower, egg, etc. Some of the illustrations and text are too small for younger readers, but the appealing format and illustrations and the simple texts make these books truly special. Also in this series:

La casa (The House), El castillo (The Castle), El color (Color), El dinosaurio (The Dinosaur), El oso (The Bear), El pájaro (The Bird), El ratón (The Mouse).

Jeunesse, Gallimard. *El bebé. (The Baby)* Illus: Danièle Bour. ISBN: 84-348-4151-7.

————. *La vista. (Vision)* Illus: Sophie Kniffke. ISBN: 84-348-4318-8.

Jeunesse, Gallimard, and Christian Broutin. *La ciudad. (The City)* Illus: Christian Broutin. ISBN: 84-348-4319-6.

Jeunesse, Gallimard, and others. *Contar. (To Count)* Illus: Donald Grant. ISBN: 84-348-4320-X.

Jeunesse, Gallimard, and Pascale de Bourgoing. *El gato. (The Cat)* Illus: Henri Galeron. ISBN: 84-348-4399-4.

Jeunesse, Gallimard, and Pierre-Marie Valat. *El agua. (Water)* Illus: Pierre-Marie Valat. ISBN: 84-348-4378-1.

Ea. vol.: 34p. Translated from the French by Paz Barroso (Mundo Maravilloso) Madrid: Ediciones SM, 1994. $10.95. Gr. 1-3.

Like previous titles in this innovative series, originally published in France, these contain transparent plastic overlays intermingled between glossy pages and brief, easy-to-understand texts. In a jocose yet straightforward manner, *El bebé* explains the life of a baby from before birth up to the toddler stage. Some adults may disapprove of a few drawings which show a mother nursing her baby and a nude boy without his diaper, yet the realistic, child-like color illustrations describe numerous facts about babies, including baby animals, with tenderness and good taste. Other titles describe the growth of a city; encourage children to count; explain the process of seeing, the special characteristics of cats, and the importance of water.

Johnson, Rebecca L. *La Gran Barrera de Arrecifes: Un laboratorio viviente. (The Great Barrier Reef: A Living Laboratory)* Translated by Isabel Guerra. Minneapolis: Lerner Publications, 1994. 96p. ISBN: 0-8225-2008-7. $22.95. Gr. 5-8.

The animal and plant life of Australia's Great Barrier Reef are described through charts, drawings, and color photographs, and a simple text. A useful glossary and index complement this well-done translation, originally published by Lerner Publications in 1991.

Johnson, Sylvia A., and Alice Aamodt. *La manada de lobos: Siguiendo las huellas de los lobos en su entorno natural. (Wolf Pack: Tracking Wolves in the Wild).* Translated by Isabel Guerra.

Minneapolis: Lerner Publications, 1994. 94p. ISBN: 0-8225-2007-9. $22.95. Gr. 4-8.

The social interaction of wolves in a pack as they share the work of hunting, maintaining their territory, and raising their young are described in a fluid Spanish narrative. Numerous color photographs of wolves in their natural habitat add interest to this well-done book, originally published by Lerner Publications in 1985.

Jones, Brian. *La exploración del espacio.* *(Space Exploration)* ISBN: 84-372-4512-5.

Parker, Steve. *Historia de la medicina.* *(History of Medicine)* ISBN: 84-372-4522-2.

Pollock, Steve. *La vida animal.* *(Animal Life)* ISBN: 84-372-4513-3.

Rowland-Entwistle, Theodore. *El tiempo y el clima.* *(Weather and Climate)* ISBN: 84-372-4521-4.

——. *La vida prehistórica.* *(Prehistoric Life)* ISBN: 84-372-4511-7.

Seidenberg, Steven. *Ecología y conservación de la naturaleza.* *(Ecology and Conservation)* ISBN: 84-372-4514-1.

——. *Fuentes de energía.* *(Fuel and Energy)* ISBN: 84-372-4520-6.

Underwood, Lynn. *Religiones del mundo.* *(Religions of the World)* ISBN: 84-372-4519-2.

Ea. vol.: 64p. Biblioteca Básica Altea. Madrid: Altea, Taurus, Alfaguara, 1991. $19.95. Gr. 5-9.

Readers are introduced to the world of science through clearly written texts, numerous excellent photographs, maps, drawings, and charts on every page as well as interesting "facts and figures" sections that provide additional relevant information on each subject discussed. Scientists-to-be will especially appreciate the brief chapters (approximately two pages), easy-to-understand explanations, and attractive design of these titles, originally published by Gareth Stevens in 1990. Useful glossaries and indexes add further to these valuable introductions to space, medicine, animals, weather, prehistoric life, ecology, energy, and religions.

Julivert, Maria Angels. *Las abejas.* *(Bees)* Illus: Carlos de Miguel. ISBN: 84-342-1187-4.

——. *Las arañas.* *(Spiders)* Illus: Estudio Marcel Socías. ISBN: 84-342-1347-8.

——. *Los castores y los topos.* *(Beavers and Moles)* Illus: Marcel Socías. ISBN: 84-342-1349-4.

——. *Las hormigas.* *(Ants)* Illus: Marcel Socías. ISBN: 84-342-1188-2.

————. *Las mariposas.* *(Butterflies)* Illus: Francisco Arredondo. ISBN: 84-342-1189-0.
Ea. vol.: 30p. (El fascinante Mundo de) Barcelona: Parramón Ediciones, 1991-1992. $7.40. Gr. 4-7.

The fascinating worlds of bees, spiders, beavers, moles, ants, and butterflies come to life in these appealing books. Full-page drawings in color and well-written narratives explain basic facts about the life cycles of these animals. Each title includes a glossary of useful terms. Also in this series: *Las aves (Birds)*.

Julivert, María Angels. *La vida de las plantas.* *(The Life of Plants)* Illus: Marcel Socías. ISBN: 84-342-1465-2.
Parramón, Mercè. *La maravilla de la vida.* *(The Wonder of Life)* Illus: Francisco Arredondo. ISBN: 84-342-1466-0.
Ea. vol.: 31p. (Mundo Invisible) Barcelona: Parramón Ediciones, 1993. $9.95. Gr. 5-9.

The purpose of this series is to explain to young readers the functions of the most important natural processes through clear and attractive drawings and diagrams in full color and easy-to-understand texts. *La vida de las plantas* describes how plants grow and the process of photosynthesis. *La maravilla de la vida* is a lucid explanation of the reproductive system. In addition, the well-done glossaries will be appreciated by scientists-to-be. Also in this series: *Como circula nuestra sangre (How Our Blood Circulates)*.

Kelly, John, and Philip Whitfield. *Robot Zoo.* *(The Robot Zoo)* Translated by Franca Jordá and Begoña Arrizabalaga. Madrid: Santillana, 1995. 49p. ISBN: 84-372-2190-0. $25.95. Gr. 5-8.

Sixteen mechanical animals are depicted following the natural body shapes of their real counterparts. Such animals as a spider, a bat, a giraffe, a whale, a fly, a turtle, and others are shown in double-page color spreads alongside color inset diagrams of the real animal. This is indeed a novel approach to the body structure of these animals and how they move, breathe, and eat.

Leggett, Jeremy. *El aire contaminado.* *(Air Pollution)* ISBN: 950-11-0975-5.
————. *Bosques en extinción.* *(Deforestation)* ISBN: 950-11-0977-1.
————. *El derroche de la energía.* *(Wasting Energy)* ISBN: 950-11-0980-1.
————. *Invasión de la basura.* *(The Invasion of Waste)* ISBN: 950-11-0979-8.

Leggett, Dennis, and Jeremy Leggett. *El agua en peligro.* *(Water in Danger).* ISBN: 950-11-0976-3.

――――. *La trampa de la humanidad.* *(Humanity's Trap)* ISBN: 950-11-0978-X.

Ea. vol.: 46p. (Operación Tierra) Illus: Rod Ferring. Translated by Edith Tálamo. Buenos Aires: Editorial Sigmar, 1994. pap. $9.95. Gr. 6-10.

The most important ecological issues of our time—deforestation, air and water pollution, misuse of energy, domestic and industrial waste, and overpopulation—are discussed in this informative and well-written paperback series with excellent color photographs, charts, drawings and maps on every page. Originally published in 1994 by Templar Publishing, Surrey, England, this series is one of the best and most up-to-date worldwide overviews about ecological issues confronting our planet in the Spanish language for young readers. Well-done glossaries and indexes add to the usefulness of this series.

Lindsay, William. *Barosaurio.* *(Barosaurus)* ISBN: 84-226-4358-8.

――――. *Tiranosaurio.* *(Tyrannosaurus)* ISBN: 84-226-4430-5.

Ea. vol.: 29p. (Todo Sobre Los Dinosaurios) Translated by Manuel Pijoan i Rotgé. Barcelona: Plaza Joven, 1992. $11.95. Gr. 5-9.

Dinosaur enthusiasts will truly enjoy these large-format publications, originally published by Dorling Kindersley in London, that describe the life of two of the largest dinosaurs that inhabited the Earth. Excellent photographs, drawings and charts in color, and brief, straightforward texts will capture the interests of all readers and viewers in this timely topic.

Mis primeros conocimientos. *(My First Knowledge)* 10 vols. Danbury, CT: Grolier International, 1989. ISBN: 968-33-0527-X. $149.00. Gr. 4-7.

Originally published in English by Franklin Watts, this series is a collection of high-interest topics that should appeal to students in the middle grades. This excellent Spanish translation (done by Editorial Cumbre in Mexico City) is easy-to-read and easy-to-understand. In addition, numerous full-color illustrations add interest to each topic. Subjects include pets, transportation, aquatic animals, astronomy, computers, selected sports, volcanoes, earthquakes, dinosaurs, and serpents. As an overview to these topics, this series is definitely worthwhile. This is not, however, a science and nature encyclopedia as stated in the publisher's catalogue.

Mota, Ignacio H. de la. *El libro del chocolate. (The Book of Chocolate)* Madrid: Ediciones Pirámide, 1992. 429p. ISBN: 84-368-0647-6. Gr. 9-adult.

The origin, legends, history, anecdotes, and other aspects of chocolate from pre-Columbian to modern times are included in this comprehensive, well-organized book. Chocolate lovers will appreciate such chapters as chocolate plantations, chocolate in literature, and the social role of chocolate as well as over 200 chocolate recipes. This is indeed a thorough overview of this delicious product.

Murphy, Bryan. *Experimentos con agua. (Experiment with Water)* ISBN: 970-10-0298-9.
————. *Experimentos con aire. (Experiment with Air)* ISBN: 970-10-0312-8.
————. *Experimentos con luz. (Experiment with Light)* ISBN: 970-10-0313-6.
————. *Experimentos con movimiento. (Experiment with Movement)* ISBN: 970-10-0311-X.
Ea. vol.: 32p. (Un Libro de Ciencia Jump!) Translated by Guadalupe Meza and Pedro Avalos. Mexico: McGraw-Hill, 1993. pap. $7.95. Gr. 3-6.

Children are introduced to basic concepts about our physical world through simple experiments and procedures. The only disappointing feature about these attractive publications are the paperback covers; otherwise, they are exactly what children need to be interested in water, air, light, and movement—excellent photographs in color, simple texts, and clear illustrations.

Murray, Peter. *El planeta tierra. (Planet Earth)* (Un Libro Visión) Chicago: Encyclopaedia Britannica Educational, 1993.   30p. ISBN: 1-56766-026-6. $15.95. Gr. 5-8.

The Earth's physical characteristics, including interactions of climate, geology, and ecology are described in a well-written text. This book also includes excellent, full-page color photographs. The problem is the concept of this *"Libro Visión"*: To allow for multilingual publishing on demand, the photographs and text are completely separated from each other—hence there are no labels or captions on any of the photographs, nor any photographs within the written narrative. Perhaps this is a cost-effective format for multilingual publishing but readers and viewers will find it difficult to relate the written information to the appropriate photograph.

Mutel, Cornelia F., and Mary M. Rodgers. *Las selvas tropicales.*
(*Tropical Rain Forests*) ISBN: 0-8225-2005-2.
Winckler, Suzanne, and Mary M. Rodgers. *La Antártida.* (*Antarctica*)
ISBN: 0-8225-2006-0.
Ea. vol.: 64p. (Nuestro Planeta en Peligro) Translated by Isabel
Guerra. Minneapolis: Lerner Publications, 1994. $21.50. Gr. 4-8.
Outstanding maps, charts, drawings and photographs in color,
and a direct text in Spanish introduce readers to the ecology of
tropical rain forests and to the world's coldest continent. Both
titles discuss their role in the global environmental balance and how
easily human activities can endanger or upset these areas of the
world. Originally published by Lerner Publications in 1991-1992,
these well-translated and attractive publications are sure to sensitize
Spanish speakers to the importance of caring for our endangered
planet.

Norton, Peter. *Introducción a la computación.* (*Introduction to
Computers*) Translated by Leslie Charles, Dawe Barnett, and
others. Mexico: McGraw-Hill, 1995. 567p. ISBN: 970-10-0667-
4. pap. $13.95. Gr. 9-adult.
This up-to-date introduction to computers is just what Spanish-
speaking computer fans need to understand the role of computers in
their lives. Through numerous photographs as well as drawings
and charts on almost every page of the original English version,
readers are exposed to a basic yet comprehensive overview of the
ubiquitous machine. A well-done glossary and index as well as
optional activities contribute further to the value of this paperback
publication to potential computer users.

Olaya, Clara Inés. *Frutas tropicales,* (*Tropical Fruits*) Illus:
Marcela Cabrera. Caracas: Banco del Libro, 1991. 77p. ISBN:
980-257-072-9. pap. $9.95. Gr. 6-10.
The history, characteristics, and special uses of thirty-one tropical fruits, most of them indigenous to Latin America, are presented
in this unassuming paperback publication. Each fruit is described
through approximately half a page of text and rather dull black-and-
white (and a few color) drawings. Despite the lackluster illustrations, this is an informative guide to tropical plants, flowers, and
fruits, emphasizing the contributions of pre-Columbian civilizations.

Panafieu, Jean-Baptiste de. *Exploremos la naturaleza.* (*Exploring
Nature*). Illus: Francois Crozat and others. Madrid: Rialp Junior,
1992. 159p. ISBN: 84-321-2882-1. $22.00. Gr. 4-8.

Scientists-to-be will find this guide most useful and informative as they learn to observe and discover nature. Through brief narratives, clear charts, and simple illustrations, readers are exposed to numerous experiments and activities that they can easily do at the seashore, in the mountains, and in the countryside such as gathering, conserving, or collecting leaves, algae, feathers, and minerals. In addition, it offers simple suggestions for fishing, camping, and others. The only weakness of this otherwise outstanding guide to exploring nature are some of the awkward illustrations of young explorers which are more condescending than cute.

Parker, Steve. *Aristoteles y el pensamiento científico. (Aristotle and Scientific Thought)* (Pioneros de la ciencia) Madrid: Celeste Ediciones, 1994. 32p. ISBN: 84-87553-63-X. $11.95. Gr. 4-7.

Like previous titles in this outstanding series, "Science Pioneers," originally published by Belitha Press, London, this includes an easy-to-read narrative and attractive drawings, photographs, and charts on every page introducing young readers to Aristotle and scientific thought. A time chart, a glossary, and an index add further to the value of this engrossing series.

Parker, Steve. *Charles Darwin y la evolución. (Charles Darwin and Evolution)* ISBN: 84-87553-14-1.

———. *Galileo y el universo. (Galileo and the Universe)* ISBN: 84-87553-15-X.

———. *Isaac Newton y la gravedad. (Isaac Newton and Gravity)* ISBN: 84-87553-37-0.

———. *Louis Pasteur y los gérmenes. (Louis Pasteur and Germs)* ISBN: 84-87553-36-2.

———. *Marie Curie y el radio. (Marie Curie and Radium)* ISBN: 84-87553-23-0.

———. *Thomas Edison y la electricidad. (Thomas Edison and Electricity)* ISBN: 84-87553-22-2.

Ea. vol.: 32p. (Pioneros de la Ciencia) Madrid: Celeste Ediciones, 1992-1993. $9.50. Gr. 4-7.

This excellent series, Science Pioneers, introduces readers to great scientists and their discoveries. It narrates the scientists' lives and how their discoveries were accomplished, as well as the social and scientific climate of their times. The easy-to-read narratives are beautifully complemented by most attractive drawings, photographs, and charts on every page that definitely make these pioneers and their accomplishments understandable to all readers. Well-done glossaries and indexes add further to the value of these books, originally published by Belitha Press.

Parker, Steve. *Cuerpo humano.* *(Human Body)* (Ciencia Visual) Translated by Dr. Rafael Lozano Guillén. Madrid: Santillana, 1994. 64p. ISBN: 84-372-4547-8. $23.95. Gr. 6-12.

This exquisite, large-format guide to the human body illustrates the ideas, processes, and discoveries that have changed our conception of the human body. Magnificent, detailed, color photographs of anatomic models and microscopic images and a brief, easy-to-understand text explain all major systems, from skeleton to skin and nerves to lungs. Like other titles in this excellent series, originally published by Dorling Kindersley, London, this volume is hard to resist. A well-done index adds to the value of this guide.

Parker, Steve. *Dime cómo funciona.* *(How Things Work)* Madrid: Ediciones Larousse, 1991. Distributed by The Millbrook Press, 1992. 157p. ISBN: 1-56294-179-8. $19.90. Gr. 6-10.

Originally published by Grisewood & Dempsey, Great Britain in 1990, this excellent translation explains in a clear and concise manner how many things work including things found at home, in the human body, animal life, various industries, and forms of recreation. The easy-to-understand explanations, clear diagrams, and well-conceived chapters certainly facilitate the understanding of simple mechanisms. A glossary and subject index add to the value of this book.

Parry, Linda. *Tú eres maravilloso.* *(You Are Wonderful)* Illus: Alan Parry. Barcelona: Editorial Molino, 1993. 13p. ISBN: 84-272-5630-2. $22.50. Gr. 2-4.

This is certainly a fun way to learn about the human body. Through colorful pop-ups and open-the-flaps, children will see that each person is different, the muscular and skeletal systems, the basic organs, the five senses, and how personalities differ. This attractive book was originally published in English by Hunt & Thorpe in 1992.

Platt, Richard. *El asombroso libro del interior de las cosas.* *(The Incredible Cross Section Book)* Illus: Stephen Biesty. Madrid: Santillana, S.A., 1992. 48p. ISBN: 84-372-4524-9. $23.95. Gr. 5-9.

Excellent, detailed cross-section drawings are in color and the brief texts describe the functions and operations of a medieval castle, an observatory, a submarine, an airplane, the Empire State Building, a car factory, a coal mine, and other architectural and technological wonders. This attractive, large-format publication is certain to appeal to any reader and viewer who has the slightest interest in the inner workings and or design of machines, buildings, factories, and mines.

Rovira Sumalia, Albert. *¿Te atreves? Electroimanes en acción. (Do You Dare? Electromagnets in Action)* ISBN: 84-342-1721-X.
————. *¿Te atreves? Imanes y corriente eléctrica. (Do You Dare? Magnets and Electricity)* ISBN: 84-342-1837-2.
Ea. vol.: 48p. (Serie Electricidad) Barcelona: Parramón Ediciones, 1994. $21.95. Gr. 5-8.

The purpose of this series is to demonstrate how technological advances are part of our daily lives. Excellent color photographs, charts and drawings, and brief texts describe simple experiments and devices that children can make. *¿Te atreves? Electroimanes en acción* demonstrates how to make a buzzer, a doorbell, an alarm mechanism, and a telegraph apparatus. *¿Te atreves? Imanes y corriente eléctrica* demonstrates how to make a compass, an experimental circuit, two electromagnets, a voltmeter, and an electric motor. Each title includes a well-done glossary.

Royston, Angela. *Gatito. (Kitten).* Photos by Jane Burton. ISBN: 84-406-3748-9.
————. *Pato. (Duck)* Photos by Barrie Watts. ISBN: 84-406-3750-0.
————. *Perrito. (Puppy)* Photos by Jane Burton. ISBN: 84-406-3747-0.
————. *Rana. (Frog)* Photos by Kim Taylor and Jane Burton. ISBN: 84-406-3749-7.
Ea. vol.: 21p. Translated by Mireia Blasco. (Mira Cómo Crecen) Barcelona: Ediciones B, 1993. $10.75. Gr. 1-3.

Through clear photographs in color and a simple, concise text, children are exposed to various stages in the growth and development of kittens, ducks, puppies, and frogs. The most appealing design, covers and photographs of this series, originally published by Dorling Kindersley, London, in 1991, should make it a real winner with children, animal lovers, and others. (It should be noted that this series also was published by Sitesa in Mexico City in 1992.)

Royston, Angela. *Gatitos. (Kittens)* Photos by Jane Burton. ISBN: 968-6579-46-X.
————. *Patitos. (Ducks)* Photos by Barrie Watts. ISBN: 968-6579-44-3.

————. *Perritos. (Puppies)* Photos by Jane Burton. ISBN: 968-6579-43-5.

————. *Ranitas. (Frogs)* Photos by Kim Taylor and Jane Burton. ISBN: 968-6579-45-1.

Ea. vol.: 21p. (Mira Cómo Crecen) Mexico: Sitesa, 1992. $9.95. Gr. 1-3.

Through clear photographs in color and a simple, concise text, children are exposed to various stages in the growth and development of kittens, ducks, puppies, and frogs. The most appealing design and covers of this series, originally published by Dorling Kindersley in Great Britain in 1991, should make it a real winner with children, animal lovers, and others. (This series is also available from Ediciones B.)

Schubert, Ingrid, and Dieter. *Sobre moscas y elefantes. (About Flies and Elephants)* Translated by Esther Tusquets. Barcelona: Editorial Lumen, 1994. 32p. ISBN: 84-264-3687-0. $13.95. Gr. 1-3.

The animal kingdom is introduced to young readers and viewers through spectacular double-page watercolor spreads and a brief, easy-to-understand text that illustrates the lifestyles, protective mechanisms, habitats, eating habits, and other characteristics of wild animals. All children definitely will want to spend time looking at the informative, detailed, eye-catching illustrations. Originally published by Lemniscaat, Rotterdam, this is indeed one of the best introductory large-format books about the world of animals for the young.

Selsam, Millicent E. *Como crecen los gatitos. (How Kittens Grow)* Photos by Neil Johnson. Translated by Teresa Mlawer. New York: Scholastic, Inc., 1992. 30p. ISBN: 0-590-45000-X. pap. $2.95. Gr. Preschool-3.

Selsam's informative text about newly born kittens and their development to eight weeks is now available in Spanish in this excellent translation. Spanish-speaking children will enjoy looking at the color photographs of kittens in familiar situations and reading or listening to the accessible text.

Sharman, Lydia. *Mi primer libro de formas. (My First Book of Shapes)* Photos by Steve Gorton. Barcelona: Editorial Molino, 1995. 37p. ISBN: 84-272-3270-5. $23.55. Gr. 2-5.

Like its predecessors, this attractive, large-format volume, originally published by Dorling Kindersley, London, includes sharp, color photographs and simple, easy-to-follow directions that assist children in understanding geometrical concepts through a wide variety of shapes and designs—from traditional cubes to computer-designed images.

Stone, Lynn M. *Caballos. (Horses)* ISBN: 0-86592-987-4.
―――. *Cerdos. (Pigs)* ISBN: 0-86592-989-0.
―――. *Ovejas. (Sheep)* ISBN: 0-86592-915-7.
―――. *Patos. (Ducks)* ISBN: 0-86592-953-X.
―――. *Pollos. (Chickens)* ISBN: 0-86592-949-1.
―――. *Vacas. (Cows)* ISBN: 0-86592-952-1.
Ea. vol.: 24p. (Animales de Granja) Translated by Aída E. Marcuse. Vero Beach, FL: Rourke Enterprises, 1991. $8.95. Gr. 2-4.

Young readers are introduced to farm animals in this easy-to-read series with clear photographs in color. Each title describes the special characteristics, customs, natural environment, and reason each animal is important to people.

Taylor, Kim. *Demasiado inteligente para verlo. (Too Intelligent to Be Seen)* ISBN: 84-263-2047-3.
―――. *Demasiado lento para verlo. (Too Slow to Be Seen)* ISBN: 84-263-2046-5.
―――. *Demasiado rápido para verlo. (Too Fast to Be Seen)* ISBN: 84-263-2048-1.
―――. *Oculto bajo el agua. (Hidden Underwater)* ISBN: 84-263-2044-9.
―――. *Oculto bajo la tierra. (Hidden Underground)* ISBN: 84-263-2043-0.
―――. *Oculto en el interior. (Hidden Inside)* ISBN: 84-263-2041-4.
―――. *Oculto en la oscuridad. (Hidden in Darkness)* ISBN: 84-263-2042-2.
Ea. vol.: 24p. (Mundos Secretos) Translated by Miguel A. Lafuente Rosales. Zaragoza: Editorial Luis Vives, 1991. $6.30. Gr. 4-7.

The secret world of nature is explained to young readers through excellent, detailed photographs in color and informative texts. Originally published in Great Britain in 1989, this appealing series discusses special characteristics of nature that are not easily observed such as how some plants eat insects, how spiders carry their infants, how butterflies see at night, and other wonders. Subject indexes complement each title.

Tison, Cindra. *Datos, relatos y divertimientos informáticos.* *(The Ultimate Collection of Computer Facts and Fun)* Translated by Andrew Cabré. Barcelona: Página Uno, 1993. 90p. ISBN: 84-88004-11-7. pap. $10.95. Gr. 4-7.

Diagrams, puzzles, labyrinths, cartoons, simple explanations, and fun activities expose young readers to basic facts about computers including their history and development, software languages, and special capabilities. This is not one more basic guide to computers but rather an appealing and well-thought-out collection of fun activities that adds to the understanding and enjoyment of computer enthusiasts. The appealing layout and design of this paperback, originally published by Macmillan Computer Publishing in 1991, is sure to please Spanish speakers.

Ventura, Piero. *Los alimentos: La evolución de la alimentación a través del tiempo.* *(Food: The Evolution of Food through Time)* ISBN: 84-241-5903-9.

————. *La comunicación: Medios y técnicas para intercambiar información a través del tiempo.* *(Communication: Means and Techniques to Exchange Information through Time)* ISBN: 84-241-5902-0.

Ea. vol.: 64p. (Historia Ilustrada de la Humanidad) Madrid: Editorial Everest, 1994. $14.50. Gr. 5-8.

In a readable and accessible manner, readers are introduced to the history of humankind's advances in and search for food and communication. Excellent, detailed pen and watercolor drawings further entice young readers and viewers to the study of food and communication from prehistoric times up to genetic biology and satellite communication. Other titles in this series are: *Las casas (Houses), La tecnología (Technology), Los transportes (Transportation), and Los vestidos (Clothing).*

Walker, Jane. *El agujero de la capa de ozono.* *(The Hole in the Ozone Layer)* ISBN: 84-7894-183-5.

————. *Atmósfera en peligro.* *(The Atmosphere in Danger)* ISBN: 84-7894-182-7.

————. *Desaparición de hábitats y especies.* *(The Loss of Habitats and Species)* ISBN: 84-7894-185-1.

————. *Marea negra.* *(Oil Spills)* ISBN: 84-7894-184-3.

Ea. vol.: 32p. (Desastres Provocados por el Hombre) Madrid: Aglo Ediciones, 1995. $15.95. Gr. 6-9.

Through excellent color photographs, drawings, maps and charts, and brief, easy-to-understand texts, readers are introduced to four man-made disasters: the hole in the ozone layer, air pollution, the loss of habitats and species, and oil spills. Each title explains how the effects of human actions around the world affect the environment and includes a glossary, an index, and a section on facts and figures. Originally published by Aladdin Books, London, this well-designed, approachable series is sure to sensitize readers to the benefits of protecting the environment.

Health and Medicine

Ball, Jacqueline A. *La higiene.* *(Hygiene)* ISBN: 0-86625-293-2.
Klare, Judy. *La autoestima.* *(Self-Esteem)* ISBN: 0-86625-292-4.
Rourke, Arlene C. *Los dientes y los frenos.* *(Teeth and Braces)* ISBN: 0-86625-291-6.
————. *La dieta y el ejercicio.* *(Diet and Exercise)* ISBN: 0-86625-295-9.
————. *Las manos y los pies.* *(Hands and Feet)* ISBN: 0-86625-290-8.
————. *La piel.* *(Skin)* ISBN: 0-86625-294-0.
Ea. vol.: 30p. (Buena Presencia) Vero Beach, FL: Rourke Publications, 1992. Gr. 5-9.

Written especially for adolescent girls, these straightforward guides instruct teenagers about proper hygiene, achieving self-esteem, the function and care of teeth and braces, diet and exercise, hands and teeth, skin care, and makeup. The approachable tone of these common-sense guides combined with the high-interest topics discussed will certainly appeal to teenage girls.

Blake, Jeanne. *Tiempos de riesgo: Entérate del SIDA para mantenerte saludable. (Risky Times: How to Be AIDS-Smart and Stay Healthy)* Translated by Aída E. Marcuse. New York: Workman Publishing, 1993. 158p. ISBN: 1-56305-436-1. pap. $5.95. Gr. 7-12.

In an approachable and straightforward manner, the author discusses the problem of AIDS and explains important issues surrounding this disease such as sexual relationships, the use of condoms, drug abuse, and ways of dealing with people infected with the AIDS virus. Adolescents will certainly appreciate the informative and nonjudgmental tone of this paperback. In addition, numerous black-and-white photographs of adolescents relating their personal experiences make this guide even more accessible.

Koplow, Lesley. *Tanya and the Tobo Man: A Story for Children Entering Therapy/Tanya y el hombre Tobo: Una historia para niños que empiezan terapia.* Illus: Eric Velasquez. Spanish

Translation: Alexander Contos. New York: Magination Press, 1991. 32p. ISBN: 0-945354-34-7. $16.95; ISBN: 0-945354-33-9. pap. $6.95. Gr. 2-4.

The purpose of this bilingual (English-Spanish) story is to help children and their parents to feel more familiar with the therapeutic process. Through Tanya's continuing fear of the Tobo Man, readers are exposed to her mother's apprehensions, her visits to a therapist, and the happy results. The black-and-white drawings of a black mother and her daughter are realistic and appropriate. The Spanish translation is adequate though marred by four typographical mistakes.

McManners, Hugh. *Manual completo de supervivencia. (The Commando Survival Manual)* Translated by Maite Rodríguez Fischer. Barcelona: Blume, 1994. 192p. ISBN: 84-8076-098-2. $38.95. Gr. 9-adult.

The purpose of this large-format publication is to guide users to master survival techniques which may be needed in any situation. Originally published by Dorling Kindersley, London, it includes numerous excellent photographs, drawings, and charts and easy-to-understand explanations on such topics as survivors, basic equipment, living with nature, searching for water and food, and getting there. This practical guide is further complemented by well-done appendices, a glossary, an index, and a survival checklist. This is indeed one of the best survival manuals in the Spanish language.

Ryan, Elizabeth A. *Hablemos francamente de las drogas y el alcohol. (Straight Talk about Drugs and Alcohol)* New York: Facts on File, 1990. 152p. ISBN: 0-8160-2496-0. $16.95. Gr. 7-12.

In a candid and easy-to-understand manner, the author discusses the physical and social effects of drug and alcohol abuse, how to recognize an addiction, and how to get help for a dependency problem. Adolescents will especially appreciate the author's efforts to avoid lecturing on the evils of these substances and yet presenting the facts so that youngsters can reflect and make their own decisions. This is indeed an excellent translation of a most useful book.

Cookery

Bosch, Magda. *Bebidas y helados. (Drinks and Ice Creams)* (¿Cómo se Hacen?) Illus: Bartolomé Seguí. Barcelona: Parramón, 1995. 32p. ISBN: 84-342-1724-4. $16.95. Gr. 5-9.

Thirteen simple, appetizing recipes for hot and cold drinks and ice creams that are fun to make and beautiful to serve are included in this easy-to-use publication with attractive color photographs and drawings. It includes such popular Hispanic favorites as stuffed pineapples, frozen avocado dessert, "*Sangría Paramí,*" and others.

Bosch, Magda. *¿Cómo se hacen? Postres (How Do You Make Them? Desserts)* Illus: Bartolomé Seguí and Sonia Delgado. Barcelona: Parramón, 1994. 32p. ISBN: 84-342-1852-6. $19.50. Gr. 5-8.

Dessert lovers will find these thirteen recipes truly irresistible. The full-page color photographs and drawings of delicious and most appealing cakes, mousse, gelatins, and other special desserts will encourage viewers to test their culinary skills. Perhaps some of the recipes require more expertise than what young people of their age generally have, but with knowledgeable adult supervision these are sure winners.

The Arts

El arte de construir. (The Art of Building) ISBN: 84-348-4505-9.
Historia de los imágenes. (History of Images) ISBN: 84-348-4716-7.
La invención de la pintura. (The Invention of Painting) ISBN: 84-348-4110-X.
¿Qué ven los pintores? (What Do Painters See?) ISBN: 84-348-4706-X.
El trabajo de los escultores. (The Work of Sculptors) ISBN: 84-348-4210-6.

Ea. vol.: 48p. Translated from the French by Fernando Bort. (Biblioteca Interactiva/Mundo Maravilloso/Artes plásticas) Madrid: Ediciones SM, 1994-1995. $12.95. Gr. 4-8.

Originally published by Gallimard Jeunesse, France, in 1993-1994, these "interactive" titles include numerous fold-outs, flaps, and transparent plastic overlays intermingled between detailed, glossy color illustrations and simple, easy-to-understand explanations. Topics include building and architecture from an Egyptian tomb up to modern skyscrapers, prehistoric pictures up to computer art, art and painting, and the work of sculptors. These well-constructed, attractive publications are sturdy enough to withstand eager hands as they admire and manipulate representations of noteworthy artistic creations. Each title includes a glossary and an index.

Delafosse, Claude, and Gallimard Jeunesse. *Bestiario.* *(Bestiary)*
ISBN: 84-348-4449-4.
_____. *Cuadros.* *(Paintings)* ISBN: 84-348-4451-6.
_____. *Paisajes.* *(Landscapes)* ISBN: 84-348-4450-8.
_____. *Retratos.* *(Portraits)* ISBN: 84-348-4448-6.
Ea. vol.: 34p. Illus: Tony Ross. Translated by Paz Barroso.
(Mundo Maravilloso/Arte) Madrid: Ediciones SM, 1994. $9.95.
Gr. 2-4.

Like comparable titles in the Mundo Maravilloso series,
originally published in France, this series introduces the young to
the great works of art of all times through brief, simple texts and
humorous watercolor illustrations on glossy pages intermingled
between transparent plastic overlays that depict before/after views of
prehistoric cave murals, Alexander Calder's abstract mobiles,
Michelangelo's Sistine Chapel, Monet's and Matisse's landscapes,
Leonardo da Vinci's *La Gioconda,* and other well-known paintings.
In contrast to other stodgy introductions to artists and their works,
this series allows children to whimsically participate in great artistic
creations.

Ditzinger, Thomas, and Asmin Kuhn. *Visión Mágica: Imágenes
ocultas en una nueva dimensión.* *(Magic Images: Hidden Images
in a New Dimension)* Translated by María Rabassa. Barcelona:
Ediciones B, 1994. 40p. ISBN: 84-406-5055-8. $25.95. Gr. 8-
adult.

Excellent color, full-page computer graphic reproductions and the
magic of optical illusions in third dimension should provide joyful
relaxation to followers of this new art form. First published by
Südwest Verlag, Munich, Germany, this edition has maintained the
exquisite quality of the original.

Érase una vez el cine. *(There Was Once a Motion Picture)* ISBN: 84-
348-4504-0.
La música y los instrumentos. *(Music and the Instruments)* ISBN:
84-348-4111-8.
Los teatros del mundo. *(The Theaters of the World)* ISBN: 84-348-
4211-4.
Ea. vol.: 48p. Translated from the French by Fernando Bort.
(Biblioteca Interactiva/Mundo Maravilloso/Música, Artes Escénicas
y Espectáculos) Madrid: Ediciones SM, 1995. $12.95. Gr. 4-8.

These "interactive" titles, originally published by Gallimard
Jeunesse, France, in 1993-1994, include numerous fold-outs, flaps,
and transparent plastic overlays intermingled between detailed,
glossy color illustrations and simple, easy-to-understand explanations. Young readers/viewers are introduced to the history and art

of motion pictures, music and musical instruments, and the theaters of the world. These attractive publications are constructed so that eager hands can view and manipulate representations of these creations. Each title includes a glossary and an index.

Fletcher, Valerie. *Crosscurrents of Modernism: Four Latin American Pioneers.* Washington: Smithsonian Institution Press, 1992. 296p. ISBN: 1-56098-206-3. $24.95. Gr. 10-adult.

Written to accompany an exhibition organized by the Hirshhorn Museum and Sculpture Garden in 1992, this bilingual (English/ Spanish) study provides an in-depth look at the efforts of four Latin American artists—Diego Rivera (Mexico), Joaquín Torres García (Uruguay), Wifredo Lam (Cuba), and Matta (Chile)—to develop pluralist modernist expressions. The excellent quality of the 128 illustrations and the erudite essays (one by Octavio Paz), which present a short account of the life and career of each artist, make this an invaluable study of the sophistication, complexity, and diversity of four Latin American pioneering artists. Serious students of modern art will enjoy.

Hayes, Ann. *Te presento a la orquesta.* *(Meet the Orchestra)* Illus: Karmen Thompson. Translated by Alma Flor Ada. San Diego: Harcourt Brace, 1995. 32p. ISBN: 0-15-200275-8. pap. $5.00. Gr. 3-5.

Like the original 1991 English version, spacious watercolors depicting animal musicians in formal evening dress enhance this charming introduction to the orchestra. The succinct one-page treatments organized by musical families and the subtle sense of color and humor should prove useful to Spanish-speaking students choosing a musical instrument.

Micklethwait, Lucy. *Mi primer libro de arte: Famosas pinturas, primeras palabras.* *(My First Book of Art: Famous Paintings, First Words)* Barcelona: Editorial Molino, 1993. 64p. ISBN: 84-272-1922-9. $21.23. Gr. K-6.

Spanish-speaking readers and viewers of all ages will enjoy this beautiful introduction to the world of art. Through simple concepts that even the very young can understand, such as the family, home, colors, fruits, farm animals, pets, and others, this large-format volume certainly achieves its purpose. This book is illustrated with outstanding color reproductions of some of the world's most admired masterpieces. Originally published in 1993 by Dorling Kindersley in London, viewers will appreciate a wonderful diversity of styles, themes, artists, and eras.

Sirett, Dawn. *Mi primer libro de pintar.* *(My First Book of Painting)*
Translated by María Millán. Barcelona: Editorial Molino, 1994.
48p. ISBN: 84-272-1711-0. $24.95. Gr. 3-6.

Using easy-to-obtain materials, children can learn how to make
and frame paintings, paint paper bags and T-shirts, apply stencils
on boxes, and other fun projects. Like other titles originally
published by Dorling Kindersley, London, this attractive, large-
format book includes sharp, life-size color photographs and easy-to-
understand explanations.

Thiel-Cramér, Bárbara. *Flamenco.* *(Flamenco)* Lidingö, Suecia:
Remark AB, 1992. Distributed by Seven Hills Distributors,
Cincinnatti, OH. 152p. ISBN: 91-9712-594-6. $22.95. Gr. 8-
adult.

The joy and exuberance so characteristic of flamenco are
described in this lovingly written and well-translated book that tells
how flamenco came into existence, its historical and social
background, important artists, and its current status as a new art
form with song, dance, and guitar music. Numerous carefully
selected black-and-white and color photographs complement this
well-done introduction to this unique Spanish artistic expression,
originally published in Sweden.

Wilkinson, Philip. *Edificios asombrosos.* *(Amazing Buildings)*
Illus: Paolo Donati and Studio Illibill. Translated by Andrés
Molina. Barcelona: Ediciones B, 1993. 48p. ISBN: 84-406-
3757-8. $22.78. Gr. 5-10.

Inside and outside views of twenty-one of the world's most
amazing buildings—such as the Coliseum in Rome, the Taj Mahal
in India, the Temple of the Inscriptions in Mexico, the Guggenheim
Museum in the United States—are beautifully reproduced in this
large-format volume. Brief introductions, simple explanations,
double-page color drawings, and photographs convey the grandeur
of these architectural masterpieces. This is indeed a fascinating
introduction to some of the world's most beautiful creations,
originally published by Dorling Kindersley, London, in 1991.

Arts and Crafts

Wilkes, Angela. *Mi primer libro de Navidad.* *(My First Christmas
Book)* Translated by Conchita Peraire del Molino. Barcelona:
Editorial Molino, 1994. 48p. ISBN: 84-272-1712-9. $17.50. Gr.
5-9.

The fun, color, and joy of the Christmas season can be anticipated through numerous ideas for decorations, gifts, cards, and recipes that children can make by following simple, detailed instructions. Like previous titles originally published by Dorling Kindersley in London, this attractive, large-format book includes excellent, life-size color photographs of cookies, candies, tree ornaments, and other manual creations to help children prepare for the holidays.

Recreation and Sports

Beisner, Monika. *Atrapa a ese gato: Libro de juegos y adivinanzas.* *(Catch That Cat: Book of Games and Riddles)* Translated by Enrique Ortenbach. Barcelona: Editorial Lumen, 1994. 30p. ISBN: 84-264-3689-7. $15.95. Gr. 3-5.

Cat lovers will be enthralled with the bold, colorful illustrations of cats as they eat, sleep, play, and hide. The well-done Spanish rendition of these games and riddles, originally published by Faber and Faber, London, will encourage children to think about and imagine what cats can and can not do.

Davis, Edmond. *¿Y qué más?: Máquinas desafiantes y labertinos disparatados.* *(What Else? Challenging Machines and Absurd Labyrinths)* Translated by Frank Schleper. Madrid: Santillana, 1995. 32p. ISBN: 84-372-2174-9. $21.95. Gr. 3-8.

Lovers of detail will enjoy these twelve incredible machines—a star factory, a science laboratory, a clock, a tart factory, a music box, and others—that challenge readers and viewers through winding passages in these hard-to-follow colorful labyrinths. Originally published by Hamlyn Children's Books, London, this large-format volume includes detailed double-page spreads with a minimum of text and lots of minutia.

Fernández Solís, Luis. *La competición de Karate: Entrenamiento de campeones.* *(Karate Competition: Training for Champions)* *(Colección Artes Marciales)* Barcelona: Editorial Paidotribo, 1994. 267p. ISBN: 84-8019-112-0. pap. $8.95. Gr. 8-adult.

Adolescents interested in karate, the Japanese system of self-defense which is characterized by sharp, quick blows with the hands and feet, will find this book difficult to resist. Numerous black-and-white photos and clear, simple explanations beginning with basic techniques up to tactical and attitude strategies make this an excellent choice for energetic teenagers.

Lewis, Brenda Ralph. *Monedas y billetes. (Coins and Bills)* ISBN: 84-7444-645-7.
Oliver, Ray. *Rocas y fósiles. (Rocks and Fossils)* ISBN:84-7444-644-9.
Ea. vol.: 76p. (Mis Aficiones) Madrid: Editorial Debate, 1993. $12.99. Gr. 7-12.

The purpose of these guides is to introduce adolescents to interesting activities through simple explanations, numerous practical suggestions, and a wonderful selection of photographs, charts, and drawings in color. These are indeed attractive, large-format publications that will encourage would-be coin and rock collectors. Previous titles in this series are: *Observación de pájaros (Bird Watching)* and *Sellos (Stamps)*.

Lineker, Gary. *Jóvenes futbolistas. (Young Soccer Players)* Barcelona: Editorial Molino, 1994. 32p. ISBN: 84-272-4962-4. $19.95. Gr. 4-8.

This is indeed the book for young soccer enthusiasts who want to learn to play soccer. Originally published by Dorling Kindersley, London, it describes through excellent color photographs and drawings and simple explanations the rules, equipment, and basic play techniques. To encourage all young people, it includes photos of girls and boys of different ethnic backgrounds learning the game as well as shots by great players.

Literature

Cervantes Saavedra, Miguel de. *El ingenioso hidalgo Don Quijote de la Mancha. (The Ingenious Nobleman, Don Quijote de la Mancha)* Vol. 1. 592p. ISBN: 84-207-5671-7.
————. *El ingenioso caballero Don Quijote de la Mancha. (The Ingenious Knight, Don Quijote de la Mancha)* Vol. 2. 608p. ISBN: 84-207-5672-5.
Ea. vol.: Illus: José Ramón Sánchez. Madrid: Anaya, 1993. ISBN: 84-207-5629-6 (for both volumes). $199.00. Gr. 8-adult.

This is indeed *the* edition to expose readers to the most loved and admired novel of the Spanish-speaking world. More than a thousand spectacular double-page watercolor spreads and black-and-white line illustrations as well as a luxurious binding and design bring to life Don Quijote's ingenious adventures which transform reality into idealistic dreams and facts into poetic fantasies. Even more important, readers will appreciate this new edition with updated punctuation and spelling which makes Cervantes's masterpiece truly accessible to contemporary Spanish speakers. A well-written introduction and more than 6,000 notes by Angel Basanta contribute further to the understanding and enjoyment of the first modern novel of all times. The only caveat that makes these large-format volumes less than absolutely perfect is that each volume weighs approximately eight pounds. Hence, readers and viewers cannot comfortably hold them on their laps to read or view.

Poetry

Aguilar, Luis Miguel, *Coleadas. (Puns)* Illus: Germán Montalvo. ISBN: 968-494-048-3.
Cross, Elsa. *El himno de las ranas. (The Frog's Hymn)* Illus: Lucía Zacchi. ISBN: 968-494-052-1.
Del Paso, Fernando. *Paleta de diez colores. (Ten-Color Palette)* Illus: Vicente Rojo. ISBN: 968-494-053-X.
Forcada, Alberto. *Despertar (To Awaken)* Illus: Hermilo Gómez. ISBN: 968-494-051-3.
Moscona, Myriam. *Las preguntas de Natalia. (Natalia's Questions)* Illus: Fernando Medina. ISBN: 968-494-049-1.
Ea. vol.: 22p. (Reloj de Versos) Mexico: Cidcli, 1991-1992. pap. $8.95. Gr. 3-6.

The purpose of this series is to encourage children into the world of poetry. Younger children will enjoy: *El himno de las ranas,* which shows frogs having fun after a rainstorm; *Despertar,* which captures children's daydreams and wishes; and *Las preguntas de Natalia,* which features children's questions about words and life. Older children will prefer: *Coleadas,* which examines, in a jocular manner, the meaning of various words and *Paleta de diez colores,* which presents colors in a poetic manner. The attractive presentation of this paperback series and the appealing, modernistic illustrations certainly contribute to all readers's and listeners's enjoyment.

Bartolomé, Efraín. *Mínima animalia. (A Few Animals)* Illus: Marisol Fernández. 24p. ISBN: 968-494-047-5.
Paz, Octavio. *La rama. (The Branch)* Illus: Tetsuo Kitora. 20p. ISBN: 968-494-046-7.
Ea. vol.: (Reloj de Versos) Mexico: Cidcli, 1991. pap. $6.95. Gr. 6-12.

Like previous titles in this series whose purpose is to encourage young readers to read poetry, these easy-to-read, yet sophisticated poems are two wonderful additions for the libraries of older children and adolescents. Especially notable is *Minima animalia,* which lyrically depicts the characteristics of selected animals loosely following the letters of the alphabet. Striking watercolor illustrations of serpents, jaguars, butterflies, and other animals add to the tone and appeal of this poem. *La rama* includes two poems by Mexico's Nobel-prize-winning author, Octavio Paz. Artfully-done collages beautifully capture the abstract mood of these poems that celebrate the joy and silence of nature.

Cardenal, Ernesto. *Apalka (Apalka)* Illus: Felipe Dávalos. ISBN: 968-494-057-2.
Parra, Nicanor. *Sinfonía de cuna. (Cradle's Symphony)* Illus: Enrique Martínez. ISBN:968-494-056-4.
Ea. vol.: 27p. (En Cuento) Mexico: Cidcli, 1992. pap. $9.95. Gr. 4-7.

The purpose of this paperback series is to expose young readers to notable Spanish-speaking authors. Colorful, witty, full-page spreads add interest to the enjoyable texts. Especially appealing is Nicanor Parra's *Sinfonía de cuna* which shows, in a lighthearted manner, why he is considered the creator of "antipoetry." Lovers of irony will relish this treat.

Dabcovich, Lydia. *The Keys to My Kingdom: A Poem in Three Languages.* Illus: the author. New York: Lothrop, Lee and Shepard Books, 1992. 30p. ISBN: 0-688-09774-X. $14.00. Gr. Preschool-2.

The traditional nursery rhyme which takes the reader through his/her kingdom and through the day in English, French, and Spanish is a joy to listen to or to read in any language. The full-page, colored pencil and crayon illustrations add a child-like quality to this personal kingdom of flowers, town, and other special things.

Domínguez, Antonio José. *Luis Cernuda para niños. (Luis Cernuda for Children)* Illus: Ginés Liébana. ISBN: 84-7960-002-0.
García Viñó, Manuel. *Manuel Machado para niños. (Manuel Machado for Children).* Illus: Pablo Isidoro. ISBN: 84-7960-003-9.
Lacarta, Manuel. *Francisco de Quevedo para niños. (Francisco de Quevedo for Children)* Illus: Jesús Aroca. ISBN: 84-86587-91-3.
Santos, Teresa de. *Luis de Góngora para niños. (Luis de Góngora for Children)* Illus: Carmen Sáez. ISBN: 84-86587-90-5.
Ea. vol.: 126p. (Serie Poesía) Madrid: Ediciones de la Torre, 1991. Gr. 8-12.

Like the previous twenty-seven titles in this series, these are not "for children." Rather, they are excellent introductions for adolescents to the life and work of these great Spanish poets. Numerous black-and-white photographs and drawings, interesting selections from their works as well as chronologies and bibliographies make these just the right point of departure for appreciating these masters.

Kingsolver, Barbara. *Another America/Otra América*. Seattle, WA: The Seal Press, 1992. 103p. ISBN: 1-878067-14-1. $14.95; ISBN: 1-878067-15-X. pap. $10.95. Gr. 9-adult.

This is a collection of powerful and moving bilingual (Spanish-English) political poems that depict the author's feelings about war, friendship, money, rape, justice, and other compelling topics. The well-done Spanish translation will be welcomed by Spanish speakers interested in reading about another America.

Martín, Susana. *Mis primeros versos de amor. (My First Love Poems)* Buenos Aires: Planeta Juvenil, 1992. 103p. ISBN: 950-742-170-X. pap. $6.00. Gr. 5-8.

This collection of candid and deeply-felt poems tells about the anxiety and happiness of love, the fear and frustration of waiting, the doubts of puberty, and other feelings common to adolescents. Adolescents around the world will enjoy and understand these special poems.

The Tree Is Older Than You Are: A Bilingual Gathering of Poems and Stories from Mexico with Paintings by Mexican Artists. Ed. by Naomi Shihab Nye. New York: Simon & Schuster, 1995. 111p. ISBN: 0-689-80297-8. $19.95. Gr. 6-12.

More than sixty Mexican poets and traditional tales are represented in this lavish, large-size volume with attractive, richly colored paintings by contemporary Mexican artists. The excellent English translations, which appear side-by-side the original Spanish, are just right to introduce English speakers to some of the great contemporary Mexican poets such as Octavio Paz, Rosario Castellanos, and Jaime Sabines. Readers will note a wide variety in the selections—from simple rhymes and tales to profoundly reflective and imaginative poems.

Geography

Bradley, Catherine. *Kazajstán (Kazakhstan)* ISBN: 84-236-38153-92.

Flint, David C. *Los estados bálticos: Estonia, Letonia, Lituania (The Baltic States: Estonia, Latvia, Lithuania)* ISBN: 84-236-38150-92.

————. *La federación Rusa (The Russian Federation)* ISBN: 84-236-38149-92.

Gosnell, Kelvin. *Bielorrusia, Ucrania y Moldavia (Belarus, Ukraine and Moldova)* ISBN: 84-236-38151-92.

Roberts, Elizabeth. *Georgia, Armenia y Azerbaiyán. (Georgia, Armenia, and Azerbaijan)* ISBN: 84-236-38154-92.

Thomas, Paul. *Los estados centroasiáticos: Tayikistán, Uzbekistán, Kirguizistán, Turkmenistán (The Central Asian States: Tajikistan, Uzbekistan, Kyrgyzstan, Turkmenistan)* ISBN: 84-236-38152-92.
Ea. vol.: 32p. (Las Ex Repúblicas Soviéticas) Barcelona: Edebé, 1993. $17.95. Gr. 5-8.

Originally published by Aladdin Books, Great Britain, in 1992, this excellent series provides a concise introduction to the fifteen prepublics of the former Soviet Union. Divided by geographic regions, each title describes each republic's history, people, geography, and current issues and perspectives. The easy-to-understand and straightforward narratives and the numerous clear, color maps, photographs, and charts make this an invaluable aid to the study of this complex region. Each title also includes an index and a facts and figures, chronology, and important people section.

Diperna, Paula. *Los secretos de los antípodas. (The Secrets of the Antipodes)* ISBN: 84-348-3530-4.

Mose, Richard. *Los secretos de Papúa Nueva Guinea. (The Secrets of Papua New Guinea)* ISBN: 84-348-3723-4.

Stacey, Pamela, and David O. Brown. *Los secretos de la amazonía. (The Secrets of the Amazons)* ISBN: 84-348-3529-0.
Ea. vol.: 44p. Translated from the French by Catherine Tussy (Cousteau y la Aventura) Madrid: Ediciones SM, 1992. $10.95. Gr. 5-8.

Spectacular, full-page color photographs and a straightforward text describe the natural environment and popular traditions of the Maoris of New Zealand, the Papuans of New Guinea, and the inhabitants of the Amazon region in South America. Especially appealing are the beautiful views of the flora and fauna of these areas. Originally published in France, these books emphasize the importance of conservation and the threats of economic development to these regions of the world.

Kalman, Bobbie. *México: Su cultura (Mexico: Its Culture)* ISBN: 0-86505-370-7; pap. ISBN: 0-86505-400-2.

————. *México: Su gente (Mexico: Its People)* ISBN: 0-86505-369-3; pap. ISBN: 0-86505-399-5.

————. *México: Su tierra (Mexico: Its Land)* ISBN: 0-86505-368-5; pap. ISBN: 0-86505-398-7.

Ea. vol.: 32p. (Serie tierra, gente y cultura) New York: Compañía Editora Crabtree, 1994. $12.76; pap. $7.16. Gr. 4-6.

Originally published in English, this generally upbeat and attractive series introduces readers to the culture, people, and land of Mexico through numerous color photographs and drawings, and a well-translated, informative text. It is important to note that this series discusses not only common tourist-type information on Mexico such as piñatas and fiestas, but also serious problems such as air pollution and unemployment. This series is only marred by several typos throughout, but the fluid Spanish rendition will be appreciated by Spanish-speaking readers.

Knight, Margy Burns. *Las paredes hablan. (Talking Walls)* Illus: Anne Sibley O'Brien. Translated by Clarita Kohen. Gardiner, Maine: Tilbury House, 1995. 36p. ISBN: 0-88448-156-5. $17.95; pap. ISBN: 0-8844-8-157-3. $8.95. Gr. 4-6.

Through a straightforward Spanish narrative and vibrant, pastel drawings on large, double-page spreads, children are introduced to the world and its diverse cultures by exploring fourteen well-known walls. From the Great Wall of China to the walls of the ancient Inca city of Cuzco and Diego Rivera's Mexican murals up to the fall of the Berlin Wall, Spanish-speaking children will experience the context and meaning of each wall. Appended world maps and notes add to the information in the text.

History

Alberro, Solange. *Estampas de la Colonia. (Images of the Colony)* Mexico: Editorial Patria, 1994. 208p. ISBN: 968-39-1084-X. pap. $11.95. Gr. 8-12.

The exquisite color reproductions and design are the best features of this paperback book that presents an intimate view of the people, customs, architecture, and lifestyles during colonial times in Mexico, 1521-1794. In addition, some readers may be interested in the six stories that attempt to portray the special concerns of the people of the times such as a love affair between a nun and a laborer, an Indian from Tlaxcala, a healer accused before the Inquisition, the effects of chocolate in the peaceful city of Real de Chiapa, and how the viceroy took advantage of Mexican society ladies. The stories are much too contrived to be appealing but the brief texts alongside each illustration provide interesting information that is difficult to find elsewhere.

Alcina Franch, José. *A la sombra del cóndor.* *(By the Shadow of the Condor)* Illus: Marina Seoane Pascual. ISBN: 84-86732-94-8.

Ciudad Ruiz, Andrés. *Así nació América.* *(Thus Was America Born)* Illus: Marina Seoane Pascual. ISBN: 84-86732-92-1.

León-Portilla, Miguel. *Encuentro de dos mundos.* *(Encounter of Two Worlds)* Illus: Marina Seoane Pascual. ISBN: 84-86732-96-4.

Lucena Salmoral, Manuel. *América inglesa y francesa.* *(British and French America)* Illus: Alicia Cañas Cortázar. ISBN: 84-86732-98-0.

Martínez Díaz, Nelson, and Eduardo L. Moyano Bozzani. *La independencia americana.* *(American Independence)* Illus: Alicia Cañas Cortázar. ISBN: 84-8673-299-9.

Vázquez Chamorro, Germán. *América hoy.* *(The Americas Today)* Illus: Alicia Cañas Cortázar. ISBN: 84-8055-000-7.

————. *Mayas, aztecas, incas.* *(Mayas, Aztecs, Incas)* Illus: Marina Seoane Pascual. ISBN: 84-86732-91-3.

————. *Los pueblos del maíz.* *(The Corn People)* Illus: Marina Seoane Pascual. ISBN: 84-86732-93-X.

Vines Azancot, Pedro A., and Josefa Vega. *Los siglos coloniales.* *(The Colonial Centuries)* Illus: Alicia Cañas Cortázar. ISBN: 84-86732-97-2.

Ea. vol.: 63p. (América Ayer y Hoy) Madrid: Cultural, S.A. de Ediciones, 1992. ISBN: 84-86732-91-3 (for the series) $100.00. Gr. 5-10.

This is a most readable and appealing overview of the history of the Western Hemisphere beginning with its early inhabitants 30,000 years ago up to America in the twentieth century in nine attractive, large-format volumes. The easy-to-understand narrative complemented by informative, pastel, watercolor illustrations presents just the right amount of information about key issues in the historical development of the Western Hemisphere. Each volume concludes with a useful, six-page "For further learning" section. Historians-to-be will not be disappointed.

La aventura de navegar. *(The Adventure of Navigating)* Translated by Fernando Bort Misol. (Biblioteca Interactiva/Mundo Maravilloso/ Ciencias) Madrid: Ediciones SM, 1995. 49p. ISBN: 84-348-4705-1. $14.95. Gr. 4-8.

Like previous titles in this attractive "interactive series" originally published in France, this one includes numerous fold-outs, flaps, and transparent plastic overlays intermingled between detailed, glossy watercolor illustrations and simple, easy-to-understand texts that introduce readers to ships from early Egyptian and Chinese vessels to submarines and the *Queen Mary.* This well-constructed book shows exciting inside/outside views of more than forty types of ships. A glossary, a chronology, and an index add to the value of this adventure in the world of navigation.

Avilés, Jaime. *Ignacio Cumplido, un impresor del siglo XIX. (Ignacio Cumplido, a Printer of the Nineteenth Century).* ISBN: 968-6382-57-7.

Escandón, Patricia. *Al servicio de su majestad imperial: Un oficial de húsares en México. (At the Service of His Imperial Majesty: A Husar Officer in Mexico)* ISBN: 968-6382-65-8.

Flores Clair, Eduardo. *Un granito de sal. (A Little Grain of Salt)* ISBN: 968-6382-60-7.

Hernandez Franyuti, Regina. *Versiones y diversiones de un cirquero. (Versions and Diversions of a Circus Performer)* ISBN: 968-6382-56-9.

Sepúlveda Otaíza, Ximena. *Un gran río: entre la selva y el mar. (A Great River: Between the Jungle and the Sea)* ISBN: 968-6382-69-0.

Ea. vol.: 48p. (El Tiempo Vuela) Mexico: Instituto de Investigaciones Dr. José María Luis Mora, 1992. pap. $6.95. Gr. 8-10.

With the exception of *Un granito de sal*, which presents the history of salt from pre-Columbian times to the nineteenth century, these titles describe various aspects of life in nineteenth century Mexico: *Ignacio Cumplido: Un hombre del siglo XIX* describes the life of the publisher of Mexico's first modern newspaper; *Al servicio de su majestad imperial: Un oficial de húsares en Mexico* tells about political struggles between two opposing groups; *Versiones y diversiones de un cirquero* shows the life of a circus performer of the times; and *Un gran río: entre la selva y el mar* describes the life along the Usumacinta River during the last century. Despite the cheap paper, unsightly covers, and some inferior black-and-white photographs, these historical narratives might serve a purpose. They present interesting views about the history of Mexico for adolescents that can not be found in other sources.

Bertoni, Lilia Ana, and Luis Alberto Romero. *Entre dictaduras y democracias. 12. (Between Dictatorships and Democracies. 12)* ISBN: 950-737-058-5.

————. *Cronología (1418-1983) Argentina y el mundo. (Chronology [1418-1983] Argentina and the World)* ISBN: 950-737-093-1.

Ea. vol.: 62p. Illus: Carlos Schlaen. (Una Historia Argentina) Buenos Aires: Libros del Quirquincho, 1992. pap. $11.95. Gr. 5-9.

Like the eleven previous titles in this excellent series on the history of Argentina, *Entre dictaduras y democracias* includes brief chapters, animated text, numerous amusing black-and-white line illustrations, and discussions of important topics. In addition, it includes photographs of the period discussed as well as brief documents or testimonies of people who lived at the time. *Cronología (1418-1983)* presents a timetable with amusing line illustrations and brief phrases of incidents in Europe and the World, America and Argentina, noting important facts as they relate to Argentina's economy, society, culture, politics, and institutions. This series is indeed a most readable and appealing manner to introduce readers to the history of Argentina.

Boixados, Roxana Edith, and Miguel Angel Palermo. *Los aztecas. (The Aztecs)* ISBN: 950-737-017-X.

—————. *Los diaguitas. (The Diaguitas)* ISBN: 950-737-104-1.

—————. *Los mayas. (The Maya)* ISBN: 950-737-057-7.

Palermo, Miguel Angel. *Los jinetes del Chaco. (The Riders of Chaco)* ISBN: 950-737-111-9.

—————. *Los tehuelches. (The Tehuelches)* ISBN: 950-737-080-3.

Ea. vol.: 64 p. Buenos Aires: Coquena Grupo Editor, 1991-1992. pap. $11.00. Gr. 5-8.

Like the previous seven titles of this informative series about the early inhabitants of America, readers will appreciate the fast-paced narrative which relates, in an easy-to-read and easy-to-understand text, important aspects about the Diaguita, Mayan, Tehuelche, and Chaco cultures. Like their predecessors, the only disappointment are the black-and-white line illustrations, which don't add much to the narrative except, at times, some humor. Despite this caveat, this series is an interesting historical overview to pre-Columbian America for this age group.

Cardini, Franco. *Europa 1492: Retrato de un continente hace quinientos años. (Europe 1492: Portrait of a Continent Five Hundred Years Ago)* Madrid: Grupo Anaya, 1989. 238p. ISBN: 84-207-3344-X. $90.00. Gr. 9-adult.

Exquisite paintings, miniatures, drawings, and engravings of the fifteenth and sixteenth centuries as well as beautiful photographs of the landscape and a most informative text describe the history, life, and culture of Europe five centuries ago. This is certainly one of the most beautiful ways to learn and appreciate the achievements, joys, and sorrows of that era. An informative chronology, bibliography, and name index complement this outstanding large-format publication, originally published in Italy in 1989.

Castelló, José Emilio. *La primera guerra mundial. (The First World War)* Biblioteca Básica de Historia. Madrid: Grupo Anaya, 1993. 96p. ISBN: 84-207-4825-0. pap. $9.95. Gr. 9-12.

The importance of World War I as well as the causes, battles, and consequences of the war are examined in a straightforward narrative. Black-and-white period photographs and maps on almost every page add interest to this historical overview. It should be noted that the small size—5 1/2 by 7 1/2 inches—of this paperback unfortunately required reducing most photographs to 3 1/2 by 4 1/2 inches, thereby reducing their effectiveness. Nonetheless, this is a useful guide to World War I.

Corbishley, Mike. *¿Qué sabemos sobre los romanos? (What Do We Know about the Romans?)* Translated by Pilar León Fiz. ISBN: 84-348-3923-7.
Defrates, Joanna. *¿Qué sabemos sobre los aztecas? (What Do We Know about the Aztecs?)* Translated by Jesús Valiente. ISBN: 84-348-3927-X.
Martel, Hazel Mary. *¿Qué sabemos sobre los vikingos? (What Do We Know about the Vikings?)* Translated by Raquel Velázquez. ISBN: 84-348-3925-3.
Pearson, Anne. *¿Qué sabemos sobre los griegos? (What Do We Know about the Greeks?)* Translated by Jesús Valiente Malla. ISBN: 84-348-3921-0.
Ea. vol.: 45p. (¿Qué sabemos sobre . . . ?) Madrid: Ediciones SM, 1993. $12.95. Gr. 3-7.

These great civilizations are introduced to young readers through excellent color photographs, maps, drawings, and charts as well as brief, straightforward texts which highlight significant people and aspects of their way of life as well as special contributions. Originally published by Simon & Schuster Young Books in 1992, these titles are just right to entice historians-to-be. Each title includes a glossary and an index. Also in this series, *¿Qué sabemos sobre los egipcios? (What Do We Know about the Egyptians?)*

Dambrosio, Mónica, and Roberto Barbieri. *El nuevo mundo: desde el descubrimiento hasta la independencia. (The New World: From Discovery to Independence)* ISBN: 84-348-3449-9.
————. *El paso al mundo moderno. (To the Modern World)* ISBN: 84-348-3448-0.
Ea. vol.: 63p. Illus: Remo Berselli (Historia del Hombre) Madrid: Ediciones SM, 1991-1992. $12.95. Gr. 5-9.

Like the previous eight titles of this series, The History of Mankind, these large-format books include full-page drawings, maps, charts, and photographs in color and half a page of text. The straightforward narrative combined with numerous illustrations on every page make this series, originally published in Italy, an appealing introduction for historians-to-be.

Elliott, J. H. ed. *El mundo hispánico: civilización e imperio, Europa y América, pasado y presente. (The Hispanic World).* Translated from the English by Jordi Ainaud and others. Barcelona: Editorial Crítica, 1991. 272p. ISBN: 84-7423-508-1. Gr. 9-adult.

The purpose of this exquisite large-format publication is to re-evaluate Spain's historical achievements as well as its contributions to the modern world. Eighteen in-depth essays, written by English-speaking and Spanish-speaking specialists in the fields of art, history, literature, politics, and culture present an overview of Hispanic cultures. Serious students of Spanish history and culture will appreciate such scholarly chapters as "Unity and Empire, 1500-1800: Spain and Europe"; others will delight in the wonderful selection of 320 illustrations in color and black-and-white with brief well-done captions that summarize the information in each essay. Readers should note that with the exception of two chapters—one on Latin America and another on Hispanics in the U.S.—this is basically about Spanish civilization. Especially interesting to non-Hispanics is the introduction, "Spain, Myth and Reality," written by the editor.

Hadley-Garcia, George. *Hollywood hispano: Los latinos en el mundo del cine. (Hispanic Hollywood: Latins in the World of Cinematography)* New York: Carol Publishing Group, 1991. 256p. ISBN: 0-8065-1208-3. $17.95. Gr. 8-adult.

The presence of Hispanic movie stars in Hollywood beginning with silent films of the 1920s up to the 1980s is amply recorded in this well-done historical overview. Black-and-white photographs on every page and a concise narrative describe the roles, themes, subject matter, and other aspects of Hispanics in the Hollywood scene. The author emphasizes the discrimination, stereotypes, and other negative experiences encountered by such stars as Dolores del Río, Antonio Moreno, Rita Cansino (Hayworth), Ramón Novarro, Anthony Quinn, Ricardo Montalbán, and many others. The author concludes with such questions as: Why are there so few Hispanic writers, directors, or producers? Why is it so difficult for successful Hispanic stars to find new successes or more Hispanic roles?

Hermano cielo, hermana águila. (Brother Sky, Sister Eagle) Illus: Susan Jeffers. Translated by Esteve Serra. Palma de Mallorca:

José J. de Olañeta, 1993. 26p. ISBN: 84-7651-169-8. $19.95. Gr. 3-6.

Susan Jeffers's extraordinary interpretation of Chief Seattle's speech regarding the purchase by the U.S. Government of the land owned by Native Americans in the 1800s is now available to Spanish speakers. The beauty of nature in all its splendor and Chief Seattle's advice to cherish and conserve the land is definitely conveyed by Jeffers's stunning, detailed double-page spreads. This is indeed a powerful and moving message in support of Native Americans' love of land and nature. Young Spanish speakers in the United States and Latin America, however, may be confused by the extensive use of the unique peninsular Spanish form of the plural you with its corresponding verb conjugation. Although recognizable, this inflected verbal form sounds old-fashioned and hence stilted to Spanish speakers outside of Spain.

Livesey, Anthony. *Enciclopedia visual de las grandes batallas: Grandes jefes militares. (Great Commanders and Their Battles)* Translated by Luis Ogg. Barcelona: Editorial Rombo, 1995. 127p. ISBN: 84-86579-64-3. $29.95. Gr. 9-adult.

Four great commanders of all times and their battles—George Washington, The Battle of Princeton; Napoleon, The Battle of Wagram; Wellington, The Battle of Arapiles; Robert E. Lee, the Battle of Chancellorsville—are described through brief, well-written narratives and spectacular, full-page color and black-and-white reproductions and drawings in this large-format visual encyclopedia, originally published by Marshall Editions, London. This series is indeed an engaging introduction to the history of great commanders and their battles.

MacDonald, Fiona. *En Babilonia con Hammurabi. (In Babylonia with Hammurabi)* Illus: Gerald Wood. ISBN: 84-207-4510-3.
————. *En Francia con Carlomagno. (In France with Charlemagne)* Illus: John James. ISBN: 84-207-4511-1.
————. *En la Roma de los papas. (In the Rome of the Popes)* Illus: Nick Harris & John James. ISBN: 84-207-4513-8.
————. *En París con el Rey Sol. (In Paris with the Sun King)* Illus: Mark Bergin. ISBN: 84-207-4512-X.
Ea. vol.: 32p. Translated by Nieves Méndez. (El Túnel del Tiempo) Madrid: Grupo Anaya, 1992. pap. $6.95. Gr. 6-9.

Like previous titles in this excellent yet unassuming paperback series, young readers are introduced to the eras of Hammurabi, Charlemagne, Pope Sixtus VI, and France's Louis XIV through fast-paced narratives and detailed, full-page illustrations which highlight important people, places, or events. The matter-of-fact narratives and the informative illustrations are just right to excite readers about the study of great civilizations. These titles were originally published in Italy in 1991.

MacDonald, Fiona. *Los exploradores: Expediciones, pioneros y aventureros. (Explorers, Expeditions and Pioneers)* ISBN: 84-207-6698-4.

──────. *La vivienda: Hábitats y vida doméstica. (Houses, Habitats and Home Life)* ISBN: 84-207-6697-6.

Morley, Jacqueline. *Las diversiones: Espectáculos y artistas. (Entertainment: Screen, Stage, and Stars)* ISBN: 84-207-6700-X.

Tames, Richard. *La comida: Banquetes, cocineros y cocinas. (Food: Feasts, Cooks, and Kitchens)* ISBN: 84-207-6699-2.

Ea. vol.: 48p. (A Través del Tiempo) Illus: Mark Bergin and others. Translated by Carlos Laguna. Madrid: Grupo Anaya, 1995. $13.95. Gr. 3-6.

The development of fundamental elements of world civilization from prehistoric times to the present is presented through full-page, color drawings and charts, and brief, simple texts. Originally published by Watts, London, this is a lighthearted approach to history through well-known innovations: *Los exploradores: Expediciones, pioneros y aventureros* tells about expeditions of discovery from prehistoric explorers in Africa up to space travel. *La vivienda: Hábitats y vida doméstica* shows the development of houses from 300,000 years ago to the house of the future. *Las diversiones: Espectáculos y artistas* presents the development of entertainment from Egyptian dancers and musicians to mini-television and holography. *La comida: Banquetes, cocineros y cocinas* describes the production of food from early hunters and food gatherers up to genetic engineering. Each volume includes a chronology, a glossary, and an index.

Maestro, Betsy, and Giulio Maestro. *El descubrimiento de las Américas. (The Discovery of the Americas)* Translated by Juan González Álvaro. Madrid: Editorial Everest, 1992. 48p. ISBN: 84-241-3327-7. $10.95. Gr. 3-5.

This well-done translation presents in a simple, easy-to-understand narrative with striking, full-page watercolor illustrations the story of the discovery of the Americas. As a general introduction to the age of exploration for young readers, this handsome large-format book is worthwhile and informative. It is a beautiful view of the Americas before and after the discovery.

Milner, Angela. *Dinosaurios. (Dinosaurs)* Illus: Simone End and others. ISBN: 84-7444-939-1.

Thomas, David Hurst, and Lorann Pendleton. *Los indios norteamericanos. (Native Americans)* Illus: Helen Halliday and others. ISBN: 84-7444-892-1.

Ea. vol.: 64p. Translated by Margarita Cavándoli. (Descubrimientos) Madrid: Editorial Debate, 1995. $19.95. Gr. 4-7.

Double-page color spreads, charts, maps, and photographs and simple descriptions characterize this appealing series of more than sixteen titles originally published by Weldon Owen, Australia. *Dinosaurios* describes numerous aspects about dinosaurs from their origins up to their extinction. *Los indios norteamericanos* provides an overview to American Indians from their arrival in North America up to their future in the U.S. Both titles include well-done glossaries and indexes.

Morley, Jacqueline, *El vestido: Ropa de trabajo, de calle y de etiqueta. (Garments: Clothes for Work, Play, and Display)* ISBN: 84-207-6262-8.

Senior, Kathryn. *La medicina: Hechiceros, médicos y medicamentos. (Medicine: Doctors, Demons, and Drugs)* ISBN: 84-207-6260-1.

Ea. vol.: 48p. (A Través del Tiempo) Translated by Juan Manuel Ibeas. Madrid: Grupo Anaya, 1994. $22.95. Gr. 4-8.

The purpose of this attractive series, originally published by Watts, London, is to show the major innovations developed by humankind in various countries as well as their historical evolution and future prospects. *El vestido: Ropa de trabajo, de calle y de etiqueta* describes the evolution of clothing from pre-historic times up to climate-controlled clothes of the future. *La medicina: Hechiceros, médicos y medicamentos* describes the evolution of medicine from primitive up to modern times, including such important developments as anesthetics, antibiotics, DNA, and others. In addition to numerous color drawings, charts, and informative texts on every page, each title includes a chronology, a glossary, and an index. Previous titles in this series are *Los barcos (Ships), Los aviones (Airplanes), Los inventos (Inventions), Los transportes (Transportation), Las ciudades (Cities), and El deporte (Sports).*

Nicholson, Robert. *Los siux. (The Sioux)* ISBN: 1-56492-092-5.

Nicholson, Robert, and Claire Watts. *La antigua China. (Ancient China)* ISBN: 1-56492-093-3.

——. *El antiguo Egipto. (Ancient Egypt)* ISBN: 1-56492-094-1.

——. *Los aztecas. (The Aztecs)* ISBN: 1-56492-091-7.

Ea. vol.: 32p. (Raíces) Translated from the English by José Ramón Araluce. Torrance, CA: Laredo Publishing, 1993. $14.95. Gr. 3-6.

The culture, history, traditions, and daily life of the Sioux, Aztecs, ancient Egypt, and ancient China are described to young readers through numerous clear and appealing photographs, drawings and maps on every page, and concise, brief narratives. Originally published in Great Britain in 1991, this well-translated series provides the right amount of information for young readers. In addition, each title includes an informative glossary, "how we know" section, and a five-page legend that highlights basic beliefs about each culture. A few undesirable features of this series are the constricted margins at the binding which make it difficult to read the text or see the complete illustration.

Nuestra bandera. (Our Flag) ISBN: 968-29-4033-8. Mexico: Consejo Nacional de Fomento Educativo, 1992. 39p. pap. $6.95. Gr. 4-7.

Through excellent historical and contemporary reproductions in color and a straightforward narrative, readers are introduced to the history of the Mexican flag and to important do's and don'ts regarding the use of the flag and other national emblems. This attractive paperback publication also could be used as a bird's-eye view of Mexican history including important dates and commemorations.

Palermo, Miguel Angel. *Los tehuelches. (The "Tehuelches") (La Otra Historia)* Illus: Huadi. Buenos Aires: Coquena Grupo Editor, 1991. 63p. ISBN: 950-737-80-5. pap. $11.00. Gr. 5-8.

Like the previous seven titles of this informative series about the early inhabitants of America, readers will appreciate the fast-paced narrative which relates, in an easy-to-read and easy-to-understand text, important aspects of the "Tehuelche" culture. Like its predecessors, the only disappointments are the black-and-white line illustrations which don't add much to the narrative except, at times, some humor. Despite this caveat, this series is an interesting historical overview to pre-Columbian America for this age group.

Platt, Richard. *El asombroso libro del interior de: Un barco de guerra del siglo XVIII. (Cross-Sections. Man-of-War)* Illus: Stephen Biesty. Translated by Juan Génova Sotil. Madrid: Santillana, 1993. 32p. ISBN: 84-372-4536-2. $22.95. Gr. 5-9.

Like its predecessor, this large-format volume includes excellent, detailed, cross-section color drawings and brief texts based on the battleship, *HMS Victory,* built in England in 1765 and used in the

Battle of Trafalgar in 1805. Readers and viewers will experience life aboard an eighteenth century ship including its battle stations, cannons, sanitary and dining facilities, storage and preparation of food, as well as the duties of the seamen and marines. A glossary and an index add to the value of this informative book, originally published by Dorling Kindersley, London, in 1993.

Sala, Virginio, and Lella Cusin. *1000 acontecimientos: ¿cuándo, cómo, porqué? (1000 Events: When, How, Why?)* Illus: Maurizio Bajetti. Translated from the Italian by Ma. Isabel Giménez Rayo. Madrid: Susaeta, 1994. 192p. ISBN: 84-305-7739-4. $29.95. Gr. 5-8.

In a question-and-answer format, this volume discusses world events from the mid–fifteenth century up to the early 1990s. This is not an in-depth historical analysis of world history, rather it is a succinct introduction to the scientists, artists, and issues of the modern era with numerous color drawings, photographs, and diagrams. Reluctant historians-to-be will be intrigued by the attractive design and the accessible information presented. It includes a subject index and an easy-to-use table of contents. Like other history manuals originally published in Italy, this one emphasizes European history.

San Souci, Robert. *Los peregrinos de N. C. Wyeth. (N. C. Wyeth's Pilgrims)* Photos by Malcom Varon. Translated by Alberto Romo. New York: Lectorum Publications, 1992. 32p. ISBN: 1-880507-03-X. $14.95. Gr. 3-7.

This is an excellent Spanish translation of *N. C. Wyeth's Pilgrims*, which recaptures the first Thanksgiving Day as practiced by the Pilgrims in Plymouth. Wyeth's original illustrations definitely depict the joy, environment, and lifestyle of the Pilgrims. Spanish speakers will delight in this historically accurate view of life on the Plymouth plantation.

Scarre, Chris. *Cronos la historia visual. (Timelines of the Ancient World)* Translated by Magdalena Ferrer and others. Barcelona: Ediciones B, 1995. 256p. ISBN: 84-406-5459-6. $35.95. Gr. 8-12.

The purpose of this exquisite, large-format publication originally published by Dorling Kindersley, London, is to present an overview of the history of humankind from prehistoric times up to 1500, covering the whole world and all types of societies. This is indeed a spectacular, in-depth panorama of the most important events in the history of the world through well-designed chronological tables, maps, and brief essays. Numerous sharp, color photographs and drawings on every page will entice even reluctant historians-to-be; a well-done index will assist others.

Spanish Pathways in Florida: 1492-1992/Los caminos españoles en La Florida: 1492-1992. Edited by Ann L. Henderson and Gary R. Mormino. Translated by Carlos J. Cano, José A. Feliciano Butler and Warren Hampton. Sarasota, FL: Pineapple Press, 1991. 364p. ISBN: 1-56164-003-4. $24.95; ISBN: 1-56164-004-2. pap. $18.95. Gr. 9-adult.

This bilingual (English and Spanish on facing pages) celebration of the quincentenary of Columbus's voyage to America includes sixteen well-written essays on the influence of the Spanish in Florida, from the first explorers to the latest Hispanic migration. Serious students, especially those interested in the history of Florida, will appreciate the diversity of topics covered, from prominent individuals, to disease and the Indians of Florida, to what turned out to be better than gold: plants of the new world. In the last essay which asks, Why celebrate the Quincentenary? Michael V. Gannon responds, "This event presents us with unparalleled opportunities for expanding understanding of our Hispanic cultural heritage" (p. 340). And this indeed sums the value of this book. Spanish-speaking readers also will appreciate the well-done Spanish translation.

Urrutia, Ma. Cristina, and Krystyna Libura. *Ecos de la conquista. (Echos of the Conquest)* Mexico: Editorial Patria, 1992. 256p. ISBN: 968-39-0774-1. pap. $24.00. Gr. 6-12.

The conquest of Mexico as viewed by Bernal Díaz del Castillo, a Spanish soldier who participated alongside Cortés, and Bernardino de Sahagún, a Spanish priest who reported on the struggle and defeat as narrated by the natives fifty years after the Conquest, is vividly recounted in this most attractive and approachable book. Readers who find the original versions too difficult to understand will find the explanatory notes alongside the narrative most useful and informative. In addition, excellent photographs, mainly in color, of original paintings, maps, and codices present both the European and indigenous representations of the conquest from two different perspectives. Also valuable are the "footprints" that direct readers to a contrasting view of the same fact under discussion. This is indeed one of the best books on the Conquest of Mexico; it will interest serious students who can read the well-selected and clearly captioned original narratives or budding historians who, through the notes and illustrations, will have a better understanding of the prejudices, beliefs, and controversies that have surrounded these civilizations for centuries.

Ventura, Piero. *Las casas: Modos formas y usos de la vivienda en el tiempo. (Houses: Styles, Forms, and Uses of Dwellings Through Time)* (Historia Ilustrada de la Humanidad) Madrid: Editorial Everest, 1993. 64p. ISBN: 84-241-5899-7. $13.99. Gr. 5-8.

In a most readable and appealing manner, young readers are introduced to the history of humankind's search for safe and comfortable houses. This book describes the design, special characteristics, and beauty of the earliest cave dwellings to contemporary high rise buildings made out of steel. The excellent, detailed, pen-and-watercolor drawings are enough to entice any reader and viewer to the study of man's search for shelter. A straightforward text and a well-done glossary add to the value of this volume. Other titles in this series, originally published in 1992 by Arnoldo Mondadori Editore in Italy, are *Los vestidos (Dress), La comunicación (Communication), Los alimentos (Food), Los transportes (Transportation),* and *La tecnología (Technology).*

Ventura, Piero. *Los transportes: Del trineo a la rueda, de la vela al vapor, de la mongolfiera al jet. (Transportation: From Sleighs to Wheels, from Sails to Steam to Jets)* Translated from the Italian by Carolina López Ballester. (Historia Ilustrada de la Humanidad) Madrid: Editorial Everest, 1995. 64p. ISBN: 84-241-5904-7. $13.99. Gr. 5-8.

The history of transportation from prehistoric up to modern times is narrated through appealing detailed pen-and-watercolor drawings and a readable, informative text. This delightful volume is sure to motivate readers to explore the development of wheels, ancient Roman roads, Leonardo da Vinci's bicycle and helicopter, up to modern trains, cars, and jets. A well-done glossary adds to the value of this publication, originally published by Arnoldo Mondadori Editore.

Biography

Adler, David A. *Un libro ilustrado sobre Abraham Lincoln. (A Picture Book of Abraham Lincoln)* Illus: John y Alexandra Wallner. ISBN: 0-8234-0980-5.

—————. *Un libro ilustrado sobre Cristóbal Colón. (A Picture Book of Christopher Columbus)* Illus: John and Alexandra Wallner. ISBN: 0-8234-0981-3.

—————. *Un libro ilustrado sobre Martin Luther King, hijo. (A Picture Book of Martin Luther King, Jr.)* Illus: Robert Casilla. ISBN: 0-8234-0982-1.

Ea. vol.: 32p. Translated by Teresa Mlawer. New York: Holiday House, 1992. pap. $5.95. Gr. K-3.

Like the original English versions, these well-done Spanish translations present information on Abraham Lincoln, Christopher Columbus, and Martin Luther King, Jr., from boyhood until death. The easy-to-read text and the attractive watercolor illustrations make these books just right for primary-age Spanish-speaking readers.

Araújo, Joaquín. *Félix Rodríguez de la Fuente: El amigo de los animales que nos mostró los secretos de la naturaleza (Félix Rodríguez de la Fuente: The Friend of Animals Who Showed Us Nature's Secrets)* ISBN: 84-348-3486-3.

Nicholson, Michael. *Mahatma Gandhi: El hombre que, mediante la no violencia, liberó a la India del dominio colonial. (Mahatma Gandhi: The Man that Liberated India from Colonial Domination through Nonviolence)* ISBN: 84-348-3484-7.

Ea. vol.: 64p. (Gente de Ayer y Hoy) Madrid: Ediciones SM, 1991. Gr. 6-10.

Like previous titles in this informative series that narrate the lives of people who have distinguished themselves for their humanitarian or scientific achievements, these include straightforward and color photographs on every page. The personal lives and contributions to humankind of Félix Rodríguez de la Fuente, a well-known Spanish naturalist, and Mahatma Gandhi, the Indian nationalist and spiritual leader, should spark the interest of adolescents in the fields of ecology and justice.

Alvarez Leefmans, Francisco Javier. *Las neuronas de don Santiago: Santiago Ramón y Cajal. (Don Santiago's Neurons: Santiago Ramón y Cajal)* 130p. ISBN: 968-6177-58-2.

Chamizo, José Antonio. *El científico de sonrisa contagiosa: Linus Pauling. (The Scientist with the Contagious Smile: Linus Pauling)* 101p. ISBN: 968-6177-62-0.

Martínez, Rafael. *El arquitecto del cosmos: Johannes Kepler. (The Cosmos's Architect: Johannes Kepler)* 105p. ISBN: 968-6177-59-0.

Rojas, José Antonio. *El sembrador de salud: Alexander Fleming. (The Sower of Health: Alexander Fleming)* 99p. ISBN: 968-6177-67-1.

Sayavedra, Roberto. *El domador de la electricidad: Thomas Alva Edison. (The Tamer of Electricity: Thomas Alva Edison)* 110p. ISBN: 968-6177-69-8.

Schmidt, Alejandro. *El astrónomo que perdió la nariz: Tycho Brahe. (The Astronomer Who Lost His Nose: Tycho Brahe)* 103p. ISBN: 968-6177-68-X.

Swaan, Bram de. *El perseguidor de la luz: Albert Einstein. (The Pursuer of Light: Albert Einstein)* 125p. ISBN: 968-6177-57-4.

Viesca, Carlos. *El evangelizador empecinado: Bernardino de Sahagún. (The Stubborn Preacher: Bernardino de Sahagún)* 111p. ISBN: 968-6177-65-5.

Ea. vol.: (Viajeros del Conocimiento) Mexico: Pangea, 1994. $8.95. Gr. 8-12.

Like the approximately thirty previous titles in this unassuming paperback series, which introduces readers to the life and work of some of the world's most renowned scientists, these describe in a clear and easy-to-understand manner important aspects in their lives as well as selected fragments of their writings. Despite the cheap paper, cluttered design, and unclear black-and-white photos, these are some of the best books in Spanish to introduce adolescents to the world of science and outstanding scientists.

Antoine, Véronique. *Picasso: Un día en su estudio. (Picasso: One Day in his Studio)* ISBN: 84-207-4763-7.

Loumaye, Jacqueline. *Van Gogh: La manchita amarilla. (Van Gogh: The Yellow Spot)* Illus: Claudine Roucha. ISBN: 84-207-4764-5.

Pierre, Michel. *Gauguin: El descubrimiento de un pintor. (Gauguin: The Discovery of a Painter)* ISBN: 84-207-4762-9.

Pinguilly, Yves. *Leonardo de Vinci: El pintor que hablaba con los pájaros. (Leonardo da Vinci: The Painter Who Talked with Birds)* ISBN: 84-207-4761-0.

Ea. vol.: 60p. (El Jardín de los Pintores) Translated by María Durante and Jesús Peribáñez García. Madrid: Grupo Anaya, 1992. 60p. $11.95. Gr. 5-8.

The best parts of this series are the attractive designs, black-and-white photos, and excellent full-color reproductions of the paintings by Picasso, Van Gogh, Gauguin, and da Vinci. These biographies, however, are marred by condescending introductions that will discourage most readers. Nonetheless, these biographies, originally published by Casterman in France in 1989, present enough information and most appealing visuals that will inspire young artists-to-be.

Cardoso, Regina. *Sor Juana Inés de la Cruz. (Sor Juana Inés de la Cruz)* Illus.: Bruno González. ISBN: 968-805-440-2.

Espejel, Laura, and Ruth Solís Vicarte. *Emiliano Zapata. (Emiliano Zapata)* Illus.: Claudia de Teresa. ISBN: 968-805-234-4.

Pérez Campa, Mario A., and Ruth Solís Vicarte. *Cuauhtémoc. (Cuauhtémoc)* Illus.: María Figueroa. ISBN: 968-805-430-5.

Ruiz Lombardo, Andrés, and Ruth Solís Vicarte. *Benito Juárez.* *(Benito Juárez)* Illus.: Rafael Barajas. ISBN: 968-805-367-8.
Trejo Estrada, Evelia, and Aurora Cano Andaluz. *Guadalupe Victoria.* *(Guadalupe Victoria)* Illus.: Rafael Barajas. ISBN: 968-805-362-7.
Ea. vol.: 35p. (Biografías para Niños) Mexico: Instituto Nacional de Estudios Históricos de la Revolución Mexicana, 1992. pap. $5.95. Gr. 6-10.

Simply and succinctly, young readers are introduced to the achievements and personal lives of four renowned Mexican heroes and one extraordinary poet and author. The easy-to-read narratives, vibrant watercolor illustrations, and appealing design make this paperback series just right to learn about Mexican history through its distinguished heroes and heroine. The only undesirable feature of this otherwise well-done biographical series are the gaudy covers which make these paperbacks look more like political propaganda brochures rather than biographies for the young.

Dahl, Roald. *Mi año.* *(My Year)* Illus: Quentin Blake. Translated by Ma. José Guitián. Madrid: Ediciones SM, 1994. 137p. ISBN: 84-348-4548-2. $12.95. Gr. 6-9.

Dahl's love for nature and empathy for children are beautifully narrated in this touching memoir that describes the passage of time. In a whimsical manner, he explains why moles are such extraordinary animals, why saffron is the most expensive food product, why golf is the best sport in the world, why the cuckoo is the most disagreeable bird, and many other personal likes and dislikes. Blake's watercolor illustrations provide the lighthearted touch these reminiscences need. Admirers and admirers-to-be of the great British author will enjoy this fluid Spanish rendition.

Delmar, Albert. *Goya: Aún aprendo.* *(I Still Learn)* ISBN: 84-406-3124-3.
————. *Leonardo: Pintor, inventor y sabio.* *(Leonardo: Painter, Inventor and Scholar)* ISBN: 84-406-3125-1.
————. *Miró: La hormiga y las estrellas.* *(Miró: The Ant and the Stars)* ISBN: 84-406-3127-8.
————. *Picasso: Yo no busco, encuentro.* *(Picasso: I Don't Seek, I Find)* ISBN: 84-406-3129-4.
————. *Rembrandt: Comerciante de Amsterdam.* *(Rembrandt: Businessman from Amsterdam)* ISBN: 84-406-3128-6.
————. *Velázquez: Un pintor de palacio.* *(Velázquez: A Painter at Court)* ISBN: 84-406-3126-X.

Ea. vol.: 29p. (Grandes Pintores para Niños). Illus: F. Salvà. Barcelona: Ediciones B, 1992. $12.95. Gr. 3-5.

Briefly and succinctly, young readers and viewers are exposed to the life and important works of six great painters: Goya, Leonardo, Miró, Picasso, Rembrandt, and Velázquez. The best part of these biographies are the well-selected reproductions and details for which these masters are revered. The narratives, however, are at times confusing and disjointed. Nevertheless, some Spanish-speaking artists-to-be might be inspired by these biographies.

Filipovic, Zlata. *Diario de Zlata.* *(Zlata's Diary)* Madrid: El País/Aguilar, 1994. 218p. ISBN: 84-03-59390-2. pap. $9.95. Gr. 5-9.

Like Anne Frank, who wrote about Nazi horrors during the Second World War, Zlata Filipovic, a twelve-year-old girl from Bosnia-Herzegovina, confides to her diary her fears, doubts, and deprivations as a result of the conflict in the former Yugoslavia. With the candor and naturalness of a teenager, she tells about the horrors of the bombings and the lack of such basics as water, electricity, heat, and food experienced by the people in Sarajevo. Readers in the United States will be intrigued by the similarities in teenagers's interests such as Zlata's fascination with MTV, pizza, Michael Jackson, Madonna, and American movies. The tragedy of the conflict in Bosnia and its effects on the people come to life in this fluid Spanish rendition which includes color photographs and excerpts from Zlata's diary.

Gray, Charlotte. *Bob Geldof.* *(Bob Geldof)* ISBN: 84-348-3483-9.
Sproule, Ana. *Thomas Alva Edison.* *(Thomas Alva Edison)* ISBN: 84-348-3520-7
White, Michael. *Isaac Newton.* *(Isaac Newton)* ISBN: 84-348-3485-5.
Ea. vol.: 64p. (Gente de Ayer y Hoy) Madrid: Ediciones SM, 1990-1991. Gr. 6-10.

Like previous titles in this series, these informative biographies narrate the lives and achievements of people who have distinguished themselves in various fields. Straightforward narratives and numerous black-and-white and color photographs on every page relate the personal lives and times in which these outstanding people contributed to humankind. There is no question that these biographies will spark the interest of adolescents in these topics.

Heslewood, Juliet. *Introducción a Picasso.* *(Introducing Picasso)* Translated by Paloma Farré Díaz. Madrid: Celeste Ediciones, 1993. 32p. ISBN: 84-87553-33-8. $15.95. Gr. 5-12.

Picasso, one of the greatest artists of this century, is introduced to young readers through excellent reproductions and photographs and a concise narrative which highlights the historical and artistic influences on his work. As a simple, informative, and well-designed book, this fluid translation is hard to beat.

Marzollo, Jean. *Feliz cumpleaños, Martin Luther King. (Happy Birthday, Martin Luther King, Jr.)* Illus: J. Brian Pinkney. Translated by Alberto Romo. New York: Scholastic, Inc., 1993. 32p. ISBN: 0-590-47507-X. pap. $4.95. Gr. Preschool-3.

Marzollo's and Pinkney's simple and effective look at King's life, which focuses on his ability to affect change and bring people together, is now available in this fluid Spanish translation. Like the original English version, this includes Pinkney's outstanding scratchboard art-bold pictures with changing perspectives that are immediate and moving.

Rachlin, Ann. *Chopin. (Chopin)* ISBN: 84-282-0998-7.
————. *Tchaikovsky. (Tchaikovsky)* ISBN: 84-282-1002-0.
Ea. vol.: 20p. Illus: Susan Hellard. Translated by Anna Tous. (Niños Famosos) Barcelona: Ediciones Omega, 1994. $9.95. Gr. 2-5.

In a simple and lighthearted manner, this series relates amusing anecdotes from the youths of well-known composers. *Chopin* highlights the composer's special relationship with his eccentric piano teacher. *Tchaikovsky* tells about Piotr's beloved governess, Fanny. Jovial watercolor and ink illustrations add a sense of mirth and reality to each composer's life. Other titles in this series, originally published by Aladdin Books, London, are: *Bach, Brahms, Haendel, Haydn, Mozart,* and *Schumann.*

Rambeck, Richard. *Kristi Yamaguchi.* Translated by Isabel Guerra. Chicago: Child's World/Encyclopedia Britannica, 1994. 31p. ISBN: 1-56766-109-2. $14.95. Gr. 3-5.

The professional career of Kristi Yamaguchi, the young ice skater who won the gold medal in women's figure skating in the 1992 Olympics, is depicted through beautiful color photos and a brief, easy-to-read text. Spanish-speaking skaters-to-be will appreciate this fluid translation that highlights the training and hard work required to become an Olympic champion.

Santiago, Esmeralda. *Cuando era puertorriqueña. (When I Was Puerto Rican)* New York: Vintage/Random, 1994. 296p. ISBN: 0-679-75677-9. pap. $11.00. Gr. 10-adult.

In a vivid and engrossing narrative, Esmeralda recounts her childhood in the poor barrios of Macui and Santurci, Puerto Rico, in the 1950s. She tells of her mother's constant pregnancies and a father who wasn't there most of the time; of her feelings about being a *jíbara*; of walking to school barefooted; of what "good" women thought about *putas*; and about her experiences upon immigrating to New York as a teenager. Mature Spanish-speaking readers will be inspired by these uplifting memoirs of a young woman who, despite growing up in a different language and cultural environment and suffering the deprivations of poverty, graduated from the prestigious Performing Arts High School and Harvard.

PUBLISHERS' SERIES

Baeza, Silvia P. *Música y baile*. *(Music and Dance)* ISBN: 0-86625-565-6.

Boswell, Bethanie L. *Hablamos dos idiomas*. *(Speaking Two Languages)* ISBN: 0-86625-562-1.

Clavin, Tracy. *Comida y cocina*. *(Food and Cooking)* ISBN: 0-86625-563-X.

Goring, Ruth. *Días festivos y celebraciones*. *(Holidays)* ISBN: 0-86625-564-8.

Jensen, Jeffrey. *Deportes*. *(Sports)* ISBN: 0-86625-566-4.

Villaseñor, Isabel B. *Vida en familia*. *(Family Life)* ISBN: 0-86625-561-3.

Ea. vol.: 48p. (Vida Latina) Translated by Argentina Palacios. Vero Beach, FL: Rourke Publications, 1995. $15.95. Gr. 4-7.

Latinos' cultural contributions to American society are explored in these fluid Spanish renditions with numerous black-and-white and color photographs. Readers are exposed to the Mexican *Bamba* and *Corrido*, Puerto Rican Rap and other popular Latino music and dance in *Música y baile*. Various aspects of bilingualism and the Spanish and English languages in Latino communities are discussed in *Hablamos dos idiomas*. Different types of Latino food and cooking are presented in *Comida y cocina*. *Días festivos y celebraciones* discusses Latino family celebrations as well as religious and national Latin American holidays. Biographical and historical information about Latino sports' stars are presented in *Deportes*. *Vida en familia* introduces readers to important aspects of traditional and contemporary Latino family life in the United States.

Baquedano, Elizabeth. *Aztecas, incas y mayas*. *(Aztecs, Incas, and Mayas)* Photos by Michel Zabé. ISBN: 84-372-3779-3.

Murdoch, David H. *Cowboys*. *(Cowboys)* Photos by Geoff Brightling. ISBN: 84-372-3781-5.

Ea. vol.: 64p. (Biblioteca Visual Altea) Madrid: Santillana, 1994. $18.95. Gr. 4-9.

Like the previous forty-three titles, originally published as Eyewitness Guides by Dorling Kindersley in London, these titles include numerous close-up color photographs and brief, clear descriptions that introduce readers to three pre-Columbian civilizations and to cowboys. *Aztecas, incas y mayas* includes details about Aztec, Inca, and Mayan history, lifestyles, agriculture, and religion. *Cowboys* begins with a brief chapter on what a cowboy is and continues with chapters on horses, law and order, guns, cowgirls, and others.

Brookfield, Karen. *La escritura. (Writing)* Photos by Lawrence Pordes. ISBN: 84-372-3780-7.

Papastavrou, Vassili. *Ballenas, delfines y otros mamíferos marinos. (Whales, Dolphins, and Other Marine Mammals)* Photos by Frank Greenaway. ISBN: 84-372-3778-5.

Redmond, Ian. *Elefantes. (Elephants)* Photos by Dave King. ISBN: 84-372-3774-2.

Ea. vol.: 64p. (Biblioteca Visual Altea) Madrid: Santillana, 1993-1994. $18.95. Gr. 4-9.

Like the previous forty-four titles in this excellent series, originally published in Great Britain under the title Eyewitness Encyclopedia in 1993, these introduce readers to whales and elephants and to writing from pre-historic times up to the twentieth century. Each title contains numerous outstanding close-up color photographs, charts, and drawings and clear, easy-to-understand descriptions.

Clarke, Barry. *Anfibios. (Amphibians)* Photos by Geoff Brightling and Frank Greenaway.

Gravett, Christopher. *Caballeros. (Knights)* Photos by Geoff Dann.

Putnam, James. *Momias. (Mummies)* Photos by Peter Hayman.

Ea. vol.: 64p. (Biblioteca Visual Altea) Madrid: Santillana, 1993. $19.95. Gr. 4-10.

Like their forty predecessors in this outstanding, large-format series, originally published in Great Britain as Eyewitness Guides, these contain excellent, close-up color photographs and drawings and concise, clear explanations about amphibians, the life and environment of medieval knights, and mummies, both those that nature has accidentally preserved by freezing and those preserved deliberately, like the Egyptian Pharaoh Ramses the Great. Certainly, these are attractive, easy-to-understand introductions to historical and scientific topics.

Clutton-Brock, Juliet. *Caballos. (Horses)* ISBN: 84-372-3766-1.

————. *Gatos. (Cats)* ISBN: 84-372-3765-3.

————. *Perros. (Dogs)* ISBN: 84-372-3763-7.

Coiley, John. *Trenes. (Trains)* ISBN: 84-372-3772-6.

Kentley, Eric. *Barcos. (Boats)* ISBN: 84-372-3769-6.

MacQuitty, Miranda. *Tiburones. (Sharks)* ISBN: 84-372-3770-X.

Matthews, Rupert. *Exploradores (Explorers)* ISBN: 84-372-3764-5.

Pearson, Anne. *La antigua Grecia. (Ancient Greece)* ISBN: 84-372-3771-8.

Rose, Susanna van. *Volcanes. (Volcanoes)* ISBN: 84-372-3773-4.

Rowland-Warne L. *Trajes. (Costumes)* ISBN: 84-372-3768-8.

Tubb, Jonathan N. *Los pueblos de la Biblia. (Bible Lands)* ISBN: 84-372-3762-9.

Ea. vol.: 64p. (Biblioteca Visual Altea) Madrid: Santillana, 1992-1993. $18.95. Gr. 4-10.

More titles from this outstanding, large-format series, originally published in Great Britain as Eyewitness Encyclopedia, contain excellent, close-up photographs, charts, and drawings in color and concise, clear explanations about horses, cats, dogs, trains, boats, sharks, explorers, volcanoes, costumes, and Bible lands. These are definitely attractive, easy-to-understand introductions to numerous topics in the fields of science and social science.

Drew, Helen. *Mi primer libro de música (My First Book of Music)* ISBN: 84-272-7080-1.

Leyton, Laurence. *Mi primer libro de magia (My First Book of Magic)* ISBN: 84-272-1710-2.

Ea. vol: 48p. Barcelona: Editorial Molino, 1993-1994. $20.55. Gr. 4-7.

Like their predecessors, these large-format volumes include clear, color photographs and simple, step-by-step directions that show children how to build simple musical instruments such as maracas, triangles, and drums, and how to do simple magic tricks such as making a handkerchief disappear and pulling a rabbit from a hat. Originally published by Dorling Kindersley, London, these easy-to-follow books are just right for musicians- and magicians-to-be.

Drew, Helen. *Mi primer libro de pastelería. (My First Baking Book)* 48p. ISBN: 84-272-1704-8.

Wilkes, Angela. *Mi primer libro de ecología. (My First Green Book)* 48p. ISBN: 84-272-1705-6.

————. *Mi primer libro de fiestas. (My First Party Book)* 48p. ISBN: 84-272-1706-4.

————. *Mi primer libro de palabras. (My First Word Book)* 64p. ISBN: 84-272-3239-X.

Ea. vol.: Barcelona: Editorial Molino, 1991. $19.55. Gr. 4-8.

Like their predecessors, these attractive, large-format publications include excellent photographs in color and simple, easy-to-follow, step-by-step directions that will encourage children to experiment.

Mi primer libro de pastelería includes simple baking recipes that children can make at home. *Mi primer libro de ecología* shows how young people can contribute to protect the environment. *Mi primer libro de fiestas* includes fun ideas for children's parties. *Mi primer libro de palabras* includes photographs and illustrations of 1,000 words commonly used by children. (This is the only title in the series for much younger children.) This outstanding series was originally published by Dorling Kindersley, London, in 1991.

Jeunesse, Gallimard, and André Verdet. *La hora.* *(Time)* Illus: Céline Bour-Chollet. ISBN: 84-348-4485-0.

Jeunesse, Gallimard, and others. *La pirámide.* *(Pyramid)* Illus: Philippe Biard. ISBN: 84-348-4487-7.

Jeunesse, Gallimard, and Pierre-Marie Valat. *El deporte.* *(Sports)* Illus: Pierre-Marie Valat. ISBN: 84-348-4486-9.
Ea. vol.: 36p. Translated by Paz Barroso. (Mundo Maravilloso) Madrid: Ediciones SM, 1995. $9.95. Gr. 2-4.

Like previous titles in this appealing series originally published in France, these include brief, simple texts and colorful illustrations on glossy pages intermingled between transparent plastic overlays that show before/after or inside/outside views of an Egyptian pyramid, the measurement and passage of time and the seasons, as well as numerous sports practiced around the world.

Platt, Richard. *Corsarios y piratas.* *(Pirate)* Photos by Tina Chambers. ISBN: 84-372-3804-8.

Taylor, Barbara. *La vida en los polos.* *(Arctic and Antarctic)* Photos by Geoff Brightling. ISBN: 84-372-3805-6.
Ea. vol.: 64p. (Biblioteca Visual Altea) Madrid: Santillana, 1995. $18.95. Gr. 4-10.

Two new titles from the outstanding large-format series, originally published in 1995 as Eyewitness Guides by Dorling Kindersley, London, these include excellent close-up color photographs, charts, and drawings and concise, clear explanations about pirates from early civilizations up to pirates in literature, movies and theater and life in the two polar regions of the Earth.

Priddy, Roger. *Libro de animales.* *(Baby's Book of Animals)* ISBN: 84-01-31540-9.

Wilkes, Angela. *Libro de números.* *(My Very First Number Book)* ISBN: 84-01-31536-0.

————. *Libro de palabras.* *(My Very First Word Book)* ISBN: 84-01-31538-7.
Ea. vol.: 22p. (Mi Primer) Barcelona: Plaza & Janés, 1993. $8.95. Ages 4-7.

Continuing with the excellence typical of this series by Dorling Kindersley these attractively designed books with excellent sharp photographs and clear labels introduce Spanish-speaking children (and those interested in learning Spanish) to the colors and sounds of animals and their young, to basic mathematical concepts, and to new words and activities. It is indeed difficult to find a better series in Spanish in which the very young can learn new words and concepts in an enjoyable and easy-to-understand manner.

FICTION

Easy Books

¡A jugar! *(Playtime)* ISBN: 0-525-44854-3.
La hora de la comida. *(Mealtime)* ISBN: 0-525-44855-1.
La hora del baño. *(Bathtime)* ISBN: 0-525-44857-8.
¡Mírame! *(Look at Me)* ISBN: 0-525-44853-5.
  Ea. vol.: 12p. (¡Asi Soy Yo!) Photos by Stephen Shott. New York: Dutton, 1992. $4.99. Ages 1-5.
  The very young will be delighted with these well-constructed board books that show babies and toddlers enjoying common activities while playing, eating, bathing, and looking. The excellent, clear photographs in color and the simple labels and sentences make this series, originally published by Dorling Kindersley in London in 1991, absolutely ideal for those just learning to speak or read Spanish.

¿A dónde volamos hoy? *(Where Do We Fly Today?)* ISBN: 84-272-7082-8.
¿A quién llamo? *(Who Should I Call?)* ISBN: 82-272-7081-X.
¡Llegan los bomberos! *(The Firemen Are Here!)* ISBN: 84-272-7083-6.
¡Ya viene la policía! *(Police Are Coming!)* ISBN: 84-272-7084-4.
  Ea. vol.: 12p. (Luz y Sonidos Mágicos) Barcelona: Editorial Molino, 1991. $12.00. Gr. Preschool-2.
  Upon pushing a button, these "magic light and sound books" activate a red light and reproduce the sound of a telephone ringing, an airplane flying, and the sirens of police cars and fire engines. These well-constructed board books with appealing colorful illustrations will delight children as they wonder who they should call to save Mimi, the kitten; where they should fly; and what happens when someone calls the fire station or the police. These combination stories and action-books should provide the right amount of fun for eager minds and fingers.

Ada, Alma Flor. *Cómo nació el arco iris.* *(How the Rainbow Came to Be)* 14p. ISBN: 1-56014-220-0.

————. *El susto de los fantasmas.* *(What Are Ghosts Afraid of?)* 14p. ISBN: 1-56014-222-7.

Ea. vol.: Illus: *Vivi Escrivá.* *(Cuentos Para Todo el Año)* Compton, CA: Santillana, 1991. pap. $9.95. Gr. 2-4.

The cheerful, full-page watercolor illustrations on each of these stories are most appealing. *Cómo nació el arco iris* explains in a lighthearted manner what each color contributes to nature and *El susto de los fantasmas* shows what ghosts are afraid of at Halloween.

Ada, Alma Flor. *¿Pavo para la Cena de Gracias?—¡No, gracias!* *(Turkey for Thanksgiving? No, Thank You!)* 22p. ISBN: 1-56014-331-2.

————. *La piñata vacía.* *(The Empty Piñata)* 16p. ISBN: 1-56014-225-1.

Ea. vol.: Illus: *Vivi Escrivá.* *(Cuentos Para Todo el Año)* Compton, CA: Santillana, 1993. pap. $9.95. Gr. K-2.

These are the best stories in this series. *¿Pavo para la Cena de Gracias?—¡No, gracias!* is an amusing imitation of *Charlotte's Web* in which a turkey is saved by an ingenious spider, and *La piñata vacía* is a story in rhyme about Elena and her empty/full piñata.

Alexander, Martha. *La bota de Lalo.* *(Billy's Boot)* ISBN: 968-16-4200-7.

————. *Buenas noches, Lola.* *(Good Night, Lily)* ISBN: 968-16-4202-3.

————. *Lola y Lalo.* *(Lily and Billy)* ISBN: 968-16-4201-5.

Ea. vol.: 16p. Translated by Francisco Segovia. México: Fondo de Cultura Económica, 1993. $5.99. Ages 2-5.

Charming colored pencil illustrations depicting toddlers putting away their toys, reading a book just before falling asleep, and mimicking each other are accompanied by brief, simple texts. Originally published by Walker Books, London, these attractive board books, which are sure to please the very young, definitely capture the moods and activities of toddlers everywhere.

Aliki. *Mis cinco sentidos* *(My Five Senses)* Translated by Daniel Santacruz. (Aprende y Descubre la Ciencia) New York: Harper Arco Iris/HarperCollins, 1995. 32p. ISBN: 0-06-025358-4. $14.95; ISBN: 0-06-445138-0. pap. $4.95. Ages 4-6.

(See review under Science and Technology.)

Animales de la granja. *(Farm Animals)* ISBN: 950-11-0901-1.
Animales de la selva. *(Jungle Animals)* ISBN: 950-11-0900-3.
Animales del zoológico. *(Zoo Animals)* ISBN: 950-11-0898-8.
Mascotas. *(Pets)* ISBN: 950-11-0899-6.
   Ea. vol.: 20p. Translated by Olga Colella. (Abre Tus Ojos)
   Buenos Aires: Editorial Sigmar, 1992. pap. $5.95. Gr. K-2.
   This excellent paperback series introduces young children to
well-known animals through vivid photographs and drawings in
color and a simple text in large, clear type. Originally published by
Dorling Kindersley in Great Britain in 1991, this series is just right
for young children as they learn basic facts about pets as well as
farm, jungle, and zoo animals. Perhaps some adults will disapprove because these books are in paperback; however, young
children will definitely appreciate and praise them.

Ashforth, Camilla. *La cama de Horacio.* *(Horatio's Bed)* Illus: the
   author.   Translated by Andrea B. Bermúdez.   Compton, CA:
   Santillana, 1995. 26p. ISBN: 1-56014-581-1. pap. $11.95. Gr.
   Preschool-2.
   Horatio, a delightful stuffed bunny rabbit has trouble sleeping at
night so he consults his friend, Jaime, a helpful teddy bear. Joyous,
double-page pastel illustrations provide a tender background to
Horatio's dilemma. This excellent Spanish rendition will enthrall
young Spanish speakers and listeners just as the original English
edition did, first published by Walker Books in Great Britain.

Así o asá: jugando al escondite. *(Thus and So: Playing Hide-and-
   Seek)* Illus: Elve Fortis de Hieronymis. Madrid: Editorial Edaf,
   1992. 8p. ISBN: 84-7640-606-1. $15.95. Gr. K-2.
   Definitely a fun pull-the-tab board book in which children can
play hide-and-seek with a duck, a frog, a hen, a fox, a pig, a bunny,
a wolf, a sheep, and other animals. The colorful illustrations, simple
rhyming texts, and clever situations will appeal to all children as
they "find" animals in hiding.   And adults will appreciate the
sturdy construction, which will resist a lot of pulling and looking.

Balzola, Sofía, and Pablo Barrena. *¿Qué animal es?* *(What Animal Is
   It?)* (Los Duros del Barco de Vapor) Madrid: Ediciones SM,
   1993. 14p. ISBN: 84-348-3964-4. $13.95. Gr. Preschool-1.
   A mouse, a fox, a swallow, and an elephant are admiring an
animal in the garden. They marvel at its beautiful colors, but don't
know what kind of animal it is. Finally the peacock smiles and
explains that it is an animal just like them. Exquisite watercolor
illustrations of animals enjoying their dilemma and the simple text
make this board book truly special.

110   *Recommended Books in Spanish for Children and Young Adults*

Barklem, Jill. *Altas colinas. (High Hills)* ISBN: 84-406-2743-2.
————. *La escalera secreta. (The Secret Staircase)* ISBN: 84-406-2744-0.
Ea. vol.: 30p. Illus: the author. Translated by Dolores Berenguer (Villa Zarzal) Barcelona: Ediciones B, 1992. $8.95. Gr. 2-4.

A family of mice lives in the countryside on the other side of the river in a place called Villa Zarzal. This beautiful location is certainly conducive to exciting adventures: *Altas colinas* shows how Alfredo, a courageous mouse, becomes a hero by saving his group during a storm.   Alfredo's discovery of a fantastic dwelling is depicted in *La escalera secreta.* Originally published in Great Britain by HarperCollins, this series includes the same outstanding pastel illustrations full of exquisite details and charm. Other titles in this series are *Cuento de primavera (Spring Story), Cuento de verano (Summer Story), Cuento de otoño (Fall Story),* and *Cuento de invierno (Winter Story).*

Bell, Clarisa. *El circo. (The Circus)* ISBN: 1-56492-078X.
————. *En las olimpíadas. (At the Olympics)* ISBN: 1-56492-051-8.
————. *El teatro. (The Theater)* ISBN: 1-56492-056-9.
————. *Vamos a jugar. (Let's Play)* ISBN:1-56492-048-8.
Ea. vol.: 24p. (Esto Es Divertidísimo) Illus: José Ramón Sánchez. Los Angeles: Laredo Publishing, 1992. pap. $9.95. Gr. 2-4.

Through delightful, witty watercolor illustrations and a rhyming text, children will read about fun activities at the circus, at the Olympics, at the theater, and at play. These are indeed a wonderful introduction to these topics or just fun to read, look at, and enjoy.

Bemelmans, Ludwig. *Madeline. (Madeline)* Illus: the author. Translated by Ernesto Livon Grosman. New York: The Viking Press, 1993. 48p. ISBN: 0-670-85154-X. $14.99. Ages 4-8.

Bemelmans's unforgettable classic about twelve little girls in two straight lines and Madeline, who must be rushed off to the hospital, has maintained the charm of the original in this jocular Spanish translation with the ever-popular three-tone line illustrations in a Parisian setting.

Bertrand, Cécile. *Víctor mira. (Víctor Looks)* ISBN: 84-87560-46-6.
————. *Víctor oye. (Víctor Hears)* ISBN: 84-87560-45-8.
————. *Víctor saborea. (Víctor Tastes)* ISBN: 84-87560-48-2.
————. *Víctor toca. (Víctor Touches)* ISBN: 84-87560-47-4.
Ea. vol.: 12p. El Masnou, Spain: Manuel Salvat Vilá Editor, 1993. $8.95. Ages 3-6.

The senses are introduced to the very young by Víctor, a good-humored toddler, who looks, hears, tastes, and touches things at home and at the playground. The most appealing, full-page watercolor illustrations are witty and charming as they contrast the likes and dislikes of toddlers everywhere. In addition, the simple, easy-to-understand text makes these board books originally published by Baronian Books, just plain fun.

Blacker, Terence. *Visto y no visto, ¿Dónde se esconde el hámster?* *(Houdini, the Disappearing Hamster)* Illus: Pippa Univin. Translated from the English by Mireia Blasco. Barcelona: Ediciones B, 1991. 29p. ISBN: 84-406-2059-4. $10.50. Gr. K-2.

Houdini, the disappearing hamster, is lost and found by numerous people in the neighborhood creating much excitement in the process. Children will delight in these full-page line and watercolor illustrations filled with action and lots of fun. The simple text is an added joy for young children. Originally published in Great Britain, this story will be loved by all.

Boase, Wendy. *Caperucita Roja. (Red Riding Hood)* Illus: Heather Philpott. ISBN: 1-56014-458-0.
————. *Tres chivos testarudos. (Billy Goats Gruff)* Illus: Carolyn Bull. ISBN: 1-56014-457-2.
————. *Los tres osos. (The Three Bears)* Illus: Carolyn Bull. ISBN: 1-56014-475-0.
Ea. vol.: 28p. (Primeros Cuentos) Translated by María Puncel. Compton, CA: Santillana, 1994. pap. $8.50. Gr. K-3.

The perennial appeal of these long-time favorites make these excellent Spanish renditions a joy to read or listen to. The well-conceived watercolor illustrations depicting a charming Red Riding Hood, three stubborn billy goats, and three kind-hearted bears add to this paperback series' obvious pleasurable intent.

Brown, Margaret Wise. *El conejito andarín. (The Runaway Bunny)* Illus: Clement Hurd. Translated by Aída E. Marcuse. New York: HarperCollins, 1995. 38p. ISBN: 0-06-025434-3. $12.95; pap. ISBN: 0-06-44339-0. $4.95. Ages 4-7.

Originally published in 1942, this engaging story about a bunny who gives up the idea of running away is now available to young Spanish speakers. The tender black-and-white line illustrations and the bright color hues are just as reassuring, especially when the bunny decides to stay home with mama instead of going to distant places.

Browne, Anthony. *Cambios. (Changes)* Illus: the author. Translated by Carmen Esteva. México: Fondo de Cultura Económica, 1993. 32p. ISBN: 968-16-4270-8. $12.95. Gr. Preschool-3.

As Papa leaves home one morning, he tells José that there will be changes at home. José visualizes all kinds of changes such as an alligator under a sofa, a chair that becomes a gorilla, a soccer ball that when kicked hatches a mature bird, and huge eyes that appear behind a wall. When the door opens, José sees his father, mother, and a baby—his new sister. The striking, full-page color illustrations and a most simple text definitely capture the spirit of the changes to come in José's life in this large-format book, originally published by Julia MacRae Books, London, in 1990.

Browne, Anthony. *Cosas que me gustan. (Things I Like)* ISBN: 968-16-3779-8.
————. *Me gustan los libros. (I Like Books)* ISBN: 968-16-3780-1. Ea. vol.: 20p. (Los Especiales) Translated by Carmen Esteva. México: Fondo de Cultura Económica, 1992. $11.99. Gr. Preschool-2.

Anthony Browne's charming chimpanzee will delight all readers and viewers as he tells about the things he likes (e.g., riding his tricycle, playing with his toys, building sand castles) in *Cosas que me gustan* and about the different types of books he likes in *Me gustan los libros.* Originally published by Julia MacRae Books in London in 1988, these books will certainly appeal to all Spanish speakers, their parents, and their teachers who won't be able to resist the chimpanzee's special allure. The ingenuous, colorful illustrations will provide unlimited joy to all viewers.

Browne, Anthony. *Willy el tímido. (Willy the Wimp)* Illus: the author. Translated from the English by Carmen Esteva. México: Fondo de Cultura Económica, 1991. 32p. ISBN: 968-16-3653-8. $13.30. Gr. K-3.

Willy does not like the fact that he is a wimp so he decides to do something about it. He exercises, eats a special diet, learns to box, lifts weights, and is delighted with the results. He also saves Millie from the town bullies and becomes her hero. The colorful, bold illustrations and an easy-to-read, fun text are just right for young readers. This story was originally published in Great Britain in 1984.

Browne, Anthony. *Willy y Hugo. (Willy and Hugh)* Illus: the author. Translated by Carmen Esteva. México: Fondo de Cultura Económica, 1993. 26p. ISBN: 968-16-4271-6. $12.95. Gr. Preschool-3.

Willy, a chimpanzee, is sad and lonely. He does not have any friends and all the big boys won't let him play. One day he meets Hugo, a big gorilla, and they become good friends. They enjoy their friendship, as well as their visit to the zoo, looking at humans in a cage, and other unexpected treats. The striking full-page illustrations in bright colors of a "little boy" confronting tough bully gorillas will warm the hearts of all listeners and readers. The simple text has been excellently translated into Spanish. Originally published by Julia MacRae Books in London in 1991.

Browne, Anthony. *Zoológico. (Zoo)* Illus: the author. Translated by Carmen Esteva. México: Fondo de Cultura Económica, 1993. 26p. ISBN: 968-16-4272-4. $12.95. Gr. 1-4.

A little boy describes a most frustrating trip to the zoo with his younger brother, father, and mother: His father argues about almost everything, the boys are hungry, and mother concludes that the zoo is really for people, not for animals. The realistic, watercolor illustrations definitely capture the excitement and ennui that many families have experienced in their trips to the zoo. This is a well-done translation of the original version, published by Julia MacRae in London in 1992.

Brunhoff, Laurent de. *Un día de Babar. (Babar's Day)* Madrid: Plaza Joven, 1986. 8p. ISBN: 84-7655-272-6. $6.75. Gr. Pre-school-1.

Through Babar, a young elephant, and his family, small children learn the principles of telling time from 6:00 o'clock in the morning until bedtime. A clock with movable hands, attractive watercolor illustrations of Babar in his daily activities, and a sturdy board construction make this book ideal to teach the concept of time or just to enjoy.

Brusca, María Cristina, and Tona Wilson. *Three Friends: A Counting Book/Tres amigos: Un cuento para contar.* New York: Holt, 1995. 32p. ISBN: 0-8050-3707-1. $14.95. Ages 3-7.

Learning to count from one to ten in English and Spanish is indeed fun in this short, succinct, bilingual southwestern adventure. Humorous, cartoon-like watercolors joyfully depict three "amigos"—a cowboy, a cowgirl, and their horse—as they jump, sing, run, tumble, and sleep in the desert. Unfortunately, however, the definite articles, which must agree in number and gender with the noun they accompany and are used very frequently in Spanish, are not included in the picture dictionary of a few extra words that cowboys or cowgirls might find handy to know.

Burningham, John. *Contrarios.* *(Opposites)* Madrid: Ediciones Altea, 1986. 26p. ISBN: 84-372-8028-1. $9.00. Gr. Preschool-1.

Delicate, pastel illustrations of children in humorous situations serve as ideal introductions to the concept of opposites, such as wet/dry, hot/cold, heavy/light, slow/fast, and others.

Burningham, John. *¿Qué prefieres . . . (Would you Rather?)* Illus: the author. Translated by Esther Roehrich-Rubio. Madrid: Kókinos, 1994. 32p. ISBN: 84-88342-05-5. $15.95. Gr. K-3.

Children won't be able to resist Burningham's choices as he asks children: Would you rather have someone pour marmalade on your head? water? or be pulled by a dog through the mud? Or, have dinner in a castle? breakfast in a balloon? or supper on a boat? All alternatives are either all wonderful or not desirable. The witty, charming watercolor illustrations are as engrossing as the simple, well-conceived text. This large-format book, originally published in Great Britain in 1978, will definitely encourage participation by eager Spanish-speaking readers and listeners.

Butterworth, Nick. *Cuando es hora de ir a la cama.* *(Bedtime)* ISBN: 84-261-2933-1.

———. *Cuando jugamos juntos.* *(Play Time)* ISBN: 84-261-2934-X. Ea. vol.: 16p. (Mis Amigos) Barcelona: Editorial Juventud, 1995. $7.95. Ages 2-5.

Just right for the very young, these delightful board books depict through gentle color illustrations and simple texts a toddler getting ready for bed and playing with his toys. Other titles in this series, originally published by HarperCollins, London, are *Cuando hay que trabajar (Chores)* and *Cuando vamos a comprar (When We Go Shopping).*

Butterworth, Nick. *Un día libre ajetreado.* *(The Rescue Party)* Illus: the author. Translated by Paulina Fariza. Barcelona: Ediciones Destino, 1993. 24p. ISBN: 84-233-2335-8. $10.95. Gr. 1-3.

Tomás, a kind-hearted forest ranger, is looking forward to a relaxing day in the forest. But his plans are abruptly changed when a bunny experiences an unexplained mishap. The soft, watercolor pastel illustrations of Tomás and his numerous animal friends working hard to assist the ingenious bunny alongside the easy flowing Spanish text make this rendition as appealing as the original first published by HarperCollins in London.

Butterworth, Nick. *Una noche de nieve.* *(One Snowy Night)* Illus: the author. Translated by Pilar Jufresa. Barcelona: Ediciones Destino, 1993. 24p. ISBN: 84-233-2276-9. $12.95. Gr. K-3.

Tomás, a forest ranger, is happy to feed the animals in the park where he lives. But one cold winter night, he discovers that his friends need more than just food. The charming, pastel watercolor illustrations of Tomás and his animal friends combined with the easy-flowing Spanish translation make this snowy night as appealing as the original published by HarperCollins in 1989.

Carle, Eric. *La oruga muy hambrienta.* *(The Very Hungry Caterpillar)* Illus: the author. Translated by Aída E. Marcuse. New York: Philomel Books, 1994. 26p. ISBN: 0-399-22780-6. $16.95. Ages 3-6.
Carle's popular story about a very hungry caterpillar who becomes a beautiful butterfly is fortunately now available in this revised Spanish-language edition with the original bold watercolor illustrations.

Charles, Donald. *Gato Galano observa los colores.* *(Calico Cat Looks at Colors)* Illus: the author. Translated by Juan Quintana. Chicago: Children's Press, 1992. 32p. ISBN: 0-516-33437-9. $11.25. Gr. Preschool-2.
Gato Galano's (Calico Cat's) adventures with the colors of the rainbow are a perfect introduction to basic colors to young Spanish speakers. The vibrant illustrations are as lively and fun as the originals in the English version.

Claverie, Jean, and Michelle Nikly. *El arte de la baci.* *(The Art of the Chamber Pot)* Translated by Maribel G. Martínez and L. Rodríguez. Salamanca: Lóguez Ediciones, 1993. 26p. ISBN: 84-85334-70-1. $15.95. Ages 2-5.
With gusto and good taste, the authors tell about the art of the chamber pot—or how to use the potty. A lively, rhyming, simple text and soft full-page, charcoal illustrations depict little boys and girls experiencing the trials and tribulations of learning how to use the potty, such as pushing hard and not succeeding and falling asleep. The point is that each child can do what he or she pleases while using the potty, including reading the newspaper, which is exactly what papa does when he uses the toilet. Squeamish adults certainly will disapprove; children, however, know all this is true.

Cole, Babette. *El libro apestoso.* *(The Smelly Book)* Translated by Francisco Segovia. México: Fondo de Cultura Económica, 1994. 32p. ISBN: 968-16-4559-6. $10.99. Ages 3-7.
With humor and imagination children will learn how many things really stink such as camels that smell like wee-wee, wild boars that smell like poo-poo, skunks that make you jump, papa's

foul feet that drive mother crazy, nauseous socks, and naughty things that children can improvise with to cause bad smells. Originally published by Jonathan Cape, London, in 1987, this charming Spanish rendition includes Cole's whimsical full-page watercolor illustrations brimming with candor and child appeal.

Cole, Babette. *¡Mamá puso un huevo! o cómo se hacen los niños.* *(Mummy Laid an Egg)* Translated by Pilar Jufresa. Barcelona: Ediciones Destino, 1993. 26p. ISBN: 84-233-2288-2. $14.95. Gr. K-3.

Originally published by Jonathan Cape in London in 1993, this amusing explanation of how children are made is sure to offend many, yet it describes the concepts of conception, reproduction, and birth in a manner that is just right for the young. The first part explains the reproductive system to children like *some* adults do: "Girls are made of sugar, vanilla, and other nice things," "Some children are delivered by dinosaurs," "Some children are found in pots" and other such nonsense. The second part shows a boy and a girl laughing at their parents' silliness and explaining to them, through simple line drawings and comments, how children are *really* made. This is not a physiological exposition but rather a direct, honest, and whimsical approach to a topic that is difficult for some adults to discuss with children. Cole's full-page watercolor illustrations will please, inform and, perhaps, provoke.

Cole, Babette. *¡Tarzana!* *(Tarzanna!)* Translated by Pilar Jufresa. Barcelona: Ediciones Destino, 1993. 30p. ISBN: 84-233-2274-2. $14.95. Gr. K-2.

Tarzana lives in the jungle with her animal friends. She is really surprised when she meets Gerald, a boy who spends his time studying spiders and who invites her to visit his country. Gerald's parents are wonderful but life in the city turns out to be hectic and dangerous. Thus, all return to live in the jungle. The full-page watercolor illustrations are witty and fun; the Spanish translation is absolutely charming.

Colmont, Marie. *Michka.* *(Michka)* Illus: Gérard Franquin. Translated by Ángel García Aller. Madrid: Editorial Everest, 1993. 32p. ISBN: 84-241-3345-5. $19.95. Gr. 1-3.

Michka, a teddy bear, is not happy with Elisabeth, his disagreeable mistress who gets rid of toys the moment she finds something else to do. Fortunately, Michka runs into the Christmas Reindeer and a sick boy receives a Christmas gift after all. The tender, full-page color illustrations make this story truly special.

Colores. (Colors) ISBN: 950-11-0904-6.
Contando. (Counting) ISBN: 950-11-0903-8.
Formas. (Shapes) ISBN: 950-11-0905-4.
Opuestos. (Opposites) ISBN: 950-11-0906-2.
Tamaños. (Sizes) ISBN: 950-11-0907-0.
Tocando. (Touch) ISBN: 950-11-0902-X.
    Ea. vol.: 18p. (Primeras Imágenes) Buenos Aires: Editorial Sigmar, 1992. pap. $5.95. Gr. K-2.
    Young children will delight in these simple concept books that explain basic colors, numbers one to ten, shapes, opposites, sizes, and the sense of touch through images and simple phrases. Vibrant color photographs of things that the very young can readily identify combined with easy-to-understand sentences make this paperback series, originally published by Dorling Kindersley in 1990, ideal to introduce children to basic math and science concepts.

Colores. (Colors) ISBN: 84-7773-397-X.
Formas. (Shapes) ISBN: 84-7773-398-8.
Números. (Numbers) ISBN: 84-7773-399-6.
    Ea. vol.: 12p. (Colección Recreo) Madrid: Grafalco, S.A., 1991. $5.50. Gr. Preschool-1.
    Bold, full-page watercolor illustrations introduce basic concepts to the very young in these attractive and durable board books. Especially noteworthy is how the authors and illustrators (unfortunately not credited in the books) conceived and executed in a most simple and direct way, the concepts of color, shapes, and numbers one to ten. Also in these series *AEIOU.*

Cowcher, Helen. *El bosque tropical. (Rain Forest)* Translated by Rita Gilbert. New York: Farrar, Straus, and Giroux, 1992. 34p. ISBN: 0-374-30900-0. $15.00. Gr. 1-3.
    Through vivid, powerful, watercolor illustrations and a direct text, children are informed about the dangers of machines that are cutting and destroying the rain forest. This is indeed a trenchant albeit fictionalized interpretation of the effects of "machines" on rain forests. Many will definitely approve. The Spanish translation conveys the author's powerful message.

Cowcher, Helen. *La tigresa. (Tigress)* Translated by Aída E. Marcuse. New York: Mirasol/Farrar, Straus, and Giroux, 1993. 34p. ISBN: 0-374-37565-8. $16.00. Ages 4-7.
    Cowcher's powerful depiction of the problem of a tigress who wanders out of her protected sanctuary and kills the livestock of local village herdsmen has been dramatically maintained in this most effective Spanish translation. Vivid color paintings of land-

scapes, people, and animals will help even the youngest readers understand the need to respect two ways of life—that of humans and that of animals.

Day, Alexandra. *Carlito en el parque una tarde.* *(Carl's Afternoon in the Park)* Translated by Carmen Malvido. New York: Mirasol/ libros juveniles Farrar, Straus, and Giroux, 1992. 32p. ISBN: 0-374-31100-5. $11.95. Gr. Preschool-1.

Day's humor and sense of adventure combined with luxuriously textured, brightly hued oil paintings of Rottweiler Carl and a happy toddler make this almost wordless picture book a joyous afternoon in the park. Six easy-to-understand sentences in Spanish are most appropriate as introduction and conclusion to this story about a reliable and attentive babysitter.

De Beer, Hans. *Al mar, al mar, osito polar.* *(To Sea, To Sea, Polar Bear)* Illus: the author. Translated by Mercedes Roffé. New York: Ediciones Norte-Sur, 1995. 26p. ISBN: 1-55858-504-4. pap. $6.95. Gr. 2-4.

Like previous Polar Bear books that related the adventures of Lars, a little polar bear, as he travels around the world, this one has gorgeous, pastel watercolor illustrations and an easy-flowing Spanish text with lots of action. Here, Lars meets Nemo, a friendly cat who shows him the big, dirty city. Of course, it's always wonderful to return home to mama and papa.

De Beer, Hans. *El oso valiente y el conejo miedoso.* *(The Brave Bear and the Fearful Rabbit)* Illus: the author. Translated from the German by Miguel Azaola. Madrid: Ediciones SM, 1995. 45p. ISBN: 84-348-4545-8. $13.95. Gr. 1-3.

Lars, a polar bear, is constantly telling Hugo that he is a fearful rabbit. Lars, on the other hand, is a very brave polar bear. Until he gets trapped in an office in the Artic and Hugo has to figure out how to rescue him. Lars admits that he was afraid and promises to never call Hugo a fearful rabbit. The double-page spreads done in gentle colors and soft lines provide a touching background to this lively story about friendship, originally published by Nord-Süd Verlag, Hamburg, in 1992.

De Beer, Hans. *El osito polar.* *(Polar Bear)* Illus: the author. Translated by Silvia Arana. New York: Ediciones Norte Sur, 1995. 26p. ISBN: 1-55858-390-4. pap. $5.95. Gr. 2-4.

Gorgeous, pastel watercolor illustrations depicting Little Polar Bear's adventures in the tropics are the most spectacular aspect of this attractive, large-format paperback book, originally published in

Switzerland. Spanish-speaking readers and listeners will rejoice with Little Polar Bear's experiences in the hot, tropical jungle and his return to a loving father.

de Paola, Tomie. *La clase de dibujo.* *(The Art Lesson)* Illus: the author. Translated by Juan González Álvaro. Madrid: Editorial Everest, 1993. 32p. ISBN: 84-241-3341-2. $11.95. Gr. K-3.

De Paola's perceptive story about Tommy, a tousle-haired little boy who is captivated by drawing and is sadly disappointed by art class in kindergarten as well as bureaucratic regimentation in first grade, will delight Spanish speakers who certainly know a lot about red tape and official do's and don'ts. De Paola's color-drenched artwork is as appealing as the original English version, published in 1989.

de Paola, Tomie. *El libro de las palomitas de maíz.* *(The Popcorn Book)* Translated by Teresa Mlawer. New York: Holiday House, 1993. 32p. ISBN: 0-8234-1058-7. $14.95; ISBN: 0-8234-1059-5. pap. $5.95. Gr. 1-3.

Spanish speakers will enjoy reading how Tony eagerly makes popcorn, and Tiny enthusiastically reads about it while two plump cats look on contentedly. De Paola's robust full-color illustrations and the easy-to-understand Spanish translation will be appreciated by popcorn lovers and other young listeners and readers.

Denou, Violeta. *La familia de Teo.* *(Teo's Family)* ISBN: 84-7722-615-6.

———. *Vamos al zoo, Teo.* *(Let's Go to the Zoo, Teo)* ISBN: 84-7722-616-4.

Ea. vol.: 10p. Barcelona: Timun Mas, 1991. $5.95. Ages 2-5.

Lively and delightful wordless board books that tell a story on every page through the expressions and activities of charming characters. The full-page, warm watercolor illustrations of things easily recognized by young children are fun and witty. These are indeed superior wordless picture books that will delight the very young as they recognize family members and visit a zoo. Fortunately, these well-constructed board books will take a lot of abuse.

Denou, Violeta. *Teo en el hipermercado.* *(Teo at the Supermarket)* Illus: the author. (Teo Descubre el Mundo) Barcelona: Timun Mas, 1992. 28p. ISBN: 84-7722-942-2. $13.95. Gr. Preschool-1.

Teo and his parents at the supermarket are realistically portrayed in Denou's amusing double-page spreads in full color. The vivacious, detailed illustrations definitely capture the bustle and confusion of a Saturday afternoon in which Teo helps Mama, another boy gets lost, and all have a good time. The simple text is easy-to-understand despite the use of the verb forms: *"os gusta," "habéis ayudado" "os gustaría"* which are only used in Spain.

Denou, Violeta. *Teo y sus abuelos. (Teo and His Grandparents)* Illus: the author. (Teo Descubre el Mundo) Barcelona: Timun Mas, 1992. 28p. ISBN: 84-7722-743-8. $9.50. Gr. K-2.

Like its predecessors in the series, "Teo Discovers the World," this attractive book includes lively, full-page illustrations in color and a simple text. In this one Teo and his brother spend a few days in the country with their grandparents picking fruit, making marmalade, riding ponies, and other fun activities.

Duckett, Elizabeth. *No os lo podéis imaginar. (You Can't Imagine)* Illus: Chiara Carrer. Barcelona: Ediciones Destino, 1994. 30p. ISBN: 84-233-2384-6. $14.95. Gr. K-3.

Trebolino is the smallest rabbit of his litter. He prefers to stay close to his burrow rather than to search for food on a faraway farm. But the other rabbits insisted that he come along. Trebolino's encounters with danger as he responds to a frightened mouse, an angry cat, a ferocious ermine, and a red fox make him a real hero. Bold double-page color spreads with attractive borders of carrots and rabbits and an ingenious mix of collages against white or black backgrounds add a sense of excitement to Trebolino's urgency to get home as fast as possible.

Dunn, Phoebe. *Los animales domésticos. (Domestic Animals)* ISBN: 0-679-84169-5. 28p. (A Chunky Book) New York: Random House, 1993. $3.25. Ages 2-5.

Originally published in English in 1984, this well-constructed, hand-sized (3 1/2 by 3 1/2 inches) board book will appeal to young Spanish speakers. The color photographs and captions of well-known domestic animals are especially attractive.

Eastman, P.D. *¡Corre, perro, corre! (Go, Dog, Go!)* Translated by Teresa Mlawer. New York: Lectorum Publications, 1992. 64p. ISBN: 1-880507-02-1. $8.95. Gr. 1-3.

Beginning Spanish-speaking readers will be able to practice their newly acquired reading skills through repetition and a predictable text in this well-done translation of Eastman's story about happy, energetic dogs who are always ready to party.

Elzbieta. *Mimí y la bruja. (Mimi's Scary Theater)* Illus: the author. Translated by Enrique Sánchez Pascual. Barcelona: Ediciones B, 1993. 20p. ISBN: 84-406-3620-2. $19.95. Gr. Preschool-2.

Attractively constructed like a portable theater—each of the nine scenes is depicted with colorful pull-out flaps highlighting significant actions, such as a little girl hitting a wolf who hides behind a bush—this is indeed a novel way to introduce young children to the theater. In addition, the entertaining play about Mimi, a brave girl, who outwits the horrible witch and escapes with Pedro, a handsome prince, is sure to appeal to readers and listeners who can participate by pulling the tabs and activating the characters. This fun theater book was originally published by Sadie Fields, London, in 1993.

Emberley, Rebecca. *Let's Go/Vamos.* ISBN: 0-316-23454-0.
——————. *My Day/Mi día.* ISBN: 0-316-23450-8.
Ea. vol.: Illus: the author. Boston: Little, Brown, and Company, 1993. 26p. $15.95. Gr. K-3.

Like previous Emberley books, these include lively, cut-paper collages, bright colors, and appealing combinations as well as simple bilingual (English and Spanish) sentences and labels. *Let's Go/Vamos* invites children to visit places such as the zoo, the aquarium, the beach, the circus, and other fun places. *My Day/Mi día* describes a child's daily activities through well-known items from unusual perspectives. In contrast to her previous books, young Spanish speakers and readers will be delighted with the Spanish translations, with two unfortunate exceptions: *"Sandwiches"* [sic] and *"la oscura"* [sic]. (This word doesn't even exist in Spanish. *"Oscura"* is an adjective; the noun is *"oscuridad."*)

Ets, Marie Hall. *Gilberto y el viento. (Gilberto and the Wind)* Illus: the author. Translated by Teresa Mlawer. New York: Lectorum Publications, 1995. 32p. ISBN: 1-880507-16-1. $11.95; ISBN: 1-8805-0719-6. pap. $5.95. Gr. K-3.

Gilberto's poetic story as he plays with the wind has maintained the lyricism of the original in this fluid rendition. Spanish-speaking readers and viewers will enjoy countless readings of Ets's playful pastels of white, browns, and pale yellow against the soft gray background.

Farris, Katherine. *Let's Speak Spanish!: A First Book of Words.* Illus: Linda Hendry. New York: Viking, 1993. 48p. ISBN: 0-670-84994-4. $11.99. Gr. 1-4.

Clearly and correctly labeled pictures in Spanish and English introduce vocabulary for familiar objects, events, concepts, numbers, and opposites. Beginning with my house and my family, Spanish-speaking or English-speaking students will enjoy learning new words as they build a vocabulary of more than 500 nouns, verbs, and phrases. The bright, watercolor illustrations add a festive touch to those learning Spanish words for clothes, the human body, breakfast time, going to school, going on a trip, animals, the city, the store, and more. A pronunication guide to Spanish words makes this easy-format book even more useful to non-Spanish-speaking adults who wish to speak Spanish immediately.

Faulkner, Keith, and Jonathan Lambert. *¡Tic Tac! (Tick! Tock! Teddy)* Translated by María Rabassa. Barcelona: Ediciones B, 1993. 10p. ISBN: 84-406-3624-5. $12.79. Gr. K-2.

Children will learn to tell time with Teddy Bear's clock by changing the position of the clock's hour hand and by moving well-constructed circles on the side of each page. Bright, watercolor illustrations and a lively, rhyming text depict Teddy Bear getting up at 8:00, having breakfast at 9:00, playing with his friends at 10:00, etc. Telling time is fun and easy with Teddy's clock.

Feder, Jane. *Table, Chair, Bear: A Book in Many Languages.* Illus: by the author. New York: Ticknor & Fields, 1995. 30p. ISBN: 0-395-65938-8. $13.95. Ages 3-7.

Bright, simple acrylic illustrations introduce children to common objects in thirteen different languages—English, Korean, French, Arabic, Vietnamese, Japanese, Portuguese, Lao, Spanish, Chinese, Tagalog, Cambodian, and Navajo. A simple pronunciation guide under each word will assist children, with the help of an adult, who are learning any of these languages. The only caveat that surely will be noted by Spanish speakers is that in this attractive vocabulary book, the author indicates that this is Mexican Spanish but neglects to specify that this is American English. If one language clarification is used, the other should be included as well.

Fowler, Allan. *Podría ser un árbol. (It Could Still Be a Tree)* ISBN: 0-516-34904-X.
————. *Podría ser un mamífero. (It Could Still Be a Mammal)* ISBN: 0-516-34903-1.
————. *Podría ser un pájaro. (It Could Still Be a Bird)* ISBN: 0-516-34901-5.
————. *Podría ser un pez. (It Could Still Be a Fish)* ISBN: 0-516-34902-3.
————. *¡Qué bueno que haya insectos! (It's a Good Thing There Are Insects!)* ISBN: 0-516-34905-8.
Ea. vol.: 32p. (Mis Primeros Libros de Ciencia) Photos by Fotos VALAN. Translated by Aída E. Marcuse. Chicago: Children's Press, 1990. $9.45. Gr. 1-2.

Through a simple text and bright full-color photographs, children are introduced to basic facts about trees, mammals, birds, fish, and insects. These well-done Spanish translations of the Rookie Read-About Science series, originally published in English in 1990, should be of special interest to young Spanish-speaking readers, who now can read about different types of trees, the characteristics of mammals, birds, and fish as well as good things about insects. Despite their small size—6 1/4 by 7 1/4 inches—the scarcity of noteworthy science books in Spanish for the young makes these titles even more welcome.

Freeman, Don. *Un bolsillo para Corduroy. (A Pocket for Corduroy)* Illus: the author. New York: Viking Children's Books, 1992. 32p. ISBN: 0-670-84483-7. $12.00. Gr. Preschool-K.

Spanish-speaking fans of the popular *Corduroy* will be satisfied with this lively Spanish translation. The full-color illustrations of the appealingly portrayed stalwart bear who wants a pocket for himself are the best part of this story.

Fröhlich, Roswitha. *El país de jauja. (Luxury Land)* Translated by María Ofelia Arruti. México: Fondo de Cultura Económica, 1994. 26p. ISBN: 968-16-4501-4. $10.99. Gr. 1-3.

Everyone is invited to Luxury Land—especially if he or she is lazy like Lisa Miranda, a liar like Mini, Mau and Moguel, and a glutton like Grandfather Panza and his friends. There the reader will find the fabulous castle of the Princes of Slack, where the walls are made of rice pudding sprinkled with raspberry syrup, traffic rules are upside down, horse manure looks like Easter eggs stuffed with marzipan, water pools rejuvenate bathers, and other treats. All readers are welcome, except those who don't believe any of this is possible. The double-page spreads, full of color and detail, and the delightful Spanish rendition make this edition as engaging as the original, first published by J. F. Schreiber, Germany, in 1994.

Gilmore, Rachna. *Mi madre es rara. (My Mother Is Strange)* Illus: Brenda Jones. Translated by Concepción Zendrera. Barcelona: Editorial Juventud, 1991. 20p. ISBN: 84-261-2600-6. $9.50. Gr. K-3.

To avoid being with her mother when she is grumpy and upset, a little girl goes to visit her neighbor, María, whose mother is always kind. Surprisingly that day, María's mother had horns on her head, sharp-pointed nails and teeth, hairs coming out of her ears, and isn't very kind. María explains that her mother didn't sleep very well last night, but not to worry: A big hug and an "I love you" message take care of Mama's bad mood. Realistic and amusing pastel watercolor illustrations warmly depict Mama's catastrophes in this candid story, originally published in Canada in 1988.

Greenfield, Eloise. *La cara de abuelito. (Grandpa's Face)* Illus: Floyd Cooper. Translated by Clarita Kohen. New York: Philomel Books, 1993. 32p. ISBN: 0-399-21525-5. $14.95; ISBN: 0-399-22511-0. pap. $5.95. Gr. K-3.

Young Spanish speakers will empathize with Tamika who loves her grandfather but is afraid of the hard, cold face she saw when he was rehearsing for a play. Grandpa's reassurances and his beautiful smile and display of affection despite her misbehavior at the dinner table will be appreciated by Spanish-speaking readers and listeners. Like the originals, the illustrations of a close-knit African American family convey the story's emotional warmth even though the secondary characters are stiff and unnatural.

Grejniec, Michael. *¿Qué te gusta? (What Do You Like?)* Illus: the author. Translated by Silvia Arana. New York: Ediciones Norte Sur, 1995. 32p. lib. ed. ISBN: 1-55858-391-2. $14.88; pap. ISBN: 1-55858-392-0. $5.95. Ages 3-5.

Just like the original English version, this delightful picture book invites young Spanish-speaking children to take turns telling what they like. The simple, bright artwork on textured paper showing how a dark-haired girl and boy interpret their special preferences will appeal to individual kids or story-hour groups.

Groening, Maggie, and Matt Groening. *El libro de las formas y los colores. (Maggie Simpson's Book of Colors and Shapes)* ISBN: 84-406-2896-X.

———. *El libro de los números. (Maggie Simpson's Counting Book)* ISBN: 84-406-2897-8.

Ea. vol.: 30p. Barcelona: Ediciones B, 1992. $5.95. Gr. Preschool-2.

In a most amusing and joyous manner, children are introduced to shapes, colors, and numbers. Bold, colorful illustrations and brief, simple texts are just right for children who will truly enjoy and learn.

Guarino, Deborah. *¿Tu mamá es una llama? (Is Your Mama a Llama?)* Illus: Steven Kellogg. Translated by Aída E. Marcuse. New York: Scholastic, Inc., 1993. 30p. ISBN:0-590-46275-X; pap. $5.95. Gr. Preschool-2.

Kellogg's engaging illustrations and Guarino's lilting verse about young animals who decide who belongs to whom are beautifully captured in a well-done Spanish translation. Young Spanish speakers will be just as reassured about the bond between mother and child as English-speakers were with the original. They also will enjoy this appealing exercise in animal classification.

Hazen, Barbara Shook. *¡Adiós! ¡Hola! (Good-Bye, Hello)* Illus: Michael Bryant. Translated by Alma Flor Ada. New York: Simon & Schuster/Atheneum, 1995. 32p. ISBN: 0-689-31952-5. $15.00. Ages 3-6.

Spanish-speaking children will empathize with a child who grieves when she moves but then settles down in her new home. She's sad about leaving her urban multicultural neighborhood until she begins to discover the riches of her new suburban world. Like the original English version, some of the rhymes fall flat, but the contemporary details, expressive watercolors, and multicultural cast make this a timely story.

Henderson, Kathy. *El libro de los bebés. (The Baby's Book of Babies)* ISBN: 84-406-3321-1.

MacKinnon, Debbie. *¿Cuántos hay? (How Many?)* ISBN: 84-406-3324-6.

————. *¿De qué color? (What Colour?)* ISBN: 84-406-3320-3.

————. *¿Qué forma tiene? (What Shape?)* ISBN: 84-406-3323-8.

Ea. vol.: 18p. (Fotolibro) Translated by Sonia Tapia. Barcelona: Ediciones B, 1993. $7.99. Gr. Preschool-1.

The very young will delight in this series, originally published in Great Britain by Frances Lincoln in 1992, with spectacular photographs in color of things young children can easily recognize. The minimal texts and simple concepts are added attractions. They include a book about all types of babies involved in everyday activities, a simple counting book, a book about colors, and another about basic shapes.

Henkes, Kevin. *Crisantemo. (Chrysanthemum)* Illus: the author. Translated by Teresa Mlawer. Madrid: Editorial Everest, 1993. 32p. ISBN: 84-241-3344-7. $11.95. Gr. K-3.

Crisantemo, a beautiful girl mouse, is delighted with her long name until she goes to school and her classmates make fun of her. The name is almost too long to write on a card and uses more than one third of the letters of the alphabet. Crisantemo's feelings of happiness, dejection, and happiness again when her music teacher decides to name her new baby Crisantemo are expressively portrayed in Henkes's lively watercolor illustrations. Children will empathize with Crisantemo's doubts, insecurities, and ultimate pride in her "strange" name.

Henkes, Kevin. *Julius, el rey de la casa. (Julius, The Baby of the World)* Translated by Teresa Mlawer. Madrid: Editorial Everest, S.A., 1993. 32p. ISBN: 84-241-3343-9. $11.95. Gr. K-3.

Henkes's humorous, persuasive story about Lily, an energetic girl mouse, who is suffering from a severe case of sibling rivalry upon the birth of her new brother, Julius, will delight all Spanish speakers. Children will empathize with Lily's feelings, which are honestly portrayed in lively watercolor illustrations, and no one should miss the clever captions that truly capture what it means to have a new baby brother. As all Spanish translations done for distribution in Spain, this one includes one verb form *"Creedme"* (p. 20) and one noun *"el zumo"* (p. 24) as used in Spain.

Henrietta. *Un ratón en casa. (A Mouse in the House)* Translated by María Puncel. Madrid: Santillana, 1992. 29p. ISBN: 84-372-6619-X. $23.95. Gr. Preschool-1.

Even though a mouse is not yet invited to a child's birthday party, he decides to go anyway. The questions are, who can find the mouse? Will the cat catch the mouse? Large close-up photographs in color of numerous things that young children can readily identify provide the background to this simple story about a mouse that delights in leftovers. This large-format book with an easy-rhyming text is just right for reading aloud to a group of Spanish speakers.

Hill, Eric. *Spot va al parque. (Spot Goes to the Park)* Translated by Teresa Mlawer. New York: G.P. Putnam's Sons, 1992. 22p. ISBN: 0-399-22345-2. $12.95. Gr. Preschool-2.

Like previous Spot books, this includes a simple text, colorful illustrations, and the especially designed flaps that children must lift to read all of the story. Here Spot goes to the park with his mother and takes his ball along. Playing ball at the park is fun but sometimes complicated. Children will enjoy.

La historia de la Creación. (The Story of the Creation) Illus: Jane Ray. New York: Dutton Children's Books, 1993. 24p. ISBN: 0-525-45055-6. $16.00. Gr. 1-3.

This gorgeous artistic interpretation of the seven days of creation is now available to Spanish speakers. Ray's folk-art style, painted in rich hues and highlighted with an iridescent gold, present a majestic view of nature, Earth, animals, plants, and all of God's creatures. The Spanish text is simple and easy to understand.

Hoban, Russell. *Pan y mermelada para Francisca. (Bread and Jam for Frances)* Illus: Lillian Hoban. Translated by Tomás

González. New York: Harper Arco Iris/HarperCollins, 1995. 31p. ISBN: 0-06-025328-2. $14.95; ISBN: 0-06-443403-6. pap. $4.95. Gr. K-3.

The diverting picture-book story about an engaging little badger, Francisca, who will not eat her lovely breakfast egg, trades her chicken-salad sandwich at school, and refuses to eat her veal cutlet at dinner is just right for fussy Spanish-speaking eaters who only want bread and jam. This gentle, amusing, and most effective message about a varied diet and the fun of eating sounds even better than the original in this joyful Spanish rendition which celebrates the rhyme, style, and tone of the Spanish language.

Holzwarth, Werner, and Wolf Erlbruch. *El topo que quería saber quién se había hecho aquello en su cabeza. (The Mole Who Wished to Know Who Had Made That on His Head)* Translated from the German by Miguel Azaola. Madrid: Altea, 1991. 22p. ISBN: 84-372-6617-3. $13.50. Gr. K-3.

Children of all ages (and most adults) will delight in a personable, near-sighted mole's quest to find out who did "that smelly thing" on his head. In the process, he learns how pigeons, horses, rabbits, goats, cows, pigs, and dogs defecate. The large lively illustrations in color provide just the right atmosphere and information to this unusual story that may offend some adults, but will be enjoyed by most young readers. Originally published in 1989 by Peter Hammer Verlag in Germany, this story was also translated and published in Mexico in 1990 by Consejo Nacional de Fomento Educativo.

Howe, James. *Hay un dragón en mi bolsa de dormir. (There's a Dragon in My Sleeping Bag)* Illus: David S. Rose. Translated by Alma Flor Ada. New York: Atheneum, 1994. 30p. ISBN: 0-689-31954-1. $14.95. Gr. K-2.

Spanish-speaking children can now enjoy this humorous and heartwarming story about two brothers, Simón and Alejandro, and their imaginary encounters with Dexter the Dragon and Calvino the Camel. The colorful and imaginative acrylic illustrations add a playful tone to the story's message: imaginary friends come and go, but brothers are forever.

Hutchins, Pat. *Llaman a la puerta. (The Doorbell Rang)* Illus: the author. Translated by Aída E. Marcuse. New York: Mulberry/ Morrow, 1994. 24p. ISBN: 0-688-13807-1. $14.93; ISBN: 0-688-13806-3. pap. $4.95. K-2.

Hutchins's mouth-watering story about Mama's freshly-baked cookies will certainly appeal to Spanish speakers. The spirited illustrations filled with cookies, interracial children, toys, and a cat, add a buoyant tone to this picture book that also teaches a thing or two about addition and subtraction in an appetizing manner.

Jeunesse, Gallimard, and others. *Atlas de las plantas. (Plant Atlas)* Illus: Sylvaine Pérols. ISBN: 84-348-4655-1.
————. *Atlas de los animales. (Animal Atlas)* Illus: René Mettler. ISBN: 84-348-4656-X.
————. *Los indios. (Indians)* Illus: Ute Fuhr and Raoul Santai. ISBN: 84-348-4654-3.
Ea. vol.: 36p. Translated by Paz Barroso. (Mundo Maravilloso) Madrid: Ediciones SM, 1995. $10.95. Gr. 2-4.

Like previous titles in this appealing series whose purpose is to introduce children into various topics, these contain transparent plastic overlays intermingled between glossy pages and brief, easy-to-understand texts. Interesting facts about plants and animals around the world are described in *Atlas de las plantas* and *Atlas de los animales*. *Los indios* discusses basic information about the daily lives of American Indians and how their lives changed with the arrival of white men.

Joly, Fanny. *¿Quién tiene miedo a la tormenta? (Who Is Afraid of Storms?)* Illus: Jean-Noël Rochut. Translated from the French by Uriel P. Eyheramonno. Madrid: Grupo Anaya, 1991. 26p. ISBN: 84-207-4304-6. $8.50. Gr. K-3.

A little girl tries to deal with her fear of storms in many ways but only succeeds when her mother takes her to mother's bed where she can cuddle between her father and mother. Thus, she learns that storms are normal and she can return to her own bed to finish reading her book and eating potato chips. Dark-toned illustrations create the right mood of a little girl and a "horrible" thunderstorm in this story originally published by Editions Rouge et Or, Paris, in 1989.

Johnson, Crockett. *Harold y el lápiz color morado. (Harold and the Purple Crayon)* Illus: the author. Translated by Teresa Mlawer. New York: Harper Arco Iris/HarperCollins, 1995. 62p. ISBN: 0-06-025332-0. $11.95; ISBN: 0-06-443402-8. pap. $3.95. Ages 4-6.

One evening Harold decides to go for a walk in the moonlight. Because there isn't any moon, he draws a moon with his purple crayon; he needs something to walk on, so he draws a path. Spanish-speaking children will be entertained by the series of adventures that Harold cleverly draws himself in and out of in this ingenious pocket-size book.

Kalan, Robert. *¡Salta, ranita, salta!* *(Jump, Frog, Jump!)* Illus: Byron Barton. Translated by Aída E. Marcuse. New York: Mulberry/Morrow, 1994. 30p. ISBN: 0-688-13804-7. $14.93; ISBN: 0-688-13805-5. pap. $4.95. Ages 3-6.

Young Spanish speakers will delight in this well-done Spanish rendition of the cumulative tale in which a frog tries to catch a fly without getting caught himself. Barton's simple and appealingly primitive illustrations done in deep colors with thick, muted outlines to define figures are just right for the young who will love to enthusiastically chant the frog's repeated escapes.

Kessler, Leonard. *¡Aquí viene el que se poncha!* *(Here Comes the Strikeout)* Translated by Tomás González. (Ya Sé Leer) New York: Harper Arco Iris/HarperCollins, 1995. 64p. ISBN: 0-06-025437-8. $13.95; ISBN: 0-06-444189-X. pap. $3.50. Gr. 1-3.

This is a zesty Spanish rendition of the popular story about Roberto, who, with the help of a friend, much practice, and hard work, improves his dismal record at bat. Just like the original English version, beginning and reluctant Spanish-speaking readers will appreciate the easy text and action illustrations.

Kessler, Leonard. *El último en tirarse es un miedoso.* *(Last One in Is a Rotten Egg)* (Ya Sé Leer) Translated by Osvaldo Blanco. New York: HarperCollins, 1995. 64p. ISBN: 0-06-444194-6. pap. $3.50. Gr. 1-3.

Freddy misses a lot of fun at the city swimming pool until he becomes a deep-water swimmer and can join his friends. This excellent Spanish rendition which maintains the easy text, lively three-tone illustrations, and theme of earned success of the original, first published in 1969, will satisfy and encourage both beginning Spanish readers and beginning swimmers.

Kozikowski, Renate. *La calle de las delicias.* *(Special Street)* Translated by María Rabassa. Barcelona: Ediciones B, 1993. 10p. ISBN: 84-406-3599-0. $16.95. Gr. Preschool-2.

Originally published by Sadie Fields Productions, London, in 1993, this attractive three-dimensional, pop-up-book with appealing pastel illustrations depicts scenes on Special Street: a vegetable store, a mailman delivering mail, a bookstore, a dairy, an ice cream shop, a flower shop, a toy store, a bakery, and a candy store. Well-constructed flaps allow little fingers to open doors and windows and observe charming scenes of cuddly animals enjoying themselves. Despite this book's somewhat fragile nature, young children will be enthralled to view the activities on *"la Calle de las Delicias."*

Krauss, Ruth. *Un día feliz. (Happy Day)* Illus: Marc Simont. Translated by María A. Fiol. New York: HarperCollins, 1995. 30p. ISBN: 0-06-025450-5. $14.95; ISBN: 0-06-443414-1. pap. $4.95. Ages 4-8.

Originally published in 1949, this exquisitely simple Spanish rendition of the popular Caldecott Honor Book is sure to please Spanish speakers. In the middle of the forest, different forest animals awake and run sniffing through the trees to discover a single yellow flower growing in the snow. The charming double-spread, two-tone illustrations, beautifully complemented by a simple repetitive text, can be used for story time, a language or science lesson, or just plain fun.

Landa, Norbert. *Alex y el amigo perdido. (Alex and the Lost Friend)* Illus: Hanne Türk. Translated by Eladio M.B. de Quirós. Madrid: Editorial Everest, 1994. 30p. ISBN: 84-241-3293-9. $9.95. Gr. K-3.

Alex, a mouse, is very fond of Tigre, his favorite toy cat. But Alex's mice friends and neighbors certainly don't like the idea of having a cat in the vicinity. Charming watercolor spreads depict Alex's misadventures with Tigre in Miceland. Young Spanish-speaking readers and listeners will sympathize with Alex's feelings about losing and later finding his special "pet."

Langley, Jonathan. *Los tres chivos Malaspulgas. (The Three Billy Goats Gruff)* Illus: the author. Barcelona: Ediciones Junior, 1992. 24p. ISBN: 84-7419-941-7. $9.95. Gr. K-3.

Originally published in Great Britain, this excellent Spanish translation of the ever-popular, *The Three Billy Goats Gruff*, has maintained all the verve of other English versions. The full-page illustrations in color of ingenious goats and a mean troll are just right for reading aloud.

Lenain, Thieny. *Mi hermanita es un monstruo. (My Little Sister Is a Monster)* Illus: Napo. Barcelona: Ediciones Junior, 1993. 29p. ISBN: 84-478-0090-3. $9.64. Gr. K-3.

Leo, a little boy, is tired of waiting in the car for his father who is in the hospital visiting his new sister. As he waits, he imagines going into the hospital and discovering that his little sister is a horrible, filthy monster who he must get rid of. Fortunately, he notices her beautiful eyes. Cartoon-like watercolor illustrations add a touch of humor and fantasy to this honest story, originally published by Editions Nathan, Paris, in 1991, about a little boy's mixed feelings concerning his new baby sister.

Lester, Alison. *La cama de Isabella.* *(Isabella's Bed)* Translated by Clarisa de la Rosa. Caracas: Ediciones Ekaré-Banco del Libro, 1992. 32p. ISBN: 980-257-118-0. $13.00. Gr. 1-3.

Ana, a little girl, and her brother, Luis, enjoy visiting Grandma and playing with the wonderful treasures stored in the sandalwood trunk in the attic. Grandma avoided the trunk because of "too many memories," until Ana and Luis realize that the sad song often sung by Grandma tells of a painful loss. Gorgeous full-page watercolor illustrations warmly depict Grandma's feelings and the children's dreams, in this tender story, originally published by Oxford University Press, Australia.

Levinson, Riki. *Mira cómo salen las estrellas.* *(Watch the Stars Come Out)* Illus: Diane Goode. Translated by Juan Ramón Azaola. New York: Puffin Unicorn/Penguin, 1995. 32p. ISBN: 0-14-055505-6. pap. $4.99. Gr. 1-3.

An immigrant's experience is recounted through a family story-within-a-story in which a little red-haired girl curls up by her grandmother to hear how, long ago, another little girl and her brother crossed the Atlantic and came to the United States. Soft, pastel illustrations including a warm portrayal of a welcoming Statue of Liberty depict the feelings and ambiance of immigrants at the end of the nineteenth century. Spanish-speaking readers and listeners will definitely relish this well-done Spanish rendition by Juan Ramón Azaola of this ALA Notable Children's Book selection.

Levy, Janice. *The Spirit of Tío Fernando: A Day of the Dead Story / El espíritu de tío Fernando: Una historia del Día de los Muertos.* Illus: Morella Fuenmayor. Translated by Teresa Mlawer. Morton Grove: Albert Whitman, 1995. 32p. ISBN: 0-8075-7585-2. $14.95; pap. ISBN: 0-8075-7586-0. $6.95. Gr. 1-3.

The Mexican Day of the Dead is beautifully recreated in this bilingual version in which Nando, a young boy, remembers all the things he liked about his favorite uncle. Soft watercolor illustrations tenderly portray Nando's joyful experiences amid the traditional Mexican festivities and ingredients—bread of the dead, sugar skulls, papier-mâché skeletons, and "cempasúchil," the special flowers of the dead, translated here as "clavelones."

Lipniacka, Ewa. *¡A dormir, o . . . !* *(To Bed . . . Or Else!)* Illus: Basia Bogdanowicz. Translated by Susana Camps. Barcelona: El Arca de Junior, 1995. 31p. ISBN: 84-478-0343-0. $10.95. Gr. K-2.

Marta and Ana, two young girls, are best friends and neighbors. They play together and, most of the time, share their toys and books. The only problem is bedtime when they both spend the night at Ana's house. After numerous attempts, Ana's mother threatens them with a serious "to bed . . . or else" and the girls finally go to sleep. Amusing watercolor illustrations provide a realistic touch to the universal issue, bedtime. This is a fluid Spanish rendition of the original, first published by Magi Publications, London.

Luenn, Nancy. *La pesca de Nessa. (Nessa's Fish)* Illus: Neil Waldman. Translated by Alma Flor Ada. New York: Atheneum, 1994. 32p. ISBN: 0-689-31977-0. $15.95. Gr. K-3.

The original luminous watercolor paintings which set the action within a remarkable variety of landscapes and snowscapes seen in the same place at different times of the day and night are the best part of this story about Nessa, an Inuit girl, and her grandmother and their ice-fishing expedition. Spanish-speaking children, however, will have to listen attentively to find Nessa's adventure in winterland a rewarding experience.

Maclean, Colin, and Moira Maclean. *¡Arriba! ¡Arriba! (Up! Up!)* ISBN: 84-243-3206-7.

————. *¿Quién se ha perdido? (Who Is Lost?)* ISBN: 84-243-3208-3.

————. *¡Sorpresa! ¡Sorpresa! (Surprise! Surprise!)* ISBN: 84-243-3207-5.

Ea. vol.: 22p. (Cuentos Activos) Illus: the authors. Translated by Araceli Ramos. Bilbao: Publicaciones Fhersal, 1994. $8.95. Gr. 2-4.

Children are encouraged to participate in fun activities that tell about a "*gobazú*" that nobody has ever seen, a kitten that is nowhere to be found, and a birthday gift whose owner cannot be determined. The delightful, busy watercolor illustrations and the simple questions alongside the narration add to the enjoyment of these "active stories" that can be used to encourage observation or for just plain fun reading or listening. It should be noted that these attractive books, originally published by Kingfisher Books in London, were translated in Spain, hence they use the second person plural verb forms and corresponding pronouns.

Macsolis. *Baile de luna. (Moon Dance)* Illus: the author. Barcelona: Editorial Juventud, 1991. 30p. ISBN: 84-261-2583-2. $12.95. Gr. 1-3.

Ramón, a lonely alley cat, becomes friendly with the moon, which helps him escape when he is in trouble, and provides him with the right amount of fun through the magic of a bright lit sky, comets, stars, and other wonders. Cat lovers will enjoy Ramón's fantasies as depicted in the sensitive full-colored illustrations of night street scenes and a lonely sky.

Marcuse, Aída E. *Caperucita Roja y la luna de papel.* *(Little Red Riding Hood and the Paper Moon)* Illus: Pablo Torrecilla. Torrance, CA: Laredo Publishing, 1993. 24p. ISBN: 1-56492-103-4. pap. $7.50. Gr. Preschool-3.

This is an appealing adaptation, in play format, of the old-time favorite with an additional character—a friendly bear—and a few added twists—a protective paper moon and a bad wolf who doesn't eat anyone but gets beaten up. The easy-rhyming dialogue and the simple color illustrations of Red Riding Hood and her mother and grandmother in modern clothes are sure to please all readers and listeners.

Marks, Burton. *Los animales.* *(Animals)* ISBN: 84-272-7235-9.
————. *Colores y números.* *(Colors and Numbers)* ISBN: 84-272-7235-4.
————. *Cuentos divertidos.* *(Amusing Stories)* ISBN: 84-272-7234-0.
————. *Vamos de viaje.* *(Let's Go on a Trip)* ISBN: 84-272-7233-2. Ea. vol.: 22p. Illus: Paul Harvey. Translated by Conchita Peraire. (Leer Es un Juego) Barcelona: Editorial Molino, 1992. $7.95. Gr. 1-3.

Through a combination of drawings and simple texts, children will "read" about animals, colors, numbers, and other fun activities. In each volume, a few key words have been replaced by amusing illustrations of characters or objects. Children will enjoy "reading" these stories as they participate in "reading" text and illustrations.

Marshak, Samuel. *¡El perrito creció! (The Pup Grew Up!)* Illus: Vladimir Radunsky. Translated by Antoni Vicens. Barcelona: Ediciones Destino, 1992. 30p. ISBN: 84-233-2143-6. $15.50. Gr. K-3.

Originally published in the Soviet Union in 1926, this preposterous story about a lost puppy and careless trainmen will appeal to sophisticated children. The bold, modernistic illustrations in color definitely capture the senselessness of some workers amid the busyness of life. The well-done Spanish translation is easy-to-read and most enjoyable.

Martí, Isabel. *Guille está enfermo. (Guille Is Ill)* Illus: Horacio Elena. (Juguemos con Guille) Barcelona: Timun Mas, 1993. 8p. ISBN: 84-7722-961-9. $8.25. Ages 2-5.

Guille, a little boy, is not feeling well, so his parents take him to the doctor where he goes through a routine examination. Later they stop at the drug store, and finally Mama gives him his medicine and puts him to bed. This wordless board book is characterized by wonderfully realistic watercolor illustrations that truly depict a sick child's day. The previous thirteen titles in this series show Guille involved in common activities such as Guille's birthday and Guille at the park.

Marzollo, Jean. *Veo navidad: Un libro de adivinanzas ilustradas.   (I Spy Christmas: A Book of Picture Riddles)* Photos by Walter Wick. Translated by Aída Marcuse. New York: Scholastic, Inc., 1995. 37p. ISBN: 0-590-50197-6. $12.95. Ages 4-8.

Featuring thirteen Christmas scenes with short rhymes, this joyful Spanish rendition challenges kids to find a variety of small objects in the purposefully crowded pictures. Like in the original English version, Wick's crisp and clear, full-color double-page spreads of seasonal scenes will provide hours of holiday fun to young Spanish speakers who love searching for details.

McBratney, Sam.   *Adivina cuanto te quiero.   (Guess How Much I Love You)* Illus: Anita Jeram. Translated by Esther Roehrich and Teresa Mlawer. Barcelona: Kókinos, 1995. 32p. ISBN: 84-88342-08-X. $11.95. Ages 3-5.

This endearing nursery game, beautifully revitalized in a gentle competition between parent and child as each avows affection in ever more expansive terms, is now available as a comforting, sleepy-time picture book for young Spanish speakers. Double-page watercolor spreads in soft shades of brown and green with delicate ink-line details warmly capture the loving relationship between parent and child as well as the comedy that stems from a little hare's awe of his wonderful dad.

Mi cuarto. (My Bedroom) ISBN: 84-7773-396-1.
Seré pintor. (I Will Paint) ISBN: 84-7773-393-7.
Soy pequeño y grande. (I Am Little and Big) ISBN: 84-7773-394-5.
Todo es distinto. (Everything Is Different) ISBN: 84-7773-395-3.

Ea. vol.: 12p. (Colección Peque-Libros) Madrid: Grafalco, S.A., 1991. $5.95. Gr. K-2.

Briefly and concisely, these appealing board books describe a child's bedroom, painting activities, the concepts of big and little, and various shapes. Unfortunately, the text is written in cursive which makes it difficult for the young to read. The simple, water-color illustrations, however, are just right for young children. Especially witty is *Soy pequeño y grande,* which concludes that a big elephant is scared of a little mouse.

Montes, Graciela. *Federico y el mar. (Federico and the Sea)* Illus: Claudia Legnazzi. Buenos Aires: Editorial Sudamericana, 1995. 16p. ISBN: 950-07-0849-3. $11.00. Ages 3-5.

Federico, a little boy, enjoys playing with the sand on the beach. But he refuses to go into the ocean—the waves are too big and there is too much water out there. He prefers to sit, watch, and play with his toys, until he decides he needs more water. The vivacious watercolor illustrations of this delightful board book and the simple text genuinely portray the joy and apprehensions of young children when they first approach the ocean.

Mosel, Arlene. *Tikki, Tikki, Tembo. (Tikki, Tikki, Tembo)* retold. Illus: Blair Lent. Translated Liwayway Alonso. New York: Lectorum Publications. 1994. 44p. ISBN: 1-880507-13-7. $14.95. Ages 4-7.

The popular presentation of an old folktale about the near-tragic fate that befalls an honored first son of a Chinese family with a long name is now available in a fluid Spanish translation. The amusing Chinese mock tragedy is retold in simple repetitive Spanish text effectively enhanced by the original, colorful pen-and-ink and wash illustrations.

Moser, Erwin. *Koko y Kiri. (Koko and Kiri)* ISBN: 84-348-4295-5.
―――. *Koko y el pájaro blanco. (Koko and the White Bird)* ISBN: 84-348-4294-7.
―――. *Koko y el paraguas mágico. (Koko and the Magic Umbrella)* ISBN: 84-348-4293-9.
―――. *Osos y ratones. (Bears and Mice)* ISBN: 84-348-4296-3.
Ea. vol.: 59p. Illus: the author. Translated from the German by Carmen Bas and Marinella Terzi. Madrid: Ediciones SM, 1994. $8.99. Gr. 1-3.

Koko, a kind mouse, experiences life in simple and marvelous ways. In *Koko y Kiri,* he and his friend Kiri dream about magic carpets, beautiful ships, and fast airplanes only to learn that not all dreams can come true. In *Koko y el pájaro blanco,* Koko wants to pick some flowers for his friend, Kiri, which he finally does, thanks to a white bird. Magic umbrellas are great to make rain, fly in the sky, provide light in the dark, and other necessary tasks as shown in *Koko y el paraguas mágico.* Polar bears like ice, brown bears like strawberries, and a friendly mouse likes his special sausage. These preferences result in a faraway trip in *Osos y ratones*. Originally published by Anette Betz, Vienna, in 1993, this delightful series with lighthearted watercolor illustrations of animals amidst nature and fantasy provides a nice balance of fun and reflection.

My First Phrases in Spanish and English. New York: Simon & Schuster Books for Young Readers, 1993. 12p. ISBN: 0-671-86595-1. $11.00. Gr. Preschool-2.

Children are exposed to their first phrases in Spanish and English through this "pull-the-tab" book with colorful illustrations of scenes they can readily identify: at a party, in the town, in the park, at the seaside, at school. This is a fun introduction to common phrases in English and Spanish for beginning Spanish speakers.

Ness, Evaline. *Sam, Bangs y hechizo de luna*. *(Sam, Bangs and Moonshine)* Illus: the author. Translated by Liwayway Alonso. New York: Lectorum Publications, 1994. 34p. ISBN: 1-880507-12-9. $14.95. Ages 5-8.

Evaline Ness's delightful story is about Sam, a fisherman's daughter with an overactive imagination. Sam comes to regret her untruths when her credulous friend Thomas almost drowns as a result of her wild tales—*hechizos de luna*. The story is beautifully rendered into Spanish. Spanish-speaking children will enjoy the original and charming two-tone drawings that beautifully portray the island scene and sensitively capture the little girl's different moods.

Nodar, Carmen Santiago. *El paraíso de abuelita*. *(Abuelita's Paradise)* Illus: Diane Paterson. Translated by Teresa Mlawer. Morton Grove, IL: Albert Whitman, 1992. 32p. ISBN: 0-8075-6346-3. $13.95. Gr. K-3.

In a tender and loving manner, Marita reminisces about her grandmother and her descriptions of life in beautiful, rural Puerto Rico. Lush watercolor illustrations of a little girl and her family enjoying life in a pastoral Puerto Rican setting and a simple, fluid Spanish text will make this story a favorite of Puerto Rican families who long for abuelita's paradise.

Numeroff, Laura Joffe. *Si le das un panecillo a un alce*. *(If You Give a Moose a Muffin)* Illus: Felicia Bond. Translated by Teresa Mlawer. New York: HarperCollins, 1995. 32p. ISBN: 0-06-025440-8. $12.95. Ages 4-7.

A pleasant boy who lures a moose to his house with a freshly baked treat sets the stage for this delightful circular story, now available in Spanish. The crisp, colorful pen-and-wash drawings, filled with mundane household objects that reinforce the comic fantasy of a large brown moose tromping around indoors, blend well with the Spanish text to convey the story's gentle underlying humor.

Numeroff, Laura Joffe. *Si le das una galletita a un ratón. (If You Give a Mouse a Cookie)* Illus: Felicia Bond. Translated by Teresa Mlawer. New York: HarperCollins, 1995. 32p. ISBN: 0-06-025438-6. $12.95. Ages 4-6.

Maintaining the affable tone of the original English version, this well-done Spanish rendition takes the reader through a young child's day through a mouse's seemingly endless string of activities and requests. The neat pen-and-wash drawings which play out the action and the similarity between mouse and child won't be lost on observant Spanish-speaking youngsters.

Oram, Hiawyn. *Alex quiere un dinosaurio. (A Boy Wants a Dinosaur)* Illus: Satoshi Kitamura. México: Fondo de Cultura Económica, 1993. 26p. ISBN: 968-16-4114-0. $12.95. Gr. K-3.

Ben has a dog, Alice has two snails, but Alex wants a dinosaur. So his kind grandfather takes him to the Dino-store where he selects Fred, a big white female dinosaur. Life in the city does not suit Fred; a walk in the country, however, performs wonders. The lively, full-page spreads in bright colors will truly satisfy all dinosaur lovers. This well-done Spanish translation has maintained the charm of the original, first published by Andersen Press, London, in 1990.

Oram, Hiawyn. *En el desván. (In the Attic)* Illus: Satoshi Kitamura. México: Fondo de Cultura Económica, 1993. 28p. ISBN: 968-16-4112-4. $12.95. Gr. Preschool-2.

A little boy relates how much fun it is to go to the attic and discover a family of mice, a colony of beetles, a busy spider, an old motor, a friendly tiger, and other amusing things even though his surprised mother insists they do not have an attic at home. The full-page colorful spreads perfectly capture the little boy's merriment. Originally published by Andersen Press, London, in 1984, this excellent Spanish translation will be treasured by all young Spanish speakers.

Oram, Hiawyn. *Un mensaje para Papá Noel.* *(A Message for Santa)*
Illus: Tony Ross. Barcelona: Timun Mas, 1995. 30p. ISBN:
84-480-1067-1. $11.95. Gr. 1-3.

Emily, a young girl, looks forward to Christmas with one
exception: She is afraid of Papá Noel's (Santa's) coming into her
home through the chimney. Her mother finally convinces her to
leave him a note with instructions where to leave the presents.
Modernistic watercolor illustrations add a contemporary touch to
Emily's fears. Spanish-speaking children will enjoy this smooth
rendition, originally published by Andersen Press, London.

Oram, Hiawyn. *¡Mío!* *(Mine!)* Illus: Mary Rees. Translated by
Carme Pol. Barcelona: Ediciones Junior, 1993. 22p. ISBN: 84-
478-0075-X. $10.95. Gr. K-3.

Two friends, Isabel and Claudia, are constantly fighting over the
same toy. Things get completely out of control when Claudia's
mother takes them to the park and they struggle over Claudia's new
tricycle. The detailed, watercolor illustrations and the wonderfully
frank text definitely capture the feelings and thoughts of two girls
who insist on taking each other's toys.

Pacheco, Miguel Ángel. *La familia de Mic.* *(Mic's Family)* Illus:
Ana López Escrivá. Barcelona: Ediciones Destino, 1993. 28p.
ISBN: 84-233-2292-0. $15.95. Gr. K-3.

Mic is a completely normal and sensible boy. His family,
however, is a little "different." His oldest sister, Parvina, lives in a
sugar bowl. His parents love animals: his father picks up stray
dogs every day and his mother will never pass a stray cat. But the
most annoying one is his grandmother, Etérea, who loves to fly out
open windows. Other family members are equally unique and Mic
obviously relishes their idiosyncrasies. The double-page watercolor
spreads are as clever and amusing as the narrative. All readers and
viewers will delight in Mic's family. This book received the
Spanish Apel-les Mestres Award in 1993.

Pacovská, Kveta. *El pequeño rey de las flores.* *(The Short Little
King of the Flowers)* Illus: the author. Translated from the
German by Esther Roehrich-Rubio. Madrid: Editorial Kókinos,
1993. 36p. ISBN: 84-88342-02-0. $20.60. Gr. Preschool-2.

A lonely king searches for a princess who he finally finds among
his beloved tulips. Modernistic, child-like watercolors and collages
add a contemporary touch to this satisfying story with a long-loved
theme: ". . . and they lived happily ever after." Originally published by Verlag Neugehauer Press, Salzburg, Austria, this book
received the Hans Christian Andersen International Award in 1992.

El parque de atracciones. (The Amusement Park) (Mundo Redondo)
Madrid: Edaf, 1992. 24p. ISBN: 84-7640-558-8. $10.95. Gr.
Preschool-2.

This well-constructed board book will delight young readers as
it describes numerous attractions that children enjoy at amusement
parks such as a Ferris wheel, roller coaster, puppet theater, candy
store, balloon seller, and others. The colorful illustrations and the
fold-out pages that can be easily assembled into a merry-go-round
are just right for eager little hands. Other titles in this series: *En la
granja (At the Farm), El arca de Noé (Noah's Ark), El jardín
público (The Public Park).*

Paulsen, Gary. *La tortillería. (The Tortilla Factory)* Illus: Ruth
Wright Paulsen. Translated by Gloria de Aragón Andújar. San
Diego: Harcourt Brace, 1995. 32p. ISBN: 0-15-200237-5.
$14.00. Gr. 1-3.

This fluid, well-done Spanish rendition has definitely maintained Paulsen's simple yet evocative language that tells how
golden corn seeds become delicious tortillas. This circular retelling
sounds even better in Spanish—"*tortillería*," of course, is a much
better word than "tortilla factory"—and the strongly textured
double-page, oil-on-linen paintings perfectly convey the genuine
ambience of Mexican food.

Pfister, Marcus. *Destello el dinosaurio. (Dazzle the Dinosaur)* Illus:
the author. Translated by José Moreno. New York: Ediciones
Norte-Sur, 1995. 32p. ISBN: 1-55858-387-4. $16.95; lib. ed.
ISBN: 1-55858-388-2. $16.88. Gr. K-3.

The reflective illustrations Pfister used in *El pez arco iris (The
Rainbow Fish)* are successfully used again in this prehistoric tale
that will charm Spanish speakers. The perennial popularity of
dinosaurs, the fast-paced and imaginative plot, the shimmering
artwork, and the fluid Spanish rendition will ensure this book a
warm reception at story time and elsewhere.

Pfister, Marcus. *El pez arco iris. (The Rainbow Fish)* Illus: the
author. Translated from the German by Ana Tortajada. New York:
Ediciones Norte-Sur, 1994. 28p. ISBN: 1-55858-361-0. $16.95.
lib. ed. ISBN: 1-55858-362-9. $16.88. Ages 4-7.

Catchy artwork in which iridescent foil is incorporated into fluid
watercolor paintings of Rainbow Fish and his shimmering silver
scales will fascinate preschoolers as they read or listen to this rather
predictable story: The more Rainbow Fish gives to others, the
happier he feels. This Spanish rendition has been as popular with

young Spanish speakers as the original German and English versions.

Pitre, Félix. *Paco y la bruja: Cuento popular puertorriqueño. (Paco and the Witch: A Puerto Rican Folktale)* Illus: Christy Hale. Translated by Osvaldo Blanco. New York: Dutton/Lodestar, 1995. 32p. ISBN: 0-525-67514-0. $13.99. Ages 4-8.

In this Puerto Rican version of Rumpelstiltskin, Paco, a little boy on the island, is trapped by a crafty witch who will not free him unless he can guess her name. Spanish-speaking youngsters will delight in this smooth Spanish rendition which does not suffer, like the original English version, by the repeated use of words in both languages. The easy-flowing Spanish narrative and the brilliant, exaggerated illustrations in bright colors are a wonderful combination.

Price, Mathew. *A la cama. (Bedtime)* ISBN: 0-553-09562-5.

————. *Amigos. (Friends)* ISBN: 0-553-09561-7.

————. *Bebés. (Babies)* ISBN: 0-553-09563-3.

————. *La ropa. (Clothes)* ISBN: 0-553-09560-9.

Ea. vol.: 8p. Illus: Moira Kemp. Translated by Teresa Mlawer. New York: Bantam Books, 1993. $4.99. Ages 2-5.

These simple texts have colorful illustrations and easy-to-use flaps that lift. The books describe fun activities that little ones experience at bedtime, with friends, with baby animals, and getting dressed in these well-constructed board books. The appealing presentation and easy-to-understand concepts make these books ideal for the very young or for those eager to learn Spanish.

Ramon, Elisa. *Todas las noches la misma historia. (Every Night the Same Story)* Illus: Gemma Sales. Barcelona: Ediciones Junior, 1994. 32p. ISBN: 84-478-0167-5. $13.95. Ages 3-6.

Despite her mother's earnest request, Leticia is not ready for bed. She still has many important things to do such as fixing a witch's broken nose, saving an evil dragon, practicing for a skating championship, and many others. But mama insists and Leticia convinces her about two things that just can't wait until tomorrow: the first—important—brushing her teeth; the second—urgent—using the toilet. Children—and their parents—will sympathize with this honest portrayal of a necessary observance. Unfortunately, some of the watercolor illustrations seem more like desperate caricatures of a mother and an active girl, but overall they are genuine renditions of nightly occurrences.

Ransome, Arthur. *Tontimundo y el barco volador; un cuento ruso.*
(The Fool of the World and the Flying Ship: a Russian Tale)
Translated by María Negroni. New York: Farrar, Straus, and
Giroux, 1991. 44p. ISBN: 0-374-32443-3. $15.95. Gr. K-3.
  The Spanish translation of the charming, Caldecott award-
winning version of the Russian folktale about a simple third son
who, through the magical powers of Listener, Swift-goer, Drinker,
and others, performs the tasks set by the czar and wins the princess.
Originally published in 1968, this version includes the same handsomely illustrated pages full of humor, animation, and gleaming
colors.

La ratita Milli y el reloj. *(Little Mouse Milli and the Clock)* ISBN:
84-272-7303-7.
La ratita Milli y los colores. *(Little Mouse Milli and Colors)* ISBN:
84-272-7302-9.
La ratita Milli y los números. *(Little Mouse Milli and Numbers)*
ISBN: 84-272-7301-0.
  Ea. vol.: 12p. Illus: Annette. Barcelona: Editorial Molino.
1992. $3.75. Gr. Preschool-2.
  Milli, a little mouse, introduces children to the concept of time,
to colors, and to numbers in these attractively conceived board
books. Through ingeniously placed cutout windows, children can
see Milli and her friends telling time, counting from one to ten, and
learning about many colors.

Reid, Margarette S. *La caja de los botones.* *(The Button Box)* Illus:
Sarah Chamberlain. Translated by: unavailable. New York:
Dutton, 1995. 24p. ISBN: 0-525-45445-4. $14.99. Gr. K-3.
  Beautiful buttons of every shape and type inspire a boy to think
about kings, queens, generals, cowboys, movie stars, and others as
he sifts through his grandmother's button box. Like the original
English version, this well-done translation will be welcomed by
Spanish-speaking young readers, parents, teachers, or librarians as a
basis for games, history lessons, and puppetry.

Rice, James. *La Nochebuena South of the Border.* Illus: the author.
Translated by Ana Smith. Gretna, LA: Pelican Publishing, 1993.
28p. ISBN: 0-88289-966-X. $14.95. Gr. K-3.
  At first glance, this looks like another burro (donkey)-siesta-
fiesta-sombrero book about poor Mexican people. Fortunately,
however, this bilingual version of "The Night Before Christmas"
where Santa is Papá Noel and his reindeer are eight burros pulling a
cart is a jovial twist with full-page color illustrations on the holiday
tale with an intrinsic Mexican appeal including the ever-popular

piñatas, *dulces*, tortillas, and others.   The Spanish version is amusing and light.

Riddell, Edwina. *100 primeras palabras. (100 First Words)* ISBN: 84-406-3781-0.
————. *Mi primera casa. (My First Home)* ISBN: 84-406-3782-9.
————. *Mi primera guardería. (My First Playgroup)* ISBN: 84-406-3779-9.
Ea. vol.: 18p. Barcelona: Ediciones B, S.A., 1993. $9.79. Ages 3-5.
    The very young will delight in these exquisitely illustrated and clearly labeled books that feature common objects and situations with charm and humor.   Each book features double-page color spreads in which babies and toddlers are depicted playing, helping, eating, bathing, and other activities at home, at the grocery store, at the nursery school, etc.   Children will especially enjoy the unexpected on each scene; for example, at the grocery store as one toddler "helps" Mama, a box of eggs is falling to the floor and another toddler is jumping out of a box.   This is indeed a joyous introduction to simple Spanish nouns and phrases, originally published by Frances Lincoln, London, in 1988.

Roddie, Shen. *¡Ábrete, huevo, ábrete! (Open! Egg Open!)* Illus: Frances Cony.   Madrid: Ediciones Beascoa, 1993.   28p.   ISBN: 84-7546-838-1. $15.95. Gr. K-2.
    Children can help mother hen open her egg and see how a baby chick comes out of its shell in this whimsical approach to a hen's dilemma.   In addition to enjoying the amusing, full-page watercolor spreads and the simple text, children will have a good time touching and lifting the appropriately placed flaps and objects.   This fun book was originally published by Sadie Fields Productions in Great Britain in 1991.

Roe, Eileen.   *Con Mi Hermano/With My Brother*.   Illus: Robert Casilla.   New York: Bradbury Press, 1991.   32p.   ISBN: 0-02-777373-6. $12.95. Gr. K-2.
    In a simple bilingual (English/Spanish) text, a little boy tells why he admires his brother and aspires to be like him.   The bold watercolor illustrations of two Latino boys beautifully capture the special relationship between the two brothers.   It must be noted, however, that even though this is a relatively good Spanish translation, the bilingual format (English and Spanish sentences on the same page) definitely has a negative effect on one language.   In this case the Spanish version is a copy of the English, thus losing the beauty and natural rhythm of the Spanish language.   In addition, an

unfortunate typo in a book with very few sentences in Spanish really
stands out.

Rosen, Michael. *Vamos a cazar un oso.* *(We're Going on a Bear
Hunt)* Illus: Helen Oxenbury. Caracas: Ediciones Ekaré, 1993.
34p. ISBN: 980-257-106-5. $15.95. Gr. K-2.

Papa, Mama, and their three children are eager to hunt a big and
dangerous bear, even if they have to walk through beautiful green
fields, deep cold rivers, dark forests, and a snowstorm. No one is
afraid of the bear until they actually find one when they rush
home to bed. Oxenbury's charming pastel watercolor and black-
and-white full-page spreads will delight Spanish-speaking young
readers and listeners. This is an excellent Spanish rendition of the
original version first published by Walker Books, London, in 1989.

Ross, Tony. *El trapito feliz.* *(The Happy Rag)* Translated by
Catalina Domínguez. México: Fondo de Cultura Económica,
1994. 28p. ISBN: 968-16-4555-3. $10.99. Ages 3-6.

Lucy is afraid of almost everything until she finds a happy rag
that cares for her all the time. Papa and Mama want to get rid of the
"dirty rag," but Lucy and a big bear won't let them. Pablo also
has a happy rag that can become a space ship and a magic carpet and
protects him when it's dark despite Aunt Carola's, Grandfather's,
and Uncle Sid's objections. The first half of the book depicts one
child; to read and view the second half, children must flip the book
over. Both stories share the center facing pages of the book with an
appropriate double-page spread of a magic carpet and a growling
bear. The bright, watercolor illustrations definitely capture all
children's feelings as they enjoy and protect their special blankets
from "concerned" adults.

Samton, Sheila White. *El viaje de Jenny.* *(Jenny's Journey)* Translated by Arshes Anasal. New York: Viking, 1993. 32p. ISBN:
0-670-84843-3. $14.99. Ages 4-7.

This imaginative interplay between fantasy and reality in which
Jenny receives a letter from her friend, Maria, who's moved far
away is now available to Spanish speakers. The colorful, primitive-
style illustrations spread across wide pages capturing Jenny's
wished-for journey and faraway friend are a beautiful complement
to this winning story of interracial friendship.

Sangberg, Monica. *El sueño de Fellini.* *(Federico's Dream)* Illus:
Letizia Galli. Translated by Xavier Lloveras. Barcelona: Editorial
Destino, 1994. 32p. ISBN: 84-233-2447-8. $14.95. Gr. 2-4.

Based on an anecdote from the life of the Italian fillmmaker, Federico Fellini, this well-written fantasy tells about Fellini's experiences as a child magician with a traveling circus accompanied by his favorite clown and friend, Gelsomina. Modernistic, double-paged spreads in full color add a sense of drama and magic to this touching tribute to the celebrated director of *La Strada* and the actress, Giulietta.

Santirso, Liliana. *Me gusta jugar con los libros.* *(I Like to Play with Books)* ISBN: 968-6465-48-0; pap. ISBN: 968-6465-47-2.
————. *Me gusta leer.* *(I Like to Read)* ISBN: 968-6465-39-1; pap. ISBN: 968-6465-38-3.
Ea. vol.: 24p. Illus: Leonid Nepomniachi. Mexico: Editorial Amaquemecan, 1991. $9.95; pap. $3.95. Gr. 1-3.

Like previous titles in this easy-to-read and easy-to-understand paperback series, a child tells why she likes to play with and read books. The amusing, two-tone illustrations convey a child's joy as she plays with and reads various types of books. The only unfortunate aspect of this upbeat series is its small size—6 by 6 inches—which limits its potential appeal.

Santirso, Liliana. *Me gustan las librerías.* *(I Like Bookstores)* ISBN: 968-6465-27-8; pap. 968-6465-26-X.
————. *Me gustan los libros de cuentos.* *(I Like Storybooks)* ISBN: 968-6465-25-1; pap. ISBN: 968-6465-24-3.
Ea. vol.: 24p. Illus: Martha Avilés. Mexico: Amaquemecan, 1991. $9.55; pap. $3.95. Gr. 1-3.

In an easy-to-read and easy-to-understand manner, a child explains why he likes to go to bookstores and to read storybooks. Fortunately, neither story moralizes to children about the values of books but rather both point out the enjoyable aspects of bookstores and storybooks, especially as they refer to young children. Amusing two-tone illustrations add the perfect childlike quality to these upbeat, informative books. It is unfortunate, however, that the small size—6 by 6 inches—of these books limits their potential use and appeal. Other titles in this series: *Me gustan la bibliotecas (I Like Libraries)*, *Me gustan los cuentos antes de dormir (I Like Stories at Bedtime)*, *Me gustan los libros (I Like Books)*.

Santirso, Liliana, and Kornelia Roth. *El globo de María.* *(María's Balloon)* Mexico: Editorial Amaquemecan, 1991. 16p. ISBN: 968-6465-29-4. pap. $7.95. Gr. K-2.

María, a little girl, has a beautiful red balloon. Her balloon is different from any other balloon. It accompanies her wherever she goes, and turns blue whenever María cries. Soft pastel watercolor illustrations depict María enjoying and crying with her special balloon. Lonely, sensitive young children may empathize with María's feelings of joy and dejection. The easy-to-read sentences and phrases are just right for beginning readers.

Schaefer, Jackie Jasina. *El día de Miranda para bailar. (Miranda's Day to Dance)* Illus: the author. Translated by Alberto Blanco. New York: Libros Colibrí/Four Winds Press, 1994. 30p. ISBN: 0-02-781112-3. $14.95. Ages 3-6.

This tribute to Carmen Miranda should also serve as an example of what a truly good translator can and should do. This excellent Spanish rendition combines the alliterative simplicity of the original English counting book with the richness, flexibility, and sense of style of the Spanish language. Despite the not very clear textured pastel drawings, young Spanish speakers will be energized by Miranda's dance and a few special South American fruits and animals in a beautiful, fluid Spanish text.

Scieszka, Jon. *¡La verdadera historia de los tres cerditos! (The True Story of the Three Little Pigs)* Illus: Lane Smith. New York: Viking, 1991. 32p. ISBN : 0-670-84162-5. $ 14.95. Gr. K-3.

This contemporary version of the ever-popular *Three Little Pigs* is now available in a fluid Spanish translation that has maintained the tongue-in-cheek telling of the original English version, published in 1989. The stylized new wave drawings and the amusing, albeit not simple text, make this retelling of special interest to the not-so-young Spanish-speaking child who will enjoy knowing how well-intentioned Mr. Wolf was framed by modern-day cops and reporters.

Seuss, Dr. *Huevos verdes con jamón. (Green Eggs and Ham)* Illus: the author. Translated by Aída E. Marcuse. New York: Lectorum Publications, 1992. 62p. ISBN: 1-880507-01-3. $8.95. Gr. 1-3.

Ms. Marcuse has done an incredible job of translating Dr. Seuss's English wordplay and nonsense humor into an easy-to-read, fluid Spanish text. Spanish speakers can now truly enjoy Dr. Seuss's original, uncluttered pictures as they relish their green eggs and ham.

Seuss, Dr. *¡Oh, cuán lejos llegarás! (Oh, the Places You'll Go!)* Translated by Aída E. Marcuse. New York: Lectorum Publications, 1993. 48p. ISBN:1-880507-05-6. $13.95. Gr. K-3.

Dr. Seuss's seriocomic ode to success is now available to Spanish speakers with its inspiring message, pajama-clad hero, busy two-page spreads, and Marcuse's easy-flowing, Spanish translation that projects zest, adventure, and hard work. Life's "Great Balancing Act" definitely will be enjoyed by Spanish speakers!

Shulevitz, Uri. *El tesoro.* *(The Treasure)* Illus: the author. Translated by Maria Negioni. New York: Mirasol/Farrar, Straus, and Giroux, 1991. 32p. ISBN: 0-374-37422-8. $16.00. Gr. 1-3.

Shulevitz's time-honored folktale about a poor old man who finds treasure in his own home after a dream directs him to look elsewhere has been appropriately translated into Spanish. The illustrations, full of well-modulated color and striking light use, are as captivating as the originals, first published in 1979.

Singer, Isaac Bashevis. *Por qué Noé eligió la paloma.* *(Why Noah Chose the Dove)* Illus: Eric Carle. Translated by Aída E. Marcuse. New York: Mirasol/Farrar, Straus, and Giroux, 1991. 32p. ISBN: 0-374-36085-5. $16.00. Gr. K-2.

Spanish speakers will enjoy this exquisite translation with Carle's expansive, full-color illustrations, which tells why Noah chose the modest dove as his messenger. The stiff, cut-out-style figures that romp gaily to the edges of each big page are as charming as the originals first published in 1974.

Slobodkina, Esphyr. *Se venden gorras.* *(Caps for Sale)* Illus: the author. Translated by Teresa Mlawer. New York: Harper Arco Iris/HarperCollins, 1995. 44p. ISBN: 0-06-025330-4. $12.95. ISBN: 0-06-443401-X. pap. $3.95. Gr. K-2.

The perennial storytime favorite about a cap seller and his encounter with the mischievous monkeys will delight Spanish-speaking young readers/listeners. Just like the original English version, youngsters will sympathize with the cap seller as he counts, organizes by color, and sells his caps.

Smith, Lane. *Las grandes mascotas.* *(The Big Pets)* Translated by Ernestina Loyo. México: Fondo de Cultura Económica, 1993. 32p. ISBN: 968-16-4113-2. $12.99. Gr. 1-3.

A little girl and a big cat enjoy traveling through space towards the Milky Way. While he drinks milk from the Milky Way, she swims alongside other children of the night. They also meet a little boy who travels on the back of a big dog as well as other children who play with huge serpents, hamsters, and crickets. Modernistic, bold, watercolor spreads provide a surreal ambiance to this fantasy (originally published by Viking Penguin) about pets and children and dreams.

Snyder, Carol. *Uno arriba, uno abajo. (One Up, One Down)* Illus: Maxie Chambliss. Translated by Alma Flor Ada. New York: Simon & Schuster/Atheneum, 1995. 32p. ISBN: 0-689-31994-0. $15.00. Gr. Preschool-2.

Older Spanish-speaking siblings will enjoy the story of a small girl who helps her parents take care of her twin baby brothers, from the time they are born until they begin to walk and talk. Jovial line-and-watercolor cartoon illustrations express the affection of the family as well as the mess and exhaustion of the domestic scene.

Solotareff, Nadia, and Grégoire Solotareff. *Bebé conejito. (Baby Bunny)* ISBN: 84-207-4423-9.

—————. *Bebé elefantito. (Baby Elephant)* ISBN:84-207-4427-1.

—————. *Bebé ratoncito. (Baby Mouse)* ISBN:84-207-4426-3.

Ea. vol.: 10p. Translated from the French by Nausica P. Eyheramonno. Madrid: Grupo Anaya, 1992. $10.95. Ages 2-5.

The very young will delight in these appealing board books with bright, watercolor illustrations introducing baby animals. Each five-by-five-inch volume shows an animal—a bunny, an elephant, and a mouse—eating, playing, and sleeping. The simple text is easy-to-understand and encourages listener and reader participation: e.g., "*me gustan las zanahorias. ¿Y a ti?*" (I like carrots. Do you?) with just the right illustration of a bunny in the middle of a carrot patch enjoying his carrots. Other titles in this series, originally published in France, are *Bebé burrito, Bebé cerdito, Bebé corderito, Bebé gatito, Bebé monito, Bebé osito, Bebé patito, Bebé perrito,* and *Bebé pollito.*

Steadman, Ralph. *¡Osito! ¿Dónde estás? (Teddy! Where Are You?)* Translated by Catalina Domínguez. México: Fondo de Cultura Económica, 1994. 26p. ISBN: 968-16-4556-1. $10.99. Gr. K-2.

Grace and her little sister have never seen a teddy bear. To please them, Grandpa searches all over his house but can't find his favorite teddy bear. In doing so, he recounts many wonderful times and decides to buy them a new one. Teddy bears, however, are not easy to find in modern toy stores, which are full of colorful plastic toys. Fortunately, there are many teddy bears in search of a home. Witty, cartoon-edged watercolors with a modernistic flair accompany the lively Spanish rendition of the original, first published by Andersen Press, London, in 1994.

Stevens, Jan Romero. *Carlos and the Cornfield/Carlos y la milpa de maíz.* Illus: Jeanne Arnold. Flagstaff, AZ: Northland Publishing, 1995. 32p. ISBN: 0-87358-596-8. $14.95. Gr. 1-3.

Richly satisfying, this well-done bilingual story tells about Carlos, who is so excited about earning money for a shiny, red pocket-knife, that he disregards his father's warning and drops too many corn seeds in many rows. When the field starts to sprout, Carlos realizes his mistake and learns that, indeed, you reap what you sow. Luscious, full-page oil paintings in deep browns warmly depict the Southwest landscape and the close feelings between father and son.

Stone, Bernard. *Operación ratón.* *(Emergency Mouse)* Illus: Ralph Steadman. Translated by Catalina Domínguez. México: Fondo de Cultura Económica, 1993. 24p. ISBN: 968-16-4033-0. $12.99. Gr. 1-3.

Enrique, a little boy, is at the hospital recovering from surgery. To avoid thinking about his painful jaw, he tries to think about pleasant things, such as Blanco, his pet mouse. He dreams that his many mice friends are truly heroic in dealing with incredible diseases, only to find out in the morning that his mother is taking him home that day. Enrique's dream and hospital fears are whimsically portrayed in lively watercolor illustrations. This is a fluid Spanish translation of *Emergency Mouse,* originally published by Andersen Press, London, in 1978.

Suárez, Maribel *¿Cuántos son?* *(How Many?)* ISBN: 970-05-0317-8.
————. *Mis primeras palabras.* *(My First Words)* ISBN: 970-05-0284-8.
Ea. vol.: 16p. (Albores) Mexico: Grijalbo, 1992. $3.50. Ages 3-6.

Like previous titles in this unassuming paperback series for young children, these include appealing watercolor illustrations of things the very young can readily identify. Despite the drab covers, *Mis primeras palabras* is a joyous introduction to a child's first words in Spanish, and *¿Cuántos son?* to the world of mathematics through the concepts of equality, more than and less than. The laminated pages feel good and will be welcomed by all readers.

Tabor, Nancy María Grande. *Somos un arco iris/We Are a Rainbow.* Illus: the author. Watertown, MA: Charlesbridge, 1995. 32p. ISBN: 0-88106-813-6. pap. $6.95. Gr. Preschool-2.

Determined seekers of bilingual books will appreciate this optimistic bilingual (Spanish/English) message that discusses the differences yet emphasizes the similarities among children from different places. It concludes: ". . . it is much more fun to be together—to share, to care, to smile, and to laugh." The colorful cut-paper art and the simple bilingual text add a festive tone to this multicultural comparison.

Talkington, Bruce. *Disney la navidad de Winnie Puh. (Disney's Winnie the Pooh's Christmas)* Illus: Alvin White Studio and others. Translated by Daniel Santacruz. New York: Disney Press/ Little, Brown and Company, 1994. 46p. ISBN: 0-7868-5007-8. pap. $13.89. Gr. 1-3.

Another Disney film adaptation that is bound to have wide popular demand. Fortunately, Spanish speakers will enjoy this fluid, well-done translation.

Thomson, Ruth. *Colores. (Colors)* Illus: Deborah War. ISBN: 84-7525-385-7.

————. *Contrarios. (Opposites)* Illus: Katy Sleight. ISBN: 84-7525-398-9.

————. *Formas. (Shapes)* Illus: Penny Ives. ISBN: 84-7525-399-7.

————. *Ruidos. (Sounds)* Illus: Mary Rees. ISBN: 84-7525-387-3. Ea. vol.: 26p. Translated by Juan Manuel Ibeas Delgado. (Mi Primer Libro) Madrid: Grupo Anaya, 1986. $6.95. Gr. K-2.

The very young are introduced to basic colors, opposite concepts, geometric shapes, and various sounds through amusing situations and charming watercolor illustrations. The only unfortunate aspect of this otherwise outstanding series is that the text is written in cursive, making it difficult to read by those for whom it is obviously intended.

Torres, Leyla. *Gorrión del metro. (Subway Sparrow)* Illus: the author. New York: Farrar, Straus, and Giroux, 1993. 30p. ISBN: 0-374-32756-3. $15.00. Gr. K-2.

A sparrow is trapped in a New York subway; fortunately, a young girl is eager to help it escape. Thanks to the concern and efforts of two Spanish-speaking young people, one English-speaking gentleman, and a Polish-speaking lady, the sparrow flies away safely. The luminous full-page watercolor spreads of four people eager to assist a lovely sparrow are hard to resist. The intermingling of three languages—Spanish, English, and Polish—sounds authentic as each person expresses his/her concern in his/her own language. This book is also available in English.

Torres, Leyla. *El sancocho del sábado. (Saturday Sancocho)* Illus: the author. New York: Mirasol/Farrar, 1995. 32p. ISBN: 0-374-31997-9. $15.00. Gr. K-3.

María Lilí spends Saturdays with her grandparents, Mamá Ana and Papá Angelino, making the popular Central and South American dish, *sancocho*. Spanish-speaking youngsters will enjoy this joyous Spanish rendition in which Mamá Ana, a shrewd and experienced barterer, bargains for the best and biggest chicken and vegetables. The bright, lively watercolors capture the action, flavor, and color of a Latin American market.

Trivizas, Eugene. *Los tres lobitos y el cochino feroz.* *(The Three Little Wolves and the Big Bad Pig)* Illus: Helen Oxenbury. Translated by, Alex Dearden. Caracas: Ediciones Ekaré, 1994. 32p. ISBN: 980-257-177-6. $18.50. Gr. 1-4.

This modern retelling with a role reversal of the classic tale is bound to please contemporary Spanish-speaking readers and listeners. Oxenbury's inimitable full-page watercolor illustrations showing the big bad pig huffing and puffing and finally resorting to pneumatic drills, sledge hammers, and dynamite to blow the house down are full of action and charm.   Especially so when beauty prevails and the big bad pig becomes a good pig and enjoys flowers and tea with his new friends. This is an excellent Spanish rendition of the original version, published by Heinemann, London, in 1993.

Tu primer libro de contar. *(Your First Counting Book)*
Tu primer libro de los colores. *(Your First Book about Colors)*
Tu primer libro de sies y noes. *(Your First Book about Yes and No)*
Tu primer libro para la hora de dormir. *(Your First Bedtime Book)*
Ea. vol.:   22p. Illus: David Anstey. (Pequeños Dinosaurios) Madrid: Susaeta, 1986.   ISBN: 84-305-1395-3 (for the series). $5.95. Gr. K-2.

In a lively and amusing manner, young children are taught basic colors, to count from one to ten, and to follow common rules.   The last title of this series, *Tu primer libro para la hora de dormir*, tells about a dinosaur's dreams.   The bold watercolor illustrations and the brief texts will appeal to young children.

Udry, Janice May. *Un árbol es hermoso.* *(A Tree is Nice)* Illus: Marc Simont.   Translated by María A. Fiol.   New York: HarperCollins, 1995. 30p. ISBN: 0-06-025317-7. $13.95; ISBN: 0-06-443405-2. pap. $4.95. Ages 4-7.

The childlike terms and enticing color and black-and-white illustrations that made this Caldecott award winner a favorite is sure to please Spanish-speaking children. Trees are nice to have around— they fill up the sky, make everything beautiful, help cats get away from dogs, and are just right to climb in, to hang a swing in, or to plant.

Van Allsburg, Chris. *La escoba de la viuda. (The Widow's Broom)*
Translated by Catalina Domínguez. México: Fondo de Cultura
Económica, 1993. 30p. ISBN: 968-16-4005-5. $12.99. Gr. K-3.

Chris Van Allsburg's fantasy about a magic broom that assists a
lonely widow and frightens strong men is now available in this
fluid Spanish translation. The striking quality of the two-tone
illustrations is certainly here. Young Spanish speakers should not
miss this wonderful artistic creation.

Velthuijs, Max. *Sapo en invierno. (Frog in Winter)* Caracas:
Ediciones Ekaré—Banco del Libro, 1992. 26p. ISBN: 980-257-
117-2. $11.50. Gr. K-2.

Frog is sad because winter has arrived. He is very cold and
cannot enjoy himself because he lacks Duck's feathers, Pig's protective fat, or Hare's fur. So, when he gets sick, his friends
immediately come to his rescue and knit a sweater with beautiful
stripes for him. Fortunately, spring's arrival warms everyone's
spirits. All children will enjoy this story about friendship with
the same stunning, simple watercolor illustrations as originally
published in 1992 in London by Andersen Press.

Velthuijs, Max. *Sapo enamorado. (Frog in Love)* Caracas:
Ediciones Ekaré—Banco del Libro, 1992. 24p. ISBN: 980-257-
112-1. $11.50. Gr. K-3.

Frog is confused. Sometimes he feels sad, sometimes he's
happy and his heart goes "tunk, tunk." After much thought, his
friend, Hare, determines that Frog is in love. But Pig explains to
him that he cannot love White Duck, because she is white and he is
green. Frog ignores Pig and continues to love Duck, who is eager
to care for him. Since then, they've loved each other tenderly
because "love knows no borders." The simple and alluring watercolor illustrations definitely capture Frog's message of love in this
story, originally published in 1989 by Andersen Press in London.

Velthuijs, Max. *Sapo y el forastero. (Frog and the Stranger)*
Caracas: Ediciones Ekaré, 1994. 26p. ISBN: 980-257-140-7.
$13.95. Gr. K-3.

Frog is the only one who approves of Rat, the stranger just
arrived in the forest. This causes great commotion among Frog's
friends who resent and criticize Rat: They believe that Rat is lazy,
dirty, adventuresome, rude, and even worse—different. But when
Pig and Hare need help, Rat is the first one there. The bright and
simple watercolor illustrations are just right as a background to this
story about differences versus kindness and generosity. This well-

done Spanish rendition of the original version was first published by Andersen Press, London, in 1993.

Velthuijs, Max. *Sapo y la canción del Mirlo. (Frog and the Bird-song)* Caracas: Ediciones Ekaré-Banco del Libro, 1992. 24p. ISBN: 980-257-112-1. $11.50. Gr. K-2.

Frog is worried that something is wrong with a blackbird that is lying on the ground and doesn't move. He consults with Pig, Duck, and Hare and concludes that the blackbird is dead. Together they give him a proper burial, remember his beautiful singing, and, later, play and laugh in the grass accompanied by a young black-bird, as Frog asks: "Isn't life wonderful?" Originally published by Andersen Press, London, in 1991, this charming story with a human message and stunning, simple watercolor illustrations is sure to appeal to nature lovers as well as other readers/listeners.

Viorst, Judith. *Alexander, que de ninguna manera—¿le oyen?—¡lo dice en serio!—se va a mudar. (Alexander, Who's Not—Do You Hear Me? I Mean It!—Going to Move)* Illus: Robin Preiss Glasser. Translated by Alma Flor Ada. New York: Simon and Schuster/Colibrí, 1995. 32p. ISBN: 0-689-31984-3. $15.00. Gr. 2-4.

Viorst's popular Alexander, who snarls and scowls here because he has to move, will appeal to Spanish speakers who have endured the pain and anguish of leaving friends, neighbors, and special places. Like in the English version, the combination of farce, immediacy, and wild exaggeration from the child's point of view, along with the crosshatched drawings, amusingly depict Alex-ander's heartfelt grief upon the inevitable move.

Waddell, Martin. *Las lechucitas. (Owl Babies)* Illus: Patrick Benson. Translated by Andrea B. Bermúdez. Compton, CA: Santillana. 1994. 26p. ISBN: 0-88272-137-2. $17.95. Gr. Preschool-2.

Sara, Perci, and Guille, three baby owls, live with their mother, Mama owl, in a hole of a tree trunk. When they wake up one morning, they notice that their mother is gone. They try to reassure each other by such thoughts as "Mother went for food." But when it gets dark, and Mother is nowhere to be seen, they really get worried. Finally, Mother returns and, of course, they jump and dance with joy. The striking, double-page spreads featuring warm, light golden baby owls against a black forest background provide a perfect setting for the concerned owls as they wait for mama. Young children will empathize and enjoy the reassuring tone of this story originally published by Walker Books, Great Britain, in 1992.

Walsh, Ellen Stoll. *Cuenta ratones.* *(Mouse Count)* Translated by Gerardo Cabello. México: Fondo de Cultura Económica, 1992. 32p. ISBN: 968-16-3766-6. $12.99. Gr. K-2.
On a beautiful day, ten mice are having fun. Things change when a hungry snake decides to put them in a jar and eat them up. The clever mice outsmart the snake and one by one run home to safety. This charming fantasy/counting book, originally published by Harcourt Brace, is enhanced by alluring watercolor illustrations and a wonderful Spanish translation.

Walsh, Ellen Stoll. *Gansa tonta.* *(You Silly Goose)* México: Fondo de Cultura Económica, 1994. 32p. ISBN: 968-16-4495-6. $10.99. Gr. K-3.
Gladys, a goose, and Max, a mouse, are good friends. But Lulú, a snoopy neighbor, mistakens Max for the bad fox and throws him in a pond. Fortunately, when the real fox appears and tries to bite Lulú, Max has already taken care of the situation. Tender watercolor double-page spreads touchingly depict friendship at its best in this smooth Spanish rendition of the original, first published by Harcourt Brace in 1992.

Walsh, Ellen Stoll. *Pinta ratones.* *(Mouse Paint)* Translated by Gerardo Cabello. México: Fondo de Cultura Económica, 1992. 32p. ISBN: 968-16-3768-2. $12.99. Gr. K-2.
Three white mice on a white piece of paper cannot be seen by a cat. While the cat sleeps, the mice play with red, yellow, and blue mouse paint producing orange, green, and purple mice. But they are careful to leave a white section, so they can hide from the cat. Children learning about primary colors will enjoy this well-translated fantasy, originally published by Harcourt Brace in 1989.

Wilhelm, Hans. *Un chico valiente como yo.* *(A Cool Kid—Like Me!)* Translated by Pilar Garriga. Barcelona: Editorial Juventud, 1992. 30p. ISBN: 84-261-2658-8. $15.95. Gr. Preschool-2.
A little boy tells how everyone thinks he is cool because he paints, brushes his teeth everyday, plays with his friend, and entertains himself when his parents are busy. Only his Grandmother knows the truth: That he sometimes is afraid of the dark or sad when he loses a ball. So when Grandmother is ready to go on a trip, she gives him a special gift—a teddy bear—who will accompany him while she is away. Young readers and listeners will enjoy comparing their fears and apprehensions with this little boy,

his understanding grandmother, and a loyal teddy bear. The soft, pastel watercolor and ink illustrations are as touching as the simple narrative that is wonderfully translated into Spanish. Originally published by Crown Publishers.

Wilkes, Angela, and Rubí Borgia. *Mi primer libro de palabras en español. (My First Book of Spanish Words)* New York: Dorling Kindersley, 1993. Distributed by Houghton Mifflin. 64p. ISBN: 1-56458-262-0. $12.95. Gr. K-2.

Like previous titles in this attractive, large-format series, originally published in London, this includes excellent photographs in color of things that children can identify from their daily lives at home, at school, in the zoo, in the park, etc. Spanish speakers (and those interested in learning Spanish) will appreciate the sharp photographs and clear bilingual (Spanish/English) labels indicating their first Spanish words.

Williams, Sue. *Salí de paseo. (I Went Walking)* Illus: Julie Vivas. Translated by Alma Flor Ada. San Diego: Harcourt Brace, 1995. 32p. ISBN: 0-15-200288-X. pap. $5.00. Ages 3-6.

Clean, oversize white pages are an excellent backdrop for the slightly stylized animals that romp across the pages while a young boy plays a guessing game as he identifies animals by name and color. The dynamic watercolors and the simple, repetitive text make this charming story an excellent story hour choice for young Spanish speakers as they learn which animal is which.

Williams, Vera B. *Algo especial para mí. (Something Special for Me)* Translated by Aída E. Marcuse. New York: Mulberry/ Morrow, 1994. 30p. ISBN: 0-688-13802-0. $15.93; ISBN: 0-688-13803-9. pap. $4.95. Gr. 1-3.

Spanish-speaking children will sympathize with Rosa's dilemma: Her birthday is almost at hand, but she can't decide what she wants for her birthday even though Mama says she can empty the half-filled penny jar for a present. Dense and bold full-page color spreads with eclectic borders show Rosa choosing wisely and looking forward to playing music with her new accordion.

Williams, Vera B. *¡Música para todo el mundo! (Music, Music for Everyone)* Illus: by the author. Translated by Aída E. Marcuse. New York: Mulberry/Morrow, 1995. 32p. ISBN: 0-688-07811-7. pap. $4.95. Ages 4-7.

Williams continues the story begun with *Un sillón para mi mamá (A Chair for My Mother);* now the family chair is often empty for Abuela is sick in bed. Rosa wonders how, with Abuela sick, they will ever be able to get the money jar full again. Rosa organizes her friends into la "Banda de la Calle Oak," which debuts with great success at a neighbor's anniversary party. Spanish-speaking children will welcome this latest installment about Rosa and her family with somewhat impressionistic rich and warm illustrations rimmed with eclectic borders.

Williams, Vera B. *Un sillón para mi mamá. (A Chair for my Mother)* Illus: the author. New York: Mulberry/Greenwillow, 1994. 32p. ISBN: 0-688-00-914-X. $4.95; lib. ed. ISBN: 0-688-00915-8. $15.95. Gr. K-2.

Spanish-speaking young readers can now share in the atmosphere of anticipation and family warmth that prevails in this story in which a young girl tells how she, her mother, and her grandmother save up all of their spare coins in a big glass jar toward the day when they will buy a much-needed easy chair. The scant plot is still here but Williams's energetic watercolor illustrations which brim with color and a cozy, indulgent expressionism will certainly vie for the attention of young Spanish-speaking readers and viewers.

Willis, Val. *El secreto en la caja de fósforos. (The Secret in the Matchbox)* Illus: John Shelley. Translated by Alma Flor Ada. New York: Mirasol/Farrar, Straus, and Giroux, 1993. 32p. ISBN: 0-374-36701-9. $16.00. Ages 5-8.

Spanish-speaking youngsters will be enthralled by the possibility of hiding a show-stopping surprise in the palms of their hands as they enjoy Paquito Pinzon's secret—a miniature dragon. The chaotic classroom scenes and the busy, detailed borders provide the right ambiance for the apathetic students and the fantasy monster.

Wood, Audrey. *La casa adormecida. (The Napping House)* Illus: Don Wood. Translated by Alma Flor Ada and F. Isabel Campoy. San Diego: Harcourt Brace, 1995. 32p. ISBN: 0-15-200053-4. pap. $5.00. Ages 3-6.

Like the original English version, this cumulative tale has the distinction of some wonderfully inventive artwork with unusual yet highly defined shapes, shadings, and perspectives that transforms a rainy, dreary day into a glorious rainbowed day. Spanish-speaking children will enjoy this perfect day for napping in which a nightcapped granny sleeps on a cozy bed followed by a somnambulant child, a dozing dog, a snoozing cat, and a slumbering mouse, who unfortunately is bitten by a wakeful flea, causing a chain of events that awakens the whole house.

Wood, Audrey. *Veloz como el grillo. (Quick Like a Cricket)* Illus: Don Wood. New York: Child's Play, 1995. 32p. ISBN: 0-8595-3-977-6. pap. $6.95. Ages 4-7.

An exuberant young child expresses his feelings about himself: He is quick like a cricket, slow like a snail, small like an ant, big like a whale, . . . sad . . . , happy . . . , lazy . . . , industrious . . . , etc. The wonderfully inventive double-page spreads coupled with the simple, direct text definitely capture a child's feelings about himself.

Wylie, Joanne, and David Wylie. *Un cuento de peces, más o menos.* *(A More or Less Fish Story)* (Fishy Fish Stories) Translated by Lada Josefa Kratky. Chicago: Children's Press, 1988. 28p. ISBN: 0-516-32984-7. $8.45. Gr. K-2.

A little girl introduces the numbers from one to ten while she explains the number of fish she caught. Bright watercolor illustrations and an easy-to-read text make learning numbers a special joy.

Zelinsky, Paul O. *El enano saltarín,* cuento de los Hermanos Grimm. *(Rumpelstiltskin)* Illus: the author. New York: Dutton Children's Books, 1992. 38p. ISBN: 0-525-44903-5. $15.00. Gr. K-2.

Zelinsky's exquisite artistic interpretation of Grimms's tale about a miller's daughter who gets unexpected help in turning hay into gold thread from a gnomelike little man can now be enjoyed by Spanish-speaking youngsters in the United States. The direct, easy-to read Spanish text, translated in Spain in 1987, is a real joy to read or to listen to and is adorned with jeweled tones and museum-quality illustrations. Note: Most Spanish speakers in the United States might object to one peninsular Spanish conjugation, *"Imaginad."* Although recognizable, this inflected verbal form sounds old-fashioned to Spanish speakers from Latin America and the United States. This minor caveat is certainly not meant to deter Spanish speakers from enjoying this most wonderful adaptation.

Zemach, Margot. *La gallinita roja: Un viejo cuento. (The Little Red Hen: An Old Story)* Translated by Aída E. Marcuse. New York: Farrar, Straus, and Giroux, 1992. 30p. ISBN: 0-374-34285-7. $14.00. Ages 2-5.

Zemach's crisp, unembellished text and whimsical watercolor illustrations are just what young Spanish speakers need. This sensitive, well-interpreted translation of the perennial favorite about an industrious little red hen and a lazy pig, cat, and goose is just perfect for the easy-story Spanish shelf.

Zemach, Margot. *Siempre puede ser peor.* *(It Could Always Be Worse)* Illus: the adapter. Translated by Aída E. Marcuse. New York: Mirasol/Farrar, Straus, and Giroux, 1991. 32p. ISBN: 0-374-36907-0. $17.00. Gr. K-3.

The immensely satisfying tale of a rabbi's response to a poor man's complaint about his terrible life is now available to Spanish-speaking readers with Zemach's original zesty, action-packed illustrations, strong colors, and careful composition. It must be noted that in this otherwise fluid Spanish translation, young Spanish-speaking readers will be confused by the regionalism *"como ser, uno o dos pollos"* (unpaged). This usage is too dialect-specific, and so fails to communicate to larger audiences of Spanish speakers. (See *Diccionario de dudas y dificultades de la lengua española* by Manuel Seco, Madrid: Espasa Calpe, 1986, p. 106.)

Zolotow, Charlotte. *El señor conejo y el hermoso regalo (Mr. Rabbit and the Lovely Present)* Illus: Maurice Sendak. Translated by María A. Fiol. New York: HarperCollins, 1995. 32p. ISBN: 0-06-025326-6. $13.95; ISBN: 0-06-443404-4. pap. $4.95. Ages 5-8.

Like the original English version, this gentle story about a little girl who asks Mr. Rabbit's help in thinking of a birthday present for her mother is told entirely in dialog, here smoothly rendered into Spanish. Sendak's lovely, full-page color illustrations perfectly match the story's quiet mood: a basket of fruit makes a lovely gift for mother.

General Fiction

Alcott, Louisa May. *Mujercitas.* *(Little Women)* Illus: Violeta Monreal. Translated by Almudena Lería. 296p. ISBN: 84-207-6547-3.

Doyle, Sir Arthur Conan. *El archivo Sherlock Holmes.* *(The Case-Book of Sherlock Holmes)* Illus: H.K. Elcock and others. Translated by Juan Manuel Ibeas. 295p. ISBN: 84-207-6536-8.

Féval, Paul. *El jorobado.* *(The Humpback)* Illus: Janet Lange and others. Translated by Megalí Martínez Solimán. 655p. ISBN: 84-207-6537-6.

Leroux, Gaston. *El fantasma de la ópera.* *(The Phantom of the Opera)* Illus: José Ma. Ponce. Translated by Mauro Armiño. 342p. ISBN: 84-207-6538-4.

Verne, Jules. *Veinte mil leguas de viaje submarino.* *(Twenty Thousand Leagues under the Sea)* Illus: Alphonse de Neuville and Edouard Riou. Translated by Miguel Angel Navarrete. 557p. ISBN: 84-207-6535-X.

Ea. vol.: (Tus Libros) Madrid: Anaya, 1995. $11.95. Gr. 8-12.

Like the previous 140 titles in this excellent series, these are wonderful, fluid Spanish renditions of popular novels with exquisite black-and-white illustrations. Spanish-speaking adolescents will be pleased with these updated editions with attractive covers and good quality paper and design of many of their favorite books. Teachers and librarians as well as serious readers will be interested in the well-written appendices and notes which provide information on the author and his or her work.

Almagor, Gila. *El verano de Aviya.* *(Aviya's Summer)* Translated from the Hebrew by Carlos Silveira. Salamanca: Lóguez Ediciones, 1994. 110p. ISBN: 84-85334-76-0. pap. $10.95. Gr. 7-12.

Aviya has one wish: She would like to live with her mother and leave the boarding school where she has spent the last five years. In a touching and engrossing manner, Gila Almagor, a well-known Israeli actress, relates in this powerful fictionalized account her sad experiences with a mother who was too sick to care for her. Set in Israel in the summer of 1951, this easy-to-read novel will affect adolescents who may share some of the same feelings of neglect or powerlessness as the protagonist. The only undesirable feature of this excellent, fluid translation is the trite cover which features an unattractive girl with her eyes closed. Unfortunately, it dissuades most readers.

Alonso, Manuel L. *Papá ya no vive con nosotros.* *(Papa Doesn't Live with Us Anymore)* Illus: Asun Balzola. Madrid: Ediciones SM, 1993. 63p. ISBN: 84-348-3968-7. pap. $6.95. Gr. 3-5.

Pablo, a little boy, is happy at home with Mama, Papa, and his toys. But one day, things change: Pablo notices that Mama is very sad and Papa doesn't come home at night. On Saturday when Papa comes home to pack his things, he holds Pablo and tells him that he loves him very much, but that he is moving to another house. This is an honest and moving story about a little boy and his parents who together experience the sad realities of separation and change. Asun Balzola's touching pen and watercolor illustrations add an even more poignant feeling to Pablo's pain. Parents or teachers looking for ways to talk to children about this difficult subject will appreciate the author's candor.

Altman, Linda Jacobs. *El camino de Amelia.* *(Amelia's Road)* Illus: Enrique O. Sánchez. Translated by Daniel Santacruz. New York: Lee and Low Books, 1993. 30p. ISBN: 1-880000-07-5. $14.95. Gr. 2-4.

Amelia, the daughter of migrant farm workers, is tired of moving around so much. She dreams of a place that belongs to her, a place where she can come back to. Spanish speakers will especially like the vivid color landscapes depicting lush farmland.

Andersen, Hans Christian. *Los cuentos más bonitos. (The Most Beautiful Stories)* Illus: Michael Fiodorov. Translated by Giovani Cantieri. Madrid: Plaza Joven, 1991. 98p. ISBN: 84-01-31328-7. $21.50. Gr. 3-6.

Seven stories by H. C. Andersen are included in this attractive, large-format publication with exquisitely detailed watercolor illustrations of beautiful princesses, courageous soldiers, vain emperors, kind animals, and others. Titles are: *"Pulgarcita," "El eslabón," "El intrépido soldado de plomo," "El traje nuevo del emperador," "El porquerizo," "El ruiseñor," "La princesa y el guisante."* Children, their parents, and teachers will rejoice with this beautiful edition of old-time favorites.

Anderson, Poul. *La espada rota. (The Broken Sword)* Translated by Javier Martín Lalanda. Madrid: Grupo Anaya, 1992. 314p. ISBN: 84-207-4827-7. $19.95. Gr. 8-12.

Skafloc, the godson of the elves, must overcome the terrible curse that befalls the broken sword. This ill-fated malediction puts Skafloc against Valgard, his shadow and main rival, in this high-action fantasy that has the allure and excitement of a Scandinavian saga full of battles and heroic deeds. This revised edition, originally published by Ballantine Books in 1971, has been excellently translated into Spanish.

Anderson, Rachel. *Los mejores amigos. (Best Friends)* Illus: Shelagh McNicholas. Translated by P. Rozarena. ISBN: 84-204-4377-8.

Ehrlich, Amy. *Leo, Zac y Emi: Tres amigos revoltosos. (Leo, Zac and Emmie)* Illus: Steven Kellogg. Translated by Pablo Lizcano. ISBN: 84-204-4372-7.

Tashlin, Frank. *El oso que no lo era. (The Bear That Wasn't)* Illus: the author. Translated by Santiago Lódanos. ISBN: 84-204-4380-8. Ea. vol.: 62p. (Infantil) Madrid: Alfaguara, 1995. pap. $4.95. Gr. 2-4.

This new paperback series by Alfaguara features attractive covers, black-and-white illustrations on every page, and easy-to-read texts. The loneliness of a girl with Down's syndrome, a congenital disease characterized by mental deficiency, is realistically depicted in *Los mejores amigos*, originally published in London. *Leo, Zac y Emi: Tres amigos revoltosos* shows the everyday life of three friends, even though at times only two can play. An occasion when a bear is not really a bear is humorously depicted in *El oso que no lo era*. These are indeed wonderful Spanish renditions of titles originally written in English with a minor caveat: Although perfectly understandable, readers will note the use of the peninsular Spanish pronoun for the second person plural "vosotros."

Anrell, Lasse. *¡Gol! (Goal!)* Illus: Mati Lepp. Translated from the German by Christiane Scheurer and Esteban Martín.   Barcelona: Editorial Juventud, 1995. 30p. ISBN: 84-261-2945-5. $13.95. Gr. 3-5.

Toni, a young boy, loves to play soccer. When he joins a real soccer team with other boys his age, Rayo, the coach, isn't exactly friendly, and Toni doesn't get to play. Fortunately, Rayo oversleeps for the big game and Toni becomes the team's hero. Amusing watercolor illustrations and an easy-to-read narrative provide a lighthearted touch to Toni's experiences as a soccer hero-to-be.

Araujo, Orlando. *Miguel Vicente, pata caliente. (Miguel Vicente "hot feet")* Illus: Morella Fuenmayor. Caracas: Ediciones Ekaré-Banco del Libro, 1992. 46p. ISBN: 980-257-102-4. $14.50. Gr. 3-5.

Miguel Vicente, a boot-black boy who lives in the outskirts of Caracas, enjoys talking to his clients and walking the streets of the city.   His special wish is to be able to travel, but his meager earnings are barely enough to buy food for himself and his mother. In a poignant and honest manner, this story relates the life of the poor in this South American city including such issues as absent fathers and illiteracy. Yet Miguel survives. Full-page watercolor illustrations perfectly capture the tone and spirit of Caracas as lived by one of its young inhabitants.

Askenazy, Ludwig. *Eres único. (You Are Unique)* Illus: Helme Heine.   Translated from the German by Juan Villoro.   México: Fondo de Cultura Económica, 1991. 64p. ISBN: 968-16-3671-6. pap. $6.95. Gr. 3-6.

In a whimsical and playful manner, this collection of ten stories tell about a porcupine that shaved his spines to please his girlfriend, Rosamunda, the cat; a forgetful elephant that knotted his trunk to remember; a deer that lent his antlers to serve as a Christmas tree, and other unique animal characters. The black-and-white line illustrations are as amusing as the stories. Originally published in 1988 by Gertraud Middelhauve Verlag in Germany.

Ayala, Lourdes, and Margarita Isona-Rodríguez. *Los niños alfa-béticos. (Children and the Alphabet)* Illus: Kathryn Shoemaker. Watertown, MA: Charlesbridge, 1995. 32p. ISBN: 0-88106-815-2. pap. $6.95. Gr. 2-5.

The Spanish-language alphabet is introduced to children through Gerardo, Isabel, and their friends who act out each letter using amusing props, colorful costumes, and delightful rhymes. The bright, colorful illustrations provide a playful background to this imaginative use of the letters of the alphabet. It also can be used for reading aloud.

Babbitt, Natalie. *Cuentos del pobre diablo. (The Devil's Storybook)* Illus: the author. Translated by Felicidad Blanco. New York: Farrar, Straus, and Giroux, 1994. 105p. ISBN: 0-374-31769-0. $13.00. Gr. 4-6.

Satan, often conniving but not always clever, is the entertaining antihero in these ten stories that are a delight to read or listen to. The author's brisk, witty style is effectively maintained in this Spanish rendition with the original, amusing black-and-white line drawings. The only caveat for Spanish speakers in Hispanic America is the repeated use of the Peninsular Spanish pronoun for the second person plural (*"vosotros"*), and its corresponding verb endings. Although recognizable, this inflected verbal form and pronoun sound awkward to Spanish speakers in Latin America and the United States.

Babbitt, Natalie. *Tuck para siempre. (Tuck Everlasting)* Translated by Narcis Fradera. New York: Farrar, Straus, and Giroux, 1993. 142p. ISBN: 0-374-48011-7. pap. $3.95. Gr. 5-7.

Babbitt's timeless story about eternal youth has maintained its serious intentions and light touch in this fluid Spanish translation. Spanish-speaking readers will identify with eleven-year-old Winnie Foster as she considers life and death decisions when she rescues her friends, the Tucks, who are charged with kidnapping and murder.

Banks, Lynne Reid. *La llave mágica. (The Indian in the Cupboard)* Translated by Pilar Salamanca Segoviano. Madrid: Editorial Everest, 1995. 203p. ISBN: 84-241-3266-1. pap. $8.95. Gr. 5-8.

This European best-seller in the English version is now available to Spanish speakers in this fluid, fast-paced rendition which maintains a boy's fascination with his plastic Indian toy, his grandmother's magic key, and his special metal chest. Readers will empathize with Omri, who is approximately nine years old, as he accepts responsibility for two tiny human beings—a brave Indian and a cocky cowboy. A wonderful combination of fantasy and adventure.

Baquedano, Lucía. *La casa de los diablos. (The Devils' House)* Barcelona: Editorial Labor, 1992. 172p. ISBN: 84-335-1202-1. pap. $8.95. Gr. 8-12.

Teresa, a teenage orphan who lives in a shelter for adolescents, can't think of a greater joy than having someone—a mother, brother, grandfather—visit her. But such things don't happen to orphans. Her life, however, is never the same after a horrible train accident. Despite a few hard-to-believe coincidences, teenagers will understand Teresa's predicament and appreciate her newly-found "grandmother." This novel was a finalist in the Spanish Infanta Elena International Award for Adolescent Literature.

Barrie, J. M., and Xavier Roca-Ferrer. *Peter Pan y Wendy. (Peter Pan and Wendy)* Illus: Marcé Llimona. Translated by Humberto Lobbosco. Barcelona: Ediciones Destino, 1994. 59p. ISBN: 84-233-2394-3. $19.95. Gr. 4-6.

The ever-popular Peter Pan is presented here in the country of Never Never Land with his friends Wendy Darling, the lost children, and Campanilla as well as the evil Captain Garfio and the courteous pirates. The full-page watercolor illustrations in soft pastels definitely capture the tone and spirit of this long-time classic. The well-done Spanish rendition is easy and light; however, some Spanish speakers from Hispanic America might object to the peninsular Spanish inflected verbal forms and the second personal plural pronoun, which are only used in Spain.

Basch, Adela, and Oscar Rojas. *Había una vez una... (There Was Once A...)* Buenos Aires: Coquena Grupo Editorial, 1993. 22p. ISBN: 950-737-127-X. $10.95. Gr. 2-4.

Children are encouraged to identify missing words through simple incomplete sentences and amusing illustrations in this well-constructed board book. This is indeed a fun way to learn the meaning and spelling of such words as *pato, zapato, bote, soldado, gato,* and others.

Base, Graeme. *El signo del Caballito de Mar: Un intenso episodio en dos actos, de codicia y aventuras. (The Sign of the Seahorse: A Tale of Greed and High Adventure in Two Acts)* Illus: the author. Translated by Juan Ramón Azaola. New York: Harry N. Abrams, Publishers, 1994. 48p. ISBN: 0-8109-4458-8. Gr. 2-4.

To adequately render rhymed couplets into another language is a rare occurrence indeed and this translator has done a masterful job of just that. Like the original English version, however, Spanish-speaking readers and listeners will find that the couplets go on and on and on. A few Spanish speakers will be able to endure this difficult form of poetry but all readers and viewers will be enthralled by the lively, detailed double-page spreads that show an underwater world complete with a café, a bar, assorted good guys, and bad guys with hearts of gold, and some real nasties who insist on poisoning the beautiful underwater reef.

Baylord, Byrd. *Halcón, soy tu hermano. (Hawk, I'm Your Brother)* Illus: Peter Parnall. Translated from the English by Tedi López Mills. México: Fondo de Cultura Económica, 1991. 46p. ISBN: 968-16-3652-X. $13.50. Gr. 3-5.

Rudi Soto, a little boy, wishes he could fly like a hawk. Everything he does is conducive to his dream, including stealing a young hawk. Finally he realizes that he must allow the young hawk to fly away even if he himself will never be able to fly. The sensitive black-and-white line illustrations and the well-done Spanish translation definitely capture the mood of the original, published by Charles Scribner's in 1976.

Berenstain, Stan and Jan Berenstain. *Los osos Berenstain en la oscuridad. (The Berenstain Bears in the Dark)* ISBN: 0-679-83471-0.
―――――. *Los osos Berenstain y el cuarto desordenado. (The Berenstain Bears and the Messy Room)* ISBN: 0-679-83470-2.
Ea. vol.: 30p. Translated by Rita Guibert. New York: Random House, 1992. pap. $2.25. Gr. 2-4.

Fans of the Berenstain bears will enjoy these lively Spanish translations. *Los osos Berenstain en la oscuridad* tells why Sister Bear's bedtime becomes ominous and threatening when Brother Bear brings home a spooky book from the library. *Los osos Berenstain y el cuarto desordenado* describes what happens when the entire Bear family becomes involved in cleaning and organizing the cubs' messy room.

Bichsel, Peter. *El hombre que ya no tenía nada que hacer. (The Man Who Had Nothing to Do)* Illus: Alfonso Ruano. Translated from the German by José A. Santiago Tagle. Madrid: Ediciones SM, 1992. 123p. ISBN: 84-348-3668. $10.95. Gr. 6-10.

The collection of seven stories full of fantasy and humor will delight readers with their unique messages and original characters. The seven protagonists question such things as the roundness of the Earth, the existence of America, new inventions, the kindness of grandmothers, and other verities. The easy-to-read text and the modernistic illustrations in color depicting incongruous situations make these stories truly different. Originally published in Switzerland, this book has been a success among European adolescents.

Blackwood, Dorian. *Un infierno en la mente.* *(A Hell in Mind)* Translated by Javier Martín Lalanda. (Ultima Thule) Madrid: Grupo Anaya, 1995. 246p. ISBN: 84-207-6696-8. $16.95. Gr. 10-adult.

Sometime in the twenty-first century, Harry O'Halloram, a literary editor, receives a puzzling manuscript written by a beautiful, mysterious lady. Thus begins this engrossing fantasy in which the protagonist travels back in time to the twelfth century in England to rescue his beloved from hell. Mature lovers of fantasy will enjoy this fast-paced novel about beautiful women and intelligent men as they travel in time.

Blanco, Alberto. *The Desert Mermaid/La sirena del desierto.* Illus: Patricia Revah. English translation by Barbara Paschke. San Francisco: Children's Book Press, 1992. 32p. ISBN: 0-89239-106-5. $13.95. Gr. 3-5.

In a lyrical and emotional manner, a desert mermaid recounts that her beautiful oasis is growing smaller and that her people are disappearing because they have forgotten the songs of their ancestors. Set in the beautiful Sonora Desert and illustrated with photographs of colorful woven tapestries that give this bilingual (English/Spanish) story a myth-like quality, readers will rejoice in the mermaid's tears of happiness as she returns to the roots of her people. The original Spanish text is a special joy to read or to listen to.

Boullosa, Carmen. *El médico de los piratas.* *(The Doctor of Pirates)* Madrid: Ediciones Siruela, 1992. 95p. ISBN: 84-7844-116-6. $15.95. Gr. 8-12.

Through Smeeks, a slave who learned the art of healing from his masters, readers are exposed to the cruelties and abuses as well as close friendships prevalent among pirates and buccaneers in the Caribbean during the seventeenth century. This is not a fast-moving adventure novel, but rather a gripping depiction of brotherhoods at the time of the Inquisition. Well-selected black-and-white reproductions of lithographs of the period add impact to the narrative.

Breve antología de cuentos.   *(Brief Anthology of Short Stories)* Buenos Aires: Editorial Sudamericana, 1991. 117p. ISBN: 950-07-0649-0. pap. $8.90. Gr. 9-adult.

An excellent collection of nine short stories includes *"Circe"* by Julio Cortázar, *"¡Embustero!"* by Isaac Asimov, *"El huésped de la maestra*" by Isabel Allende, "*Un canasto junto al Tiber*" by Alberto Moravia, and five others by lesser-known Argentine authors. The diversity of authors and topics as well as the variety of lengths of each story—the longest is thirty-three pages and a few are one page—provide readers with a great deal of choice.

Browne, Anthony. *Gorila. (Gorilla)* Illus: the author. Translated from the English by Carmen Esteva. México: Fondo de Cultura Económica, 1991. 30p. ISBN: 968-16-3651-1. $13.30. Gr. 3-5.
 Ana, a little girl, loves gorillas. She reads about gorillas, paints gorillas, and watches TV programs about gorillas. But her father was too busy to take her to the zoo to see a live gorilla. After a wonderful dream with her favorite gorilla, Ana wakes up on her birthday with her father's invitation to go to the zoo. The bold, watercolor illustrations of Ana with her gorillas are sure to satisfy all young readers. The fluid translation is an added delight. This story, originally published in Great Britain in 1983, was awarded the Kate Greenaway Award in 1984.

Browne, Anthony. *El libro de los cerdos. (Piggybook)* Illus: the author. Translated from the English: Carmen Esteva. México: Fondo de Cultura Económica, 1991. 32p. ISBN: 968-16-3651-1. $14.40. Gr. 3-5.
 All family members will enjoy this story, originally published in Great Britain in 1986, which tells how mama finally liberated herself from her Piggy family—a demanding husband and two sons—and taught them to help out with the household chores. Now they all have fun cooking together and mama sometimes even fixes the car. The bold, watercolor illustrations are as direct as the forthright text.

Brusca, María Cristina. *En la pampa. (On the Pampas)* Illus: the author. Buenos Aires: Primera Sudamericana, 1995. 32p. ISBN: 950-07-0944-9. pap. $13.80. Gr. 2-4.
 The excitement of life on a ranch in Argentina is definitely captured in this well-done Spanish rendition of the original English version, originally published by Henry Holt in 1991. Charming and lively watercolor illustrations and an animated text recount a fun-filled summer on the pampas which includes gauchos, horses, *zamba, ñandú* eggs, and big family celebrations.

Burgess, Melvin. *El aullido del lobo. (The Cry of the Wolf)* Translated by María Isabel Butler de Foley. Madrid: Ediciones SM, 1994. 152p. ISBN: 84-348-4404-4. pap. $8.95. Gr. 7-10.

A heartless hunter is committed to his search and ultimate goal: to exterminate English wolves. Packed with action and excitement, this fast-paced novel describes the desire for glory of a zealot who is eager to destroy a unique animal. Adolescents will share in the author's love and respect of animals and will be moved by this fictionalized account of the demise of the last pack of English wolves. Originally published by Andersen Press, London, this novel was included in the 1991 honor list by the Carnegie Award.

Byars, Betsy. *Bingo Brown, amante gitano.* *(Bingo Brown, Gypsy Lover)* Illus: Tino Gatagán.   Translated by Miguel Angel Mendizábel. Madrid: Espasa Calpe, 1994. 164p. ISBN: 84-239-7158-9. pap. $8.95. Gr. 6-8.

Twelve-year-old Bingo Brown continues to be an expert on long-distance romance but this achievement is now threatened by his role as the oldest brother of a new-born baby boy. Spanish-speaking adolescents will appreciate this straightforward novel that presents a real-life situation: the birth of a sibling. Like its predecessor— *Bingo Brown y el lenguaje del amor*—, the cover and black-and-white illustrations are not appropriate for adolescents; they depict a much younger boy rather than Bingo Brown, Gypsy lover, the adolescent protagonist.

Byars, Betsy. *Bingo Brown y el lenguaje del amor.* *(Bingo Brown and the Language of Love)* Illus: Tino Gatagán.   Translated by Miguel Angel Mendizábel. Madrid: Espasa Calpe, 1994. 164p. ISBN: 84-239-7158-9. pap. $8.95. Gr. 6-8.

Twelve-year-old Bingo Brown is suddenly confronted with the problems of love. At the same time, his parents are facing their own personal dilemmas, such as his mother's unexpected pregnancy. Spanish-speaking adolescents will empathize with Bingo's humorous yet honest responses to life's major and minor quandries. It is unfortuante, however, that the cover and the black-and-white illustrations will deter adolescents from approaching this book as they portray a much younger boy, rather than a normal adolescent.

Cansino, Eliacer. *Yo, Robinsón Sánchez, habiendo naufragado.* *(I, Robinson Sánchez, Having Been Shipwrecked)* Barcelona: Ediciones Toray, 1992. 159p. ISBN: 84-310-3406-8. pap. $8.95. Gr. 7-10.

A teenage boy relates in an honest and frank manner his experiences at home and at a new school as his father is assigned from Salamanca to a new job in Seville. Adolescents will sympathize with his infatuation with the most beautiful girl in town, who happens to be older and taller than he; his questions about

God; his problems with the school's principal; and other concerns. It is no wonder that this novel was awarded the 1992 Infanta Elena International Prize for Adolescent Literature in Spain.

Cardenal, Ernesto. *Apalka.* *(Apalka)* Illus: Felipe Dávalos. ISBN: 968-494-057-2.

Parra, Nicanor. *Sinfonía de cuna.* *(Cradle's Symphony)* Illus: Enrique Martínez. ISBN: 968-494-056-4.
  Ea. vol.: 27p. (En Cuento) Mexico: Cidcli, 1992. pap. $9.95. Gr. 4-7.
  The purpose of this paperback series is to expose young readers to notable Spanish-speaking authors. Colorful, witty, full-page spreads add interest to the enjoyable texts. Especially appealing is Nicanor Parra's *Sinfonía de cuna* which shows, in a lighthearted manner, why he is considered the creator of "antipoetry." Lovers of irony will relish.

Castañeda, Omar S. *El tapiz de abuela.* *(Abuela's Weave)* Illus: Enrique O. Sánchez. Translated by Aída E. Marcuse. New York: Lee and Low Books, 1993. 32p. ISBN: 1-880000-08-3. $14.95. Gr. 2-4.
  The sights, people, and culture of rural Guatemala are beautifully portrayed in this exquisitely illustrated book. The bright, rich acrylic-on-canvas paintings convey an intimate view of market day in Guatemala that Spanish-speaking readers/listeners will appreciate.

Cazarré, Lourenço. *La espada del general.* *(The General's Sword)* Illus: Rafael Barajas. Translated from the Portuguese by Mónica Mansour. México: Fondo de Cultura Económica, 1991. 164p. ISBN: 968-16-3661-9. pap. $7.95. Gr. 7-12.
  General Ahmed Salim El Kathib and his important wife, Doña Francisca, were having a big party at their summer house. The party was most enjoyable. But even more fun was looking for the general's lost sword. Adolescents searching for an entertaining novel with delightful characters, amusing black-and-white line illustrations, set in a town in Brazil, should not miss this one. It is easy to see why the Children's Literature Association of Brazil recommends this book so highly: It was originally published in Brazil in 1988 with great success. The author has received several literary awards in his native country.

Cela, Camilo José. *Santa Balbina, 37, gas en cada piso.* *(Santa Balbina, 37, Gas on Each Floor)* ISBN: 84-03-60262-6.

Chejov, Anton. *La dama del perrito y otros relatos.* *(The Lady of the Little Dog and Other Stories)* ISBN: 84-03-60267-7.

Doyle, Arthur Conan. *El tren especial desaparecido y otros relatos.* *(The Missing Special Train and Other Tales)* ISBN: 84-03-60255-3.

Pardo Bazán, Emilia. *Un destripador de antaño y otros relatos.* *(The Ripper of Long Ago and Other Tales)* ISBN: 84-03-60266-9.

Stevenson, Robert Louis. *El extraordinario caso del doctor Jekyll y Mr. Hyde.* *(The Strange Case of Dr. Jekyll and Mr. Hyde)* ISBN: 84-03-60257-X.

Wilde, Oscar. *El crimen de Lord Arthur Savile y otros relatos.* *(Lord Arthur Savile's Crime and Other Stories)* ISBN: 84-03-60256-1.

Yourcenar, Marguerite. *Ana, Soror . . .* *(Anna, Soror . . .)* ISBN: 84-03-60260-X.

Ea. vol: 79p. Miami: Santillana, 1994. pap. $6.95. Gr. 9-adult.

Reader appeal and literary merit are marvelously combined in this superior paperback collection. Adolescents are introduced to some of the world's best writers through brief novels and short stories that are distinguished by strong plots, deft characterizations, and stimulating dialogues. If the goal is to get adolescents to read and enjoy great authors, these selections will certainly encourage readers to approach imaginative literature. Each volume includes a two-page introduction to the author and his or her works and easy-to-understand footnotes that clarify meaning.

Cisneros, Sandra. *La casa en Mango Street.* *(The House on Mango Street)* Translated by Elena Poniatowska. New York: Vintage/Random House, 1994. 112p. ISBN: 0-679-75526-8. pap. $9.00. Gr. 6-12.

Elena Poniatowska's talents as a writer and as a translator make a difficult job seem easy. Translating Cisneros's vignettes from her Chicago Latino neighborhood in which she tells about the poverty, racism, and tribulations experienced by her family and friends is certainly not an easy task. Yet Poniatowska has managed to capture Cisneros's humorous and piercing descriptions in this fluid Spanish translation with a masterful command of the vernacular of Mexico. It must be emphasized that translating colloquialisms is the bane of most translators; hence, this Poniatowska translation could be used as an efficient model when translating English colloquialisms to one of the most important colloquialisms of Hispanic America. Spanish speakers, especially those from Mexico, will enjoy it.

Cleary, Beverly. *La escapada de Ralph.* *(Runaway Ralph)* Illus: Louis Darling. Translated by Ester Donato. Barcelona: Noguer, 1994. 121p. ISBN: 84-279-3424-8. pap. $5.95. Gr. 4-6.

The popular talking and enterprising young mouse, Ralph, and his ever-present motorcycle will entertain Spanish-speaking readers in this animal fantasy that is great fun. Darling's original black-and-white illustrations combined with the joyous Spanish rendition make this paperback version a sure winner.

Climent, Paco. *Sissi no quiere fotos.* *(Sissi Doesn't Want Any Photos)* Barcelona: Ediciones Toray, 1993. 159p. ISBN: 84-310-3515-3. pap. $6.95. Gr. 8-12.

This novel recreates the murder of Sissi, the Empress of Austria and beloved wife of the Emperor Francis Joseph, in 1898 through the eyes of Leticia, an eighteen-year-old journalist. The first part brims with the excitement and expectations of a young journalist eager to succeed in her chosen profession rather than follow her mother's desires: to find a "suitable husband." After that, only devotees of travel books will care to follow Empress Sissi's journey through Seville, Cádiz, and Geneva, where she was murdered by a young Italian anarchist. It is important to note that this novel won the Infanta Elena International Award for adolescent literature in Spain.

Coerr, Eleanor. *Josefina y la colcha de retazos.* *(The Josefina Story Quilt)* Illus: Bruce Degen. Translated by Aída E. Marcuse. (Ya Sé Leer) New York: Harper Arco Iris/HarperCollins, 1995. 64p. ISBN: 0-06-025319-3. $13.95; ISBN: 0-06-444190-3. pap. $3.50. Gr. 2-4.

The beginning-to-read format of the original English version is maintained in this emotional story which shows Esperanza, her pet hen, Josefina, and her family traveling west in 1850. Spanish speakers will empathize with Esperanza's effort to include Josefina on the trip despite her father's objections. Degen's charcoal and color-wash drawings will add to the understanding of a period of U.S. history that may be new to many Spanish-speaking young readers.

Cohen, Barbara. *Molly y los Peregrinos.* *(Molly's Pilgrim)* Illus: Michael J. Deraney. Translated by María A. Fiol. New York: Lectorum, 1995. 32p. ISBN: 1-880507-17-X. $12.95. Gr. 3-5.

Molly's need to belong and to be accepted in school by her classmates, despite her status as a new immigrant who doesn't even speak English well, are touchingly depicted in this well-done translation. The original, realistic two-tone illustrations and a glossary of Yiddish words add to the universal appeal of this story.

Cole, Babette. *El libro tonto.* *(The Silly Book)* Translated by Antoni Vicens. Barcelona: Ediciones Destino, 1992. 34p. ISBN: 84-233-2120-7. $12.95. Gr. 2-4.

A little boy points out many silly things that people do such as wearing silly eyeglasses, underwear, and hats; trying to fly; and eating things with wings and hair. Of course, when the little boy prefers to wear his silly warm costume, *that* is not a silly thing to do. Some adults may object to this amusing depiction of the adult world, but the ludicrous, full-page watercolor illustrations and the witty, simple text are indeed fun.

Cole, Babette. *Los problemas con mi tío.* *(The Trouble with Uncle)* Translated by Antoni Vicens. Barcelona: Ediciones Destino, 1992. 32p. ISBN: 84-233-2126-6. $10.95. Gr. 2-4.

The trouble with Uncle is that he is a pirate, owns a club, and has his own ways of doing things. These factors result in wonderful achievements but cause trouble with Aunt. Lovers of the absurd will delight in Uncle's adventures. The witty illustrations certainly complement the lighthearted text.

Cole, Brock. *Celine.* *(Celine)* Translated by Pedro Barbadillo. Madrid: Alfaguara, 1992. 172p. ISBN: 84-204-4711-0. pap. $11.50. Gr. 9-12.

Sixteen-year-old Celine wants to be a painter. While her father is on a business trip to Europe, she lives with her young stepmother. Things at home aren't going too well especially when she must redo a literature assignment, care for Jake, her neighbor's son, and deal with her own daydreams about Jake's father. Adolescents will enjoy this honest novel that tells about the worries and fantasies of a frank teenager.

Collodi, Carlo. *Pinocho.* *(Pinocchio)* Adapted by Mercè Escardó Bas. Illus: Lluïsot. Translated into Spanish by Noemí Sobregués. ISBN: 84-246-1942-1.

Grimm, J.W. *Hansel y Gretel.* *(Hansel and Gretel)* Adapted by Elisabet Abeyà. Illus: Cristina Losantos. Translated into Spanish by Jesús Ballaz. ISBN: 84-246-1941-2.

Los tres cerditos. *(The Three Little Pigs)* Adapted by Mercè Escardó i Bas. Illus: Pere Joan. Translated by Jesús Ballaz. ISBN: 84-246-1939-0.

Ea. vol.: 24p. (Popular) Barcelona: La Galera, 1995. $9.95. Gr. 3-5.

Readable and engaging narratives characterize these updated versions of these well-known favorites. The modernistic full-page watercolor illustrations on the right page face the easy-to-read text on the left page and add a contemporary touch to Pinocchio, Hansel and Gretel, and The Three Little Pigs.

Cooney, Barbara. *La señorita Emilia.* *(Miss Rumphius)* Illus: the author. Translated by Carmen Diana Dearden. Caracas: Ediciones Ekaré-Banco del Libro, 1992. 32p. ISBN: 980-257-110-5. $13.00. Gr. 2-4.

Barbara Cooney's tender story about the Lady of the Lupines, and how this determined lady succeeded in adorning the countryside with the beautiful plant with long spikes of purple, rose, and blue flowers is now available to Spanish speakers in this well-done translation. The joyous, detailed illustrations of faraway places are definitely special as well as Señorita Emilia's gift which will be appreciated by all readers and listeners.

Corona, Sarah. *El misterio del tiempo robado.* *(The Mystery of Stolen Time)* Illus: Martha Avilés. México: Consejo Nacional para la Cultura y las Artes, 1991. 26p. pap. ISBN: 968-6465-16-2. $7.25. Gr. 3-5.

In a lighthearted manner, a group of children tells what happens when the only clock in town mysteriously disappears: people don't know whether to eat lunch or dinner, teachers arrive late to class, and children have longer rest periods. Finally the children come up with a bright idea and the clock is found. The charming and sensitive watercolor illustrations of a Mexican town bustling with activity make this story even more special and fun.

Cortázar, Julio. *Manual de cronopios.* *(Manual of "Cronopios")* Illus: José Luis Largo. Madrid: Ediciones de la Torre, 1992. 126p. ISBN: 84-86587-99-9. pap. $10.95. Gr. 9-adult.

This manual of *cronopios* (one *cronopio* is a flower; two are a garden) is the perfect introduction for adolescents to Cortázar's wonderful imagery in which new worlds are transformed into flowers, unusual realties, or pleasant surprises. Admirers of the Argentine writer will appreciate the well-written introduction by his close friend, Francisco J. Aris, which highlights Cortázar's life and achievements. Others will prefer to read samples from this collection of brief—from one paragraph to three pages—stories, vignettes, and political statements. Six pages of black-and-white photographs of the late author complement this laudatory collection.

Cortázar, Julio, and others. *16 cuentos latinoamericanos.* *(16 Latin American Short Stories)* Caracas: Ediciones Ekaré. 1992. 221p. ISBN: Unavailable. pap. $9.95. Gr. 9-12.

This anthology of sixteen short stories by well-known and a few lesser-known contemporary Latin American authors will definitely appeal to adolescents. The brevity of each story—from one page to twenty-four pages—and the editors's concern in selecting stories with a high degree of interest to adolescents result in engaging stories that deal with such issues as growing up, sexual relationships, drugs, feelings of inadequacy, and other topics that will surely engage this age group. It is important to note that all of these stories have been published since the 1960s and that each story is preceded by biographical and bibliographical information about each author. Some of the authors represented are Gabriel García Márquez (Colombia), Antonio Skármeta (Chile), José Emilio Pacheco (México), Mario Benedetti (Uruguay), and Julio Cortázar (Argentina). This is indeed a wonderful introduction to contemporary Latin American authors.

Côté, Denis. *Viaje en el tiempo.* *(Travel through Time)* Illus: Francisco Nava Buchaín. Translated from the French by Gabriela Peyrón. México: Fondo de Cultura Económica, 1991. 60p. ISBN: 968-16-3536-1. pap. $6.95. Gr. 6-8.

Maximino, a thirteen-year-old boy, and his girlfriend, Jo, decide to go for a walk after lunch. Upon returning to his home, they find a pair of old-fashioned boots. Thus begins their incredible adventure through time which takes them to 1889 and to a time when an intelligent woman who was also a scientist was considered a witch. Unfortunately, the black-and-white illustrations are neither exciting nor appealing. This fast-paced fantasy novel was originally published in Canada in 1989.

Cross, Gillian. *La hija del lobo.* *(Wolf)* Translated by Jacobo Mendioroz. Madrid: Ediciones SM, 1993. 175p. ISBN: 84-348-3905-9. pap. $8.95. Gr. 8-12.

Cassy is almost fourteen years old. Suddenly, her grandmother decides to send her to live with her mother, who neither she nor her grandmother respect nor admire. Life and Cassy's fears begin to make sense when she learns the sad truth about her father—a heartless IRA terrorist. Originally published in London, this well-translated novel depicts the sad reality of an adolescent girl who must confront an immature mother and a violent father.

Dahl, Roald. *Los Mimpins.* *(The Minpins)* Illus: Patrick Benson. Translated by María Puncel. Madrid: Santillana, 1992. 48p. ISBN: 84-372-6618-1. $19.95. Gr. 3-5.

Billy is bored listening to his mother telling him what he can or cannot do. Hence, he ventures into the forbidden forest and finds what he truly fears. Spectacular, full-page color illustrations provide the perfect atmosphere to this well-translated fantasy, originally published in English.

Danziger, Paula. *¿Seguiremos siendo amigos? (Amber Brown Is Not a Crayon)* Illus: Tony Ross. Translated by Javier Franco. Madrid: Alfaguara, 1994. 105p. ISBN: 84-204-4857-5. pap. $7.95. Gr. 3-5.

Ámbar and Justo have been best friends since preschool. So when Justo's parents decide to move to another city, Ámbar is almost as sad as when her parents told her they were going to get a divorce. The sadness and pain of separation are movingly depicted in this well-done Spanish rendition with realistic black-and-white line illustrations.

Derennes, Charles. *El pueblo del polo. (The People of the Pole)* Translated by Javier Martín Lalanda. 167p. ISBN: 84-207-6267-9.
Sheffield, Charles. *Erasmus Darwin Magister. (Erasmus Magister)* Translated by María Ulloa. 197p. ISBN: 84-207-6540-6.
Sherrell, Carl. *El torneo sombrío. (The Dark Tournament)* Translated by Magalí Solimán. 184p. ISBN: 84-207-6539-2.
Ea. vol.: (Ultima Thule) Madrid: Grupo Anaya, 1994-1995. $15.95. Gr. 8-12.

Like the previous twelve titles in this excellent science fiction/ fantasy collection, these novels emphasize the adventure of exploring the unknown, and the fascination of seeing another world and its inhabitants. Appealing covers and design and smooth Spanish renditions will engage all readers of this genre. *Un pueblo de polo* tells how a French aristocrat and an engineer attempt to conquer the North Pole in a dirigible. Based on three studies by Erasmus Darwin, the grandfather of the well-known scientist, *Erasmus Darwin Magister* combines the supernatural with scientific principles. And, *El torneo sombrío* is an exciting novel where love and honor are as important as magic and strength.

Echeverría, Eugenia. *La noche que Chillanene salió a vender su alma. (The Night that Chillanene Went Out to Sell his Soul)* Illus: Fernando Aceves. Mexico: Editorial Grijalbo, 1991. 36p. ISBN: 970-05-0312-7. pap. $6.95. Gr. 6-9.

Chillanene, a teenager, has no money, nothing to eat, and is too lazy to get a job. He spends his time thinking how to get money without working. He concludes that selling his soul to the devil is the only way out of his predicament. So, he embarks on his search only to discover that devils have the same problems he does. Chillanene's dilemma and actions, though predictable, are interesting to read and definitely enjoyable.

Eco, Umberto. *Los gnomos de Gnu. (The Gnomes of Gnu)* Illus: Eugenio Carmi. Translated from the Italian by Esther Tusquets.

Barcelona: Editorial Lumen, 1994. 36p. ISBN: 84-264-3685-4. $13.95. Gr. 3-5.

A powerful emperor is eager to discover new territories on planet Earth, but his ministers convince him that the only place left to discover is space. So, he sends Galactic Explorer in search of a planet he could civilize. The gnomes of Gnu can't understand what is so special about a planet where cities are contaminated, oceans are dirty, trees have been cut, and people get stuck in horrible traffic jams. Instead they offer to go to Earth to care for its parks and gardens, clean its valleys, and teach its inhabitants to enjoy long walks. But the Prime Minister notes that the gnomes of Gnu will need to have a passport, pay immigration taxes, and obtain special permits from the forest rangers and other authorities. Striking full-page, geometric collages against black or white backgrounds provide a surrealistic tone to this fantasy whose message readers and listeners will definitely understand.

Egli, Werner J. *Tarantino.* *(Tarantino)* Translated from the German by José A. Santiago Togle. Madrid: Ediciones SM, 1992. 182p. ISBN: 84-348-3773-3. pap. $10.95. Gr. 8-12.

Tarantino, Marcelo, and Jacinto, three young adults from Guatemala, arrive in San Diego, California, in truly difficult circumstances. They left their native country in search of a better life, free from misery and political persecution. But life is not easy for poor undocumented immigrants who unwittingly get involved in gangs, drug traffic, and crime in the United States. One has to question several coincidences in Tarantino's new life that assist him in overcoming seemingly insurmountable odds, yet this fast-paced novel provides a glimpse of a truly difficult social problem of our times. Tarantino's courage and honesty are indeed laudable.

Ende, Michael. *El secreto de Lena.* *(Lena's Secret)* Illus: Jindra Capek. Madrid: Ediciones SM, 1991. 124p. ISBN: 84-348-3357-3. $11.00. Gr. 4-7.

Lena, a little girl, is a very kind girl especially if her parents behave and do exactly what she asks them to do. But this doesn't happen very often. Hence, she decides to take drastic action which results in a complicated family situation. Lena's contradictions, however, have a satisfying conclusion in this story by a popular German author, originally published in Germany in 1991.

Erburu, Lourdes, and José Morán. *Muchos chistes chistosos.* *(Many Funny Jokes)* Illus: Margarita Menéndez. Madrid: Susaeta, 1990. 139p. ISBN: 84-305-1772-3. $12.50. Gr. 4-10.

Collection of over two hundred brief jokes about animals, soldiers, school, doctors, telephones, and other well-known topics that will amuse and delight all readers/listeners. The witty, pastel watercolor illustrations make these jokes even more enjoyable.

Erlbruch, Wolf. *Leonardo.* *(Leonard)* Translated by Silvia Eugenia Castillero. ISBN: 968-6445-02-1. Mexico: Petra Ediciones, 1992. 30p. pap. $9.95. Gr. 2-4.

Leonardo, a little boy, loves dogs; he knows all about dogs and, through a kind fairy, he can become a dog, then a boy and, when necessary, a dog again. Dog lovers as well as those who are afraid of dogs will sympathize with Leonardo's incredible talent. Modernistic illustrations with a strong European flavor definitely capture the mood of this story, originally published in 1991 by Peter Hammer Verlag, Germany.

Fernández Paz, Agustín. *Cuentos por palabras.* *(Stories from Words)* ISBN: 84-348-3458-8. Madrid: Ediciones SM, 1991. 139p. Gr. 8-12.

Based on newspaper classified ads, the author has written nine engaging short stories that tell about the keys to happiness, a unique commercial artist, a mother and TV ads, super heroes, and other fantastic stories. The brevity of each story, appealing characters, and contemporary or high-interest topics make these stories sure winners for reluctant as well as habitual readers. Appropriately, this author was awarded the Spanish Premio Lazarillo in 1990.

Ferrer Bermejo, José. *Silvestre y los ladrones de sueños.* *(Silvestre and the Dream Thieves)* Madrid: Grupo Anaya, 1995. 131p. ISBN: 84-207-6545-7. pap. $8.95. Gr. 8-12.

Silvestre, a teenager, lives with his incredibly impulsive father, who always defends the rights of the less privileged. Set in Barcelona and its environs, this fast-paced novel exposes the problems of racism and illegal immigration in Spain through the adventures of Silvestre and his father who together solve the mystery of the missing jewels. Adolescents will appreciate the unaffected first-person point of view and the amusing dialogues between a mature, "philosophical" teenager and his athletic, youthful father.

Ferro, Beatriz. *Ramiro.* *(Ramiro)* Illus: Clara Urquijo. Barcelona: Editorial Lumen, 1991. 28p. ISBN: 84-264-3651-X. $13.95. Gr. 2-4.

Ramiro, a Spanish mouse, is eager to get away from cats who make his life most unpleasant. After careful thought and investigation, he decides that the only place where cats are still not a problem is in a new continent that eventually became known as America. This is not only an enjoyable story about cats with wonderfully amusing full-page watercolor illustrations, but it is also a witty introduction to life in pre-Columbian America and Spain.

Fiedler, Christamaria. *El verano de los animales. (The Summer of the Animals)* Illus: Siglint Kessler. Translated from the German by Ma. Dolores Ábalos. Madrid: Santillana, 1994. 155p. ISBN: 84-204-4819-2. pap. $8.95. Gr. 5-7.

Hugo is used to Alfi's jokes, but this one really surprises him. Alfi announces in school that he and Hugo have a business caring for animals during the summer. So in Hugo's small apartment, they care for four dogs, seven rabbits, six guinea pigs, four turtles, one parrot, three hamsters, one rooster, and several cats. The situation is not easy with Hugo's parents, but they are convinced that the boys are participating in a study on animal behavior. Originally published by K. Thienemann Verlag, Stuttgart, in 1993, this ingenious, well-translated novel should appeal to animal lovers in particular.

Fine, Anne. *Madame Doubtfire. (Mrs. Doubtfire)* Translated by Flora Peña. Madrid: Alfaguara, 1992. 165p. ISBN: 84-204-4680-7. $12.95. Gr. 5-8.

Lidia, Christopher, and little Natalia are always in the middle of their divorced parent's arguments. The father, an unemployed actor, is unhappy because his successful wife severely limits the time he can spend with the children. Enter Mrs. Doubtfire, a housekeeper, alias their father. This is a humorous adaptation of a realistic novel about a modern family who must adapt to life after divorce.

Fine, Anne. *Ojos saltones. (Goggle-Eyes)* Translated by Javier Franco Aixelá. Madrid: Alfaguara, 1995. 166p. ISBN: 84-204-4758-7. pap. $6.95. Gr. 7-10.

Kitty and Helly have one thing in common: Their divorced mothers are dating two men who they utterly dislike—or so they think at first. Originally published in London and winner of the 1989 Carnegie Medal, this well-translated novel confronts in a straightforward manner the fears and apprehensions of two girls with a contemporary problem.

Froissart, Bénédicte. *La cena con el Tío Enrique. (Dinner with Uncle Enrique)* Illus: Pierre Pratt. Translated by Francisco Segovia.

México: Fondo de Cultura Económica, 1992. 32p. ISBN: 968-16-3942-1. $12.99. Gr. 2-5.

Uncle Enrique is different. Especially when he goes to dinner at the home of a little boy, his nephew, and his family wearing a loud print shirt embellished with hundreds of hens—yellow, white, red, and orange. Sophisticated children will appreciate the fantasy and humor in this story, originally published by Annick Press in Canada. The modernistic, full-page illustrations of a family at the dinner table where incongruous things happen reflect the same worldly-wise humor as the narrative.

Gabán, Jesús. *El gran libro de los laberintos.* *(The Big Book of Labyrinths)* Illus: the author. Barcelona: Ediciones B, 1992. 26p. ISBN: 84-406-2754-8. $13.95. Gr. 3-6.

Readers are encouraged to find their way through twelve different winding passages, thereby helping Sito and his friend, Sandra, escape serious situations. Lovers of mazes will enjoy reading the introductory paragraphs which explain each labyrinth—e.g., Treasure Hunt, The Ghost Castle, A Sunken Ship—and figuring out how to arrive at their correct destinations. The twelve colorful double-page spreads of labyrinths are the focal point of this large-format publication.

Gándara, Alejandro. *Falso movimiento.* *(False Movement)* Madrid: Ediciones SM, 1992. 182p. ISBN: 84-348-3708-0. $12.95. Gr. 9-12.

It is almost midnight and, Carlota, a fifteen-year-old girl, should have been home by ten. Her mother worries and finally convinces Carlota's father to look for her. Carlota's parents's fears and anxieties intermingled with their own doubts about their marriage and the world of drugs in downtown Madrid result in a potent realistic novel. The author's wit and honesty in describing Carlota's logic will be enjoyed by adolescents.

Gándara, Alejandro. *Nunca seré como te quiero.* *(I Shall Never Become What You Want)* Madrid: Ediciones SM, 1995. 146p. ISBN: 84-348-4673-X. $12.95. Gr. 9-12.

Set in Santander, a fishing village in northern Spain, this powerful, engrossing novel tells about Jacobo, a seventeen-year-old whose life has never been easy. Abandoned by a mother he can't even remember and ignored by his alcoholic father, his only source of encouragement is Roncal, a wise father substitute, who knows when to push and when to let go. Christine, a beautiful teenager with problems of her own, adds a special joy to his life. The vivid vernacular of Spanish adolescents makes this novel even more appealing and real.

Garavaglia, Juan Carlos, and Raúl Fradkin. *Hombres y mujeres de la colonia.* *(Men and Women from Colonial Times)* Buenos Aires: Editorial Sudamericana, 1992. 282p. ISBN: 950-07-0780-2. pap. $17.50. Gr. 9-12.

Through the daily lives of fifteen Argentine men and women of the eighteenth and nineteenth centuries, adolescents are exposed to the thoughts and feelings of common citizens during Colonial times. Each chapter includes a fictional biography, a map, and approximately one page of text about different occupations, industries or institutions. Students of Argentine history will enjoy.

García Domínguez, Ramón. *Renata toca el piano, estudia inglés y etcétera, etcétera, etcétera.* *(Renata Plays the Piano, Studies English, Etcetera, Etcetera, Etcetera)* Illus: Javier Zabala. Zaragoza: Editorial Luis Vives, 1992. 137p. ISBN: 84-263-2407-X. pap. $8.95. Gr. 6-9.

Renata is a happy and easy-going girl who is eager to do what other girls do. But Renata's mother has decided that after school, Renata should learn to play the piano, study the English language, practice her singing exercises, do her homework and, to learn to relax, she should go to counseling sessions with a psychologist three afternoons a week. Many adolescents will truly sympathize with Renata's "obligations." This delightfully honest novel also is appropriate for the parents of numerous adolescents who are convinced of the "value" of extracurricular activities. Appropriately modern watercolor illustrations add the perfect touch to this jocose novel about a middle-class Spanish family.

García Márquez, Gabriel. *Doce cuentos peregrinos.* *(Strange Pilgrims: Twelve Stories)* Translated by Edith Grossman. Mexico: Editorial Diana, 1992. 245p. ISBN: 968-13-2308-4. $8.95. Gr. 9-adult.

García Márquez states in the prologue that this is the closest to the book of short stories that he always wished to write. Hence, these stories, written during the last eighteen years, relate in the author's inimitable, fluid style his dreams, memories, and thoughts sprinkled with his own magic and intuition. My favorites are *"Buen viaje, Señor Presidente"* and *"El avión de la bella durmiente"* but every reader will certainly find several that he/she will especially relish and never forget. Despite the fact that some will question the "adult" themes of some of these stories, Spanish-speaking adolescents should not miss being exposed to this most wonderful contemporary author.

Geller, Mark. *Raymond.* *(Raymond)* Translated by Alvaro Forqué. Barcelona: Noguer y Caralt, 1994. 91p. ISBN: 84-279-3215-4. pap. $7.95. Gr. 5-8.

Thirteen-year-old Raymond is intelligent and shy and devoted to his mother. Together they suffer the consequences of an abusive father, who beats mother and son at the slightest provocation. The fast pace and tension of the original, first published by HarperCollins in 1988, is definitely present. This fluid Spanish rendition, which is a best seller in Spain, resonates with the pain and fear of an adolescent boy who is caught between a weak mother and a tyrannical father.

Gisbert, Joan Manuel. *El misterio de la mujer autómata.* *(The Mystery of the Female Robot)* Madrid: Ediciones SM, 1991. 255p. ISBN: 84-348-3457-X. Gr. 8-12.

Hans Helvetius, a well-known robot designer, receives a strange request: to build a secret female robot based on a wax model of an unknown woman. Set in Paris in 1817, this fast-paced mystery includes excitement and interesting characters. It was awarded the Spanish Premio El Barco de Vapor in 1990.

Gómez Cerdá, Alfredo. *La princesa y el pirata.* *(The Princess and the Pirate)* Illus: Teo Puebla. México: Fondo de Cultura Económica, 1991. 28p. ISBN: 968-16-3654-6. $14.38. Gr. 5-8.

This modern fairy tale tells of a beautiful princess, Filomena, who lives in a high tower made of ivory and silver in a faraway country and waits for that special moment that destiny has reserved for all princesses. After rejecting numerous suitors, including Snow White's and Cinderella's princes, this brave princess decides to embark with an old pirate who only promises her a long journey. Thus, Princess Filomena lives her own life outside of her own fairytale. The sometimes delicate and sometimes ironic full-page illustrations in color are a perfect complement to this fairy tale with a twist. Perhaps some adults will object to Filomena and her pirate enjoying life by drinking a bottle of rum together, but this is a fitting conclusion to this story about a liberated princess.

Gómez Cerdá, Alfredo. *Sin billete de vuelta.* *(Without a Return Ticket)* Illus: Teo Puebla. Madrid: Alfaguara, 1994. 117p. ISBN: 84-204-4855-9. pap. $8.95. Gr. 7-9.

Six adolescents from various parts of rural Spain relate their reasons for immigrating to the big city—Barcelona—in search of jobs and a better life. There is not a lot of action and excitement in these six vignettes, rather these tender sketches portray the hard lives of poor rural workers in postwar Spain who at an early age must confront their present realities and make the difficult decision to go to the big city in search of a better future. Spanish-speaking adolescents in the United States will empathize with the feelings of sorrow and longing as well as hope and optimism that these six immigrants evoke.

González, Lola. *Brumas de octubre.* *(October Fog)* Madrid: Ediciones SM, 1994. 155p. ISBN: 84-348-4274-2. pap. $10.95. Gr. 7-9.

Life in a Spanish junior high school is depicted through the fears, anxieties, and hopes of Vero, Leti, and Miguel, three adolescents, who know exactly what parents ask and wish to hear, and what is truly important to learn and discover in school. The author's lighthearted style is perfectly suited for this novel that presents a humorous and universal view of school and adolescents.

González, Lola. *Guárdate de los idus.* *(Beware of the Ides)* Madrid: Ediciones SM, 1995. 166p. ISBN: 84-348-4743-4. pap. $7.95. Gr. 8-12.

Patrician seventeen-year-old Druso, and Porcia, his thirteen-year-old sister, live with their uncle, Senator Mario Dimitio, during the last days of the Roman Republic. Shortly after Caesar's murder, treason and murder surrounds them, their family, and friends. Druso and Porcio must rely on their own intelligence and courage to survive the intrigue and passions so prevalent in Rome of the times. This fast-paced novel offers an exciting plot with appealing characters and an engrossing setting—historical fiction at its best.

Hagemann, Marie. *Lobo Negro, un skin.* *(Schwarzer, Wolf, Skin)* Translated by Rosa Pilar Blanco. Madrid: Alfaguara, 1994. 141p. ISBN: 84-204-4818-4. pap. $8.95. Gr. 8-12.

Black Wolf is a strong and dangerous young man who delights in the companionship of other "Skins"—radical groups from the extreme right. Set in contemporary Germany, this easy-to-read novel depicts the violence, hatred, and racism prevalent among young people who reject all foreigners and enjoy seeing the fear they cause in their victims. This powerful novel invites readers to ponder on the issues that cause young people to join violent groups.

Hamilton, Virginia. *Plain City.* *(Plain City)* Translated by Amalia Bermejo y Ma. Teresa Marcos. Madrid: Ediciones SM, 1995. 167p. ISBN: 84-348-4686-1. pap. $6.95. Gr. 7-10.

Thirteen-year-old Buhlaire lives with her beautiful mother, Bluezy Sims, and her aunts and uncles in the outskirts of Plain City. She is rejected in school, perhaps because of her uncommon vanilla color. But even more painful is to find out that her father did not really die in Vietnam. This smooth Spanish rendition poignantly conveys the stark realism of the original novel, first published by Hamilton Arts in 1993.

Hamilton, Virginia. *Primos.* *(Cousins)* Translated by Amalia Bermejo. Madrid: Santillana, 1993. 125p. ISBN: 84-204-4747-1. pap. $12.50. Gr. 6-10.
Camy lives with her mother and brother but is lonely most of the time. She misses her grandmother, who now lives at a nursing home. But the real problem in her life is one of her cousins, Patty Ann, who is beautiful and very smart. Hamilton's powerful novel about conflicts within families is now available in this fluid Spanish translation.

Handford, Martin. *¿Dónde está Wally? en Hollywood.* *(Where's Wally? in Hollywood)* Translated by Jaume Ribera. Barcelona: Ediciones B, 1993. 26p. ISBN: 84-406-3798-5. $13.95. Gr. 3-8.
Like the previous five Wally large-format books originally published by Walker Books, London, busy, detailed, colorful illustrations depict scenes of Hollywood specials, such as silent movies, musicals, westerns, dinosaurs, and others. Lovers of detail will enjoy accompanying Wally as he explores Hollywood.

Hastings, Selina. *Sir Gawain y la abominable dama.* *(Sir Gawain and the Loathly Lady)* Illus: Juan Wyngaard. Translated by Clara Ardenay. Madrid: Altea, Taurus, Alfaguara, 1988. 29p. ISBN: 84-372-6604-1. $13.95. Gr. 3-6.
Sir Gawain, one of the knights in King Arthur's court, demonstrates his valor and chivalry when he swears to save his King's honor by wedding the loathly lady. Spectacularly detailed watercolor illustrations reminiscent of the era set the perfect stage for this wonderful tale with a happy, satisfying ending. The well-done translation captures the mood and the times.

Hauff, Wilhelm. *Cuentos completos.* *(Complete Stories)* Illus: Alicia Cañas Cortázar. Translated from the German by Elena Bombín Izquierdo. Madrid: Grupo Anaya, 1994. 285p. ISBN: 84-207-6285-7. $64.95. Gr. 5-8.
This luxurious, large-format edition includes the eighteen stories written by the great German storyteller of the nineteenth century, Wilhelm Hauff. A fluid Spanish rendition and numerous full-page,

exuberant, color and black-and-white illustrations echo the joyous whimsy of these tales of magic and adventure, merchants and slaves, sheiks and caliphs. Like all books published in Spain, this excellent translation uses the Peninsular Spanish pronoun and corresponding verb endings for the second person plural, which are not used, although perfectly understood, by Spanish speakers in Hispanic America.

Henry, Marguerite. *Misty de Chincoteague.* *(Misty of Chincoteague)* Barcelona: Editorial Noguer, 1994. 127p. ISBN: 84-279-3218-9. pap. $8.95. Gr. 5-7.

This is a fluid Spanish rendition of Marguerite Henry's popular adventure about a herd of wild horses descendants of Arabian stallions and mares brought to America by the Spaniards. Horse fans will relish the special relationship between Misty, a colt, and Paul, a boy who saved Misty from drowning.

Holden, L. Dwight. *El mejor truco del abuelo.* *(Gran-Gran's Best Trick)* Illus: Michael Chesworth. Translated by Laureana López Ramírez. México: Fondo de Cultura Económica, 1993. 48p. ISBN: 968-16-4032-2. $12.99. Gr. 3-5.

Dealing with the sickness and death of a loved one is never easy; especially so if the person is one's beloved grandfather. In this tender, well-done translation, a girl recounts her memories and feelings of those special times and what it means to always remember what grandfather saw and shared. The delicate black-and-white illustrations and the carefully designed margins provide a touching background to a girl's loving tribute to her grandfather, originally published by Magination Press, in 1989.

Hörger, Marlies. *La princesa que no sabía reír.* *(The Princess Who Didn't Know How to Laugh)* Illus: Guernadi Spirin. Translated by Alberto Jiménez Rioja. Madrid: Grupo Anaya, 1992. 24p. ISBN: 84-207-4835-8. $16.95. Gr. 3-5.

The popular French tale about a beautiful princess who didn't know how to laugh has been beautifully adapted into German and gracefully translated into Spanish in this gorgeous, large-format publication. The exquisite, full-page spreads depict the magic of olden times when a young and courageous blacksmith achieves his objectives and consequently marries the princess.

Howker, Janni. *Isaac Campion.* *(Isaac Campion)* Illus: Mauricio Gómez Morín. Translated by Laura Emilia Pacheco. México: Fondo de Cultura Económica, 1992. 128p. ISBN: 0-86203-270-9. pap. $7.49. Gr. 7-10.

In a gripping and touching manner, Isaac tells about life with a stern and intransigent father whose hatred toward one of his competitors caused the death of Isaac's beloved eighteen-year-old brother, Daniel. Originally published in Great Britain by Julia MacRae in 1986, this realistic, coming-of-age novel presents an honest depiction of the feelings and thoughts of an adolescent who must contend with a difficult father, a weak but loving mother, and a seemingly hopeless situation. This is indeed a powerful novel set in England in the late 1890s.

Ingoglia, Gina. *Disney el rey León (Disney's The Lion King)* Illus: Marshall Toomey and Michael Humphries. Translated by Daniel Santacruz. New York: Disney Press/Little Brown, 1994. 96p. ISBN: 0-7868-3021-2. $14.95; lib. bdg. ISBN: 0-7868-5011-6. $14.89. Gr. 3-6.

This film adaptation of *The Lion King* is certain to be popular among Spanish speakers worldwide. Kudos are due to Disney Press for respecting the grammatical, syntactic, and structural character of the Spanish language by selecting first-rate translators.

Jennings, Paul. *El embuste de las coles. (The Cabbage Patch Fib)* Illus: Enrique Martínez. Translated by Paloma Villegas. México: Fondo de Cultura Económica, 1992. 42p. ISBN: 968-16-3894-8. pap. $6.45. Gr. 5-8.

Nothing is peaceful during dinnertime, especially in a family with six children, a busy mother, and a father who won't turn off the TV until he sees the last episode of his favorite program. Finally mother insists that during dinnertime, there must be interesting conversation. Eight-year-old Chris is ready with a question: "Papa, where do babies come from?" Papa becomes flustered, hesitates, and blurts out that babies come from the cabbage patch. When this results in mass confusion, father explains to Chris that babies are delivered by storks. Finally, Chris's older brother tells the truth to Chris who feels obligated to explain the facts of life to "poor" papa. This delightful story about adults' muddled explanations was originally published by Penguin Books, Australia, in 1988. Spanish speakers will enjoy the fluid translation and the ludicrous, black-and-white illustrations.

Joyce, James. *El gato y el diablo. (The Cat and the Devil)* Illus: Mabel Piérola. Translated by Julián Ríos. Barcelona: Editorial Lumen, 1993. 36p. ISBN: 84-264-3549-1. $22.95. Gr. 2-5.

The devil offers to build a much-needed bridge for the inhabitants of Beaugency. The mayor accepts and in payment he promises to give the devil the first person who crosses the bridge.

The excitement and fear in all the townspeople and the devil's anger as he is outwitted by the mayor are exquisitely portrayed in double-page black-and-white illustrations. In addition, the fluid Spanish rendition of James Joyce prose and the spirited action make this large-format book a perfect selection for storytime or elsewhere.

Knight, Margy Burns. *¿Quién es de aquí? Una historia americana. (Who Belongs Here? An American Story)* Illus: Anne Sibley O'Brien. Translated by Clarita Kohen. Gardiner, Maine: Tilbury House, 1995. 40p. ISBN: 0-88448-158-1. $16.95; pap. ISBN: 0-88448-159-X. $8.95. Gr. 4-7.

After escaping the killing fields of Cambodia and living in a refugee camp in Thailand, ten-year-old Nary is now adjusting to his new home in the United States. The amount of food in the grocery stores amazes him, and he likes eating pizza and ice cream. But sometimes his classmates are mean to him, calling him names and telling him to go back home. Spanish-speaking children will sympathize with Nary's story as they ponder difficult questions about immigration, racism, and multiculturalism raised by the author alongside the narrative. O'Brien's original full-color pastel illustrations personalize the experiences of Nary and other new Americans.

Kraatz, David. *La canción del geco. (The Gecko's Song)* Illus: Mauricio Luengas. Miami: Santillana, 1995. 16p. ISBN: 1-56014-579-X. pap. $8.95. Gr. 2-4.

Chaco, a newly-born gecko—a small lizard of warm regions—enjoys his life in a South American jungle where his mother searches for delicious gnats and he plays among the high trees. But one dark night mother is nowhere to be found and Chaco can't communicate with toads, ocelots, monkeys, or parrots. Suddenly, he hears his mother's lovely crackle—the most beautiful sound in the world. Vividly colored double-page spreads of lush South American flora and fauna provide the ideal ambiance to this satisfying story. An informative note at the end on South American jungles is also included.

Lalana, Fernando. *Scratch. (Scratch)* Madrid: Ediciones SM, 1992. 189p. ISBN: 84-348-3709-X. $15.95. Gr. 8-12.

Sofía, an eighteen-year-old girl, is involved in a car accident as she tries to solve her own frustrations and indecisions. She is a copilot, a feminist, and a devoted friend, but the dangerous world of car races provides more excitement than she expected. This fast-paced mystery was awarded the 1991 Premio Gran Angular in

Spain. Adolescents eager for action in a contemporary setting will enjoy.

Langley, Jonathan. *Ricitos de oro y los tres osos.* *(The Three Bears and Goldilocks)* ISBN: 84-7419-916-6.
————. *Rumpelstiltskin, el enano saltarín.* *(The Story of Rumpelstiltskin)* ISBN: 84-7419-918-2.
Ea. vol.: 24p. Illus: the author. Translated from the English by Alfred Sala. Barcelona: Ediciones Junior, 1991. $13.50. Gr. 2-5.
Children of all ages will enjoy reading or listening to these simply-written large-format versions of two of their favorite stories. The amusing full-page watercolor illustrations can be followed or "read" by younger children as the illustrations do a wonderful job of telling the stories through wit and action. Originally published by HarperCollins, Great Britain, in 1991, the Spanish translations are lively, humorous, and fun to read. It is difficult to find better written and illustrated versions of these stories in Spanish.

Larreula, Enric. *La navidad de la Bruja Aburrida.* *(The Bored Witch's Christmas)* Illus: Roser Capdevila. (Las Memorias de la Bruja Aburrida) Barcelona: Editorial Planeta, 1991. 28p. ISBN: 84-320-9577-X. $11.50. Gr. 2-4.
Like the previous ten titles in this series, the delightfully witty, pastel illustrations of a bored witch and her unique experiences at Christmas alongside a refreshing narrative make this a different Christmas Story.

Lluch, Víctor Angel. *Las pinturas de arena. (Sand Paintings)* Illus: Bruno Mallart. Translated from the French by Pilar Ruiz-Va Palacios. Madrid: Alfaguara, 1993. 103p. ISBN: 84-204-4725-0. pap. $5.95. Gr. 6-9.
Nehn, an orphan boy, experiences the pain and fear of immigration despite his uncle's understanding manner. Set in a poor town amidst a canyon and mesas, this powerful, incisive novel will touch adolescents as they deal with their own anxieties about rejection, acceptance, and feelings of belonging. Two teenage bullies provide enough action to ensnare reluctant readers.

Madinaveitia, Horacio. *La gran aventura de Don Roberto. (Sir Roberto's Great Adventure)* Illus: the author. Fort Lee, NJ: W. W. Publishers, Inc., 1991. 29p. ISBN: 1-879567-02-4. $13.95. Gr. 3-5.
Don Roberto, an unconventional and brave knight, sets out in search of adventure. In his special way, he defeats the fearsome dragon, saves the kingdom, marries the beautiful princess, and

returns home where he and his princess live happily ever after. The three-tone, humorous, albeit tiny, illustrations are a beautiful complement to this slightly ironic story of chivalry and courage. Unfortunately, the "conversation pieces"—questions framed to help readers express their own thoughts about the themes and issues explored in the story—are unnecessary at best and will encourage well-meaning adults to turn this story into a dull lesson about courage, friendship, teamwork, and other noble topics.

Madrid, Juan. *Cuartos oscuros. (Dark Rooms)* Madrid: Ediciones SM, 1993. 191p. ISBN: 84-348-4079-0. pap. $10.95. Gr. 9-12.

Seventeen-year-old Tomás is looking forward to seeing his father who plans to escape from the prison in Málaga. In the ten years his father has been confined, he never once wrote to him or tried to communicate with his alcoholic mother. Life has not been easy for kind-hearted Tomás whose trip to meet his father results in a life-threatening nightmare. Appealing adolescent protagonists and lots of action make this an exciting coming-of-age adventure novel despite some hard-to-believe coincidences.

Manushkin, Fran. *101 Dálmatas: libro para contar. (101 Dalmatians: A Counting Book)* Illus: Russell Hicks. Translated by Daniel M. Santacruz. New York: Disney Press, 1994. 32p. ISBN: 1-56282-697-2. $13.89; pap. ISBN: 1-56282-568-2. $5.95. Gr. 2-4.

Disney fans will enjoy searching with Pongo and Perdita for their ninety-nine missing puppies in this well-done translation. Familiar Disney characters encourage children to count to 101 Dalmatians.

Mariño, Ricardo. *Cuentos espantosos. (Frightening Stories)* Illus: Ana Camusso. Buenos Aires: Coquena Grupo Editor, 1991. 46p. ISBN: unavailable. pap. $8.50. Gr. 5-10.

This is a collection of seven fast-paced horror stories that tell about strange customs, horrible sensations, incredible feats, and others that will scare and amuse all readers. The brevity and directness of these well-told stories make them ideal for reading aloud or for reluctant readers to enjoy.

Martin, Ann. *Ma y pa Drácula. (Ma and Pa Dracula)* Illus: Antonio Helguera. Translated from the English by Monica Mansour. México: Fondo de Cultura Económica, 1991. 118p. ISBN: 968-16-3667-8. pap. $7.95. Gr. 5-8.

Jonathan, a nine-year-old boy, is the adopted son of two vampires. His parents sleep during the day and "work" at night.

His life feels normal until he meets Tobi, a friendly neighbor, who introduces him to school, fourth graders, and other aspects of a "normal" lifestyle. The fast-paced fantasy is about a Dracula family.

Martin, C. L. G. *Tres mujeres valientes.* *(Three Brave Women)* Illus: Peter Elwell. Translated by Alejandro Fernández Susial. Madrid: Editorial Everest, 1993. 32p. ISBN: 84-241-3340-4. $11.95. Gr. 3-5.

Cathy complains to Mother and Grandma that she hates Billy because he scared her with a spider and also because he saw her panties. The three brave women carefully plan to teach Billy a lesson, which they do so with convincing results. The amusing pastel illustrations of Cathy with her Mother and Grandmother planning her revenge are indeed convincing and fun. Spanish speakers in the United States should be aware that this translation uses the word *bragas* for panties and the verb forms *acordáis* (p. 10), *ayudaréis* (p. 18, 30), *fijaos* (p. 25) as used in Spain.

Masters, Susan Rowan. *La vida secreta de Hubie Hartzel.* *(The Secret Life of Hubie Hartzel)* Illus: Patricia Acosta. Translated by Patricia Acosta. Bogota: Grupo Editorial Norma, 1992. 175p. ISBN: 958-04-1900-0. pap. $4.95. Gr. 4-6.

Hubie Hartzell's highly amusing dream world in which he deals with his middle-grade problems—the class bully, a demanding teacher, and his daydreams that often get him into trouble—is now available in Spanish in a fluid translation. Like the original English version, Spanish-speaking kids will see something of themselves in this likable protagonist. The flat black-and-white illustrations included in this homely paperback edition don't do justice to the story.

McKee, David. *Elmer.* *(Elmer)* Translated by María Puncel. Madrid: Altea, Taurus, Alfaguara, 1990. 32p. ISBN: 84-372-6614-9. $13.95. Gr. 2-4.

Elmer, a most unique elephant, is a joy to be with. All elephants enjoy his company and friendship, but he worries about his multicolored appearance. So, he decides to do something about it and becomes an elephant-colored elephant. Fortunately, nature prevails and Elmer remains Elmer except once a year. Festive, full-page watercolor illustrations provide just the right gusto to this amusing fantasy. The easy-flowing Spanish translation is a delight as well.

Mendo, Miguel Ángel. *Un museo siniestro.* *(An Evil Museum)*
Madrid: Ediciones SM, 1992. 141p. ISBN: 84-348-3803-6. pap.
$8.95. Gr. 8-12.

Alfredo, a slightly disorganized college student, and his ana-
lytical and beautiful girlfriend, Elvira, can not explain the mysteries
surrounding a strange gift he received in the mail: a small
Styrofoam cube. In their efforts to solve this mystery, they become
guinea pigs in an experiment that was supposed to be innocuous
and heroic. The author's lighthearted style makes this mystery
truly fun reading.

Merino, José María. *La edad de la aventura.* *(The Age of Adventure)*
Illus: José Ramón Sánchez. ISBN: 84-372-2195-1.
Rodríguez Almodóvar, Antonio. *Animales de aventura.* *(Animals of
Adventure)* Illus: Francisco Meléndez. ISBN: 84-372-2196-X.
Ea. vol.: 64p. (El Viaje Imaginario) Madrid: Santillana, 1995.
$22.95. Gr. 4-8.

The heroes and heroines of some of the world's best-loved
literature for children and adolescents are introduced in these
spectacular large-format publications with exquisite full-page color
illustrations and three-page, easy-to-read narratives. *La edad de la
aventura* presents fourteen well-known characters of world literature,
such as *Heidi* by Johanna Spyri, Jim Hawkins from Robert Louis
Stevenson's *Treasure Island*, Huck Finn, Tom Sawyer, Oliver
Twist, Dick Sand, Kim, and others. Nineteen well-known animal
protagonists, such as Herman Melville's *Moby Dick*, Miyax from
Jean Craighead George's *Julie and the Wolves*, Top from Jules
Verne's *Mysterious Island,* and others are also presented. These
are brief, tantalizing invitations to young Spanish speakers to
experience some of the greatest books of all times.

Merino, José María. *Los trenes del verano.* *(Summer Trains)*
Madrid: Ediciones Siruela, 1992. 212p. ISBN: 84-784-4121-1.
$16.95. Gr. 8-10.

Three adolescents from Madrid, Spain—Juan Luis, Marta, and
Piri—are eager to start their summer vacations. They are planning
a trip by train in which they will visit several cities in Europe. The
trip is certainly not what they expected: They are overwhelmed by
unintelligible languages, strange occurrences, and alien people,
apparently a result of three nuclear explosions from another planet.
Science fiction fans will be thrilled. This book received the
National Award for Creation in Spain in 1993.

Miles, Miska. *Ani y la anciana.* *(Annie and the Old One)* Illus:
Peter Parnall. Translated by Katy Torre. México: Fondo de

Cultura Económica, 1992. 48p. ISBN: 958-9093-66-3. $10.99. Gr. 3-5.

Spanish-speaking children will empathize with Ani, a little Navaho girl who doesn't want to accept the approaching death of her loving grandmother. The original, sensitive black-and-white illustrations and the smooth Spanish rendition touchingly depict Ani's special relationship with her grandmother.

Mills, Claudia. *Después del quinto año, el mundo. (After the Fifth Grade, the World)* Illus: Ana Zoebisch. Translated by Paloma Villegas. México: Fondo de Cultura Económica, 1991. 137p. ISBN: 968-16-3663-5. pap. $7.95. Gr. 4-7.

Heidi, a ten-year-old girl, cannot understand why Mrs. Richardson, her fifth grade teacher, insists on making fun of her best friend in front of the whole class. On the other hand, Mrs. Richardson is also the best math teacher Heidi has ever had. In a cheerful manner, this appealing novel, originally published in the United States by Macmillan in 1989, relates Heidi's ambivalent feelings about a difficult teacher.

Mochizuki, Ken. *El béisbol nos salvó. (Baseball Saved Us)* Illus: Dom Lee. Translated by Tomás González. New York: Lee and Low Books, 1995. 32p. ISBN: 1-880000-21-0. $14.95. Gr. 3-5.

In a touching, first-person narrative, smoothly rendered into Spanish, Pulga tells how he and his Japanese American family are suddenly moved from their home and set down behind barbed wire in a desert concentration camp during World War II. Fortunately, his father organizes the building of a baseball field and Pulga learns to play and to hit home runs at crucial times to gain social acceptance. Lee's moving illustrations, in shades of brown, evoke the bleak desert isolation and Pulga's loneliness in school.

Molina, Ma. Isabel. *De Victoria para Alejandro. (From Victoria to Alejandro)* Illus: Francisco Solí. Madrid: Alfaguara, 1994. 135p. ISBN: 84-204-4861-3. pap. $9.95. Gr. 7-10.

In Palestine, sixteen-year-old Victoria, the daughter of a Roman senator, is suddenly exposed to her Jewish mother's family. She has never met them and is overwhelmed by the differences in cultures—especially by the attitudes of intensely religious Jewish people toward women. This fast-paced historical novel set in the first century amidst Christians, Romans, and Jews depicts how money and an inheritance can be major sources of conflict.

Molina Llorente, Pilar. *La sombra de la daga.* *(The Dagger's Shadow)* Illus: Esmeralda Sánchez-Blanco. Madrid: Ediciones Rialp, 1993. 126p. ISBN: 84-321-3024-9. pap. $8.95. Gr. 6-9.

Upon his father's sudden death, fifteen-year old Ludovico becomes the head of the Santostefano Palace. Unexpectedly, he is confronted with difficult decisions that affect his whole family. Set in Florence during the Renaissance, readers will experience the danger and treason that money and power often engender. Appealing characters amid thrilling suspense make this readable historical novel with sensitive black-and-white watercolor illustrations a perfect introduction to the Renaissance period.

Montardre, Hélène. *Al final de la cometa.* *(At the End of the Kite)* Translated from the French by Sonia Tapia. Barcelona: Ediciones B, 1992. 125p. ISBN: 84-406-2903-6. $10.89. Gr. 4-7.

Mathieu, a ten-year-old boy, must accept the fact that his father is dead and his mother is too "sick" to attend to his and his five-year-old brother's needs. Intermingling reality and fantasy, this powerful, well-written novel, originally published in France, tells how Mathieu with the help of a beautiful kite deals with his present sad existence. This is not a lighthearted novel, but some readers will understand and perhaps empathize.

Monterroso, Augusto, and others. *Breve antología de cuentos 3, Latinoamérica y España.* *(Brief Anthology of Short Stories 3: Latin America and Spain)* Buenos Aires: Editorial Sudamericana, 1993. 79p. ISBN: 950-07-0821-2. pap. $9.95. Gr. 9-adult.

This excellent collection of seven short stories will appeal to adolescents eager for excitement and action. The authors are Augusto Monterroso (Guatemala), Ricardo Piglia (Argentina), José María Arguedas (Perú), Leo Maslíah (Uruguay), Mercé Rodoreda (Spain), Carlos Drummond de Andrade (Brazil), and Antonio Skármeta (Chile). Some adults may object to "*La loca y el relato del crimen*" by R. Piglia, which tells about the murder of a prostitute and police corruption in Argentina. Most adolescents, however, will be intrigued and entertained and will certainly enjoy the variety and brevity of these well-selected short stories.

Moseley, Keith. *La puerta oculta.* *(The Hidden Door)* Illus: Andy Everitt-Stewart. Barcelona: Plaza & Janés, 1991. 10p. ISBN: 84-01-31310-4. $11.50. Gr. 2-4.

Children of all ages will enjoy exploring the dark secrets hidden in this pop-up book with scary, three-dimensional settings and figures. Ghosts, skeletons, mummies, and spiders are some of the "horrible" characters concealed behind the hidden door. Also in this series, *La mansión misteriosa (The Mysterious Dwelling)*.

Muñiz, Enriqueta. *Memorias de un peón de ajedrez. (Memories of a Chess Pawn)* Illus: Carlos Manso. Buenos Aires: Editorial Fraterna, 1992. 63p. ISBN: 950-714-018-2. pap. $17.00. Gr. 5-8.

Through the vivid memories of a chess pawn, readers are exposed to the rules of chess, the characteristics of each piece, chess masters, and other important aspects of the game. Chess lovers will relive key moments of the game that have enthralled players for many centuries. Ten questions and answers by the chess master, Oscar Panno, a brief chess dictionary, and appealing chess-like watercolor illustrations add further to this story which is just right for chess devotees.

Needle, Jan. *El ladrón. (The Thief)* Illus: Luis Fernando Enríquez. Translated from the English: Juan José Utrilla. México: Fondo de Cultura Económica, 1991. 115p. ISBN: 968-16-3680-5. pap. $7.95. Gr. 6-10.

Kevin Pelham, an adolescent, is the son of a convict and needs money for his mother's birthday. So, when he misses class the day someone stole money from Miss Smith, everyone suspects he is the thief. Realistic novel about injustice that will touch all adolescents. Originally published in 1989 by Hamish Hamilton Books in Great Britain.

¿No será puro cuento...? (Pure Fiction!) ISBN: 968-29-3725-6. (Fomento Cultural) Mexico: Consejo Nacional de Fomento Educativo, 1991. 82p. pap. $7.95. Gr. 6-9.

Despite the homely presentation—cheap paper, prosaic black-and-white illustrations, unappealing cover—of this paperback publication, readers and listeners of all ages will thoroughly enjoy this collection of twenty tales from the oral tradition of Mexico. The brevity of each tale—from two to six pages—combined with fast pace, ingenious characters, and amusing situations are truly an irresistible delight. They tell about devils and goblins, peasants and animals, brave men and beautiful women. Pure fun!

Nöstlinger, Christine. *Mini, ama de casa. (Mini as Housewife)* Illus: Christine Nöstlinger, Jr. Translated by Carmen Bas. Madrid: Ediciones SM, 1995. 63p. ISBN: 84-348-4684-5. pap. $5.95. Gr. 3-5.

After their mother's car accident, Mini and her brother, Moritz, must help with housekeeping chores. But Moritz makes life difficult, especially for Mini, who must clean the house, do the dishes, and shop for food while Moritz complains and refuses to help. Upon mother's return home from the hospital, things change and Moritz finally has to do his share. Nöstlinger's easy-to-read narrative and the colorful cartoon-like illustrations make this story about sibling relationships fun and real.

Nöstlinger, Christine. *Mini va a esquiar. (Mini Goes Skiing)* Illus: Christine Nöstlinger, Jr. Translated from the German by Carmen Bas Alvarez. Madrid: Ediciones SM, 1995. 55p. ISBN: 84-348-4731-0. pap. $4.95. Gr. 3-5.

Mini, an eight-year-old girl, hates to ski and yet every vacation her father, mother, and brother are eager to spend time in the mountains practicing their favorite sport. In Nöstlinger's amusing and lighthearted style, readers are exposed to Mini's exploits as she tries to convince them that there can be fun in the snow without skiing. This is not only an amusing story with witty, color, cartoon-like illustrations, but an honest depiction about family disagreements with a happy resolution.

O'Dell, Scott. *No me llamo Angélica. (My Name Is Not Angelica)* Barcelona: Editorial Noguer, 1994. 125p. ISBN: 84-279-3222-7. pap. $9.95. Gr. 5-7.

Scott O'Dell's last novel, a riveting fictional account of the Virgin Island slave revolt of 1733-34, is now available to Spanish speakers. This excellent Spanish translation has maintained the suffering, horror, and utter degradation experienced by Raisha and her betrothed, Konje, during their capture and bondage.

Peña G., Joaquín, ed. *Cuentos fantásticos. (Fantastic Short Stories)* 107p. ISBN: 958-20-0019-8.
Peña Gutiérrez, Joaquín, ed. *Cuentos picarescos. (Humorous Short Stories)* 105p. ISBN: 958-20-0015-5.
Ea. vol.: Bogota: Cooperativa Editorial Magisterio, 1992. pap. $6.95. Gr. 9-adult.

Despite the prosaic covers and trite, black-and-white illustrations, these collections of brief short stories include outstanding selections by some of the best contemporary Latin American writers: Julio Cortázar, Juan José Arreola, Gabriel García Márquez, Carlos Fuentes, Augusto Monterroso, Mario Benedetti, and others. Their brevity—from one page to eight pages—make them ideal for adolescents and their genres—fantasy and humor—are sure to please most tastes. In addition, the two-to-three page introduction to each author is just right to acquaint adolescents with the lives and achievements of these writers. Some adults may object to the sensual themes in several of these short stories (e.g., *"Anuncio"* by

Juan José Arreola, which tells about women made out of *"Pastisex"*), but readers eager for high-interest short stories need look no further.

Picó, Fernando. *La peineta colorada.* *(The Red Shell-Comb)* Piedras, Puerto Rico and Caracas: Ediciones Ekaré/Ediciones Huracán, 1991. 46p. ISBN: 980-257-098-2. $14.50. Gr. 3-5.
 Based on historical facts, this story tells about the daring escape of a beautiful young slave woman in Puerto Rico in the mid-1800s. Readers will be touched by the spirit and determination of Vitita, a little girl, and Siña Rosa, a widow, whose wit, wisdom, and courage saved the fugitive slave woman. Bold, watercolor illustrations beautifully recreate life in rural Puerto Rico in the 1800s. A most useful glossary will assist readers who are unfamiliar with Puerto Rican regionalisms.

Pratchett, Terry. *Sólo tú puedes salvar a la Humanidad.* *(Only You Can Save Mankind)* Translated by Miguel Martínez-Lage. Madrid: Santillana, 1994. 177p. ISBN: 84-204-4840-0. pap. $9.95. Gr. 6-9.
 Johnny is an expert on computers and is certainly enjoying his new computer game, "Only You Can Save Mankind." As he is ready to save mankind by destroying the Scree Wees's space ships, he realizes they are ready to surrender. In addition to an exciting space adventure, adolescents will be exposed to such issues as war, peace, violence, and gender equity in this well-translated novel, originally published in London.

Preussler, Otfried. *El cuento del unicornio.* *(The Tale of the Unicorn)* Illus: Guennadi Spirin. Translated from the German by Alberto Jiménez Rioja. Madrid: Grupo Anaya, 1992. 24p. ISBN: 84-207-4836-6. $17.95. Gr. 3-5.
 Three brothers are eager to hunt the unicorn. Its ivory horn, gold hoofs, and a large ruby embedded in its forehead certainly promise wealth and fortune. Along the way, the fat brother marries a wealthy young woman; the skinny brother finds gold and builds himself a beautiful house; only Hans continues his search. But he is captivated by the unicorn's beauty and, many years later, when he returns home, children are delighted to hear how he walked through fire and water, night and ice, but chose not to kill the unicorn. The double-page, watercolor spreads in autumnal colors depicting rich scenes of far-away and a-long-time-ago are sure to appeal to children who will be happy to read that the unicorn is still alive. This is a fluid Spanish translation of the original, published by K. Thienemanns, Stuttgart, in 1988.

Pullman, Philip. *Aladdin y la lámpara maravillosa. (The Wonderful Story of Aladdin and the Enchanted Lamp)* Illus: David Wyatt. Barcelona: Parramón, 1993. 46p. ISBN: 84-342-1687-6. $13.95. Gr. 3-6.

This excellent rendition with a Far Eastern flavor is the popular story about Aladdin, the poor boy from the *Arabian Nights,* who finds a magic lamp and marries Badr-al-Badur, the beautiful Chinese princess. The bright, colorful illustrations and the especially designed parchment-like margins with jeweled motifs make this Aladdin version, originally published in 1993 by Scholastic Publications, London, memorable.

Quiroga, Horacio. *Cuentos para mis hijos. (Stories for My Children)* Montevideo: Arca Editorial, 1991. 131p. ISBN: Unavailable. pap. $8.70. Gr. 6-10.

Delightful collection of ten stories by the well-known Uruguayan author that reflect his love and understanding of nature. In a lively and straightforward manner, he tells about hunting dogs, fierce tigers, gentle deer, lazy serpents, and other animals that should interest all readers. These hunting stories are a wonderful introduction to Horacio Quiroga. However, the "literary exercises" at the end of the book are definitely not recommended.

Rauprich, Nina. *Una extraña travesía. (Strange Voyage)* Translated from the German by Ma. Dolores Abalos. Madrid: Ediciones SM, 1994. 176p. ISBN: 84-348-4422-2. pap. $7.95. Gr. 9-12.

Set in New Zealand in the 1800s, this engrossing adventure novel tells about Carl, a young man, who is rejected by everyone in his native town in Germany and flees to try his luck at sea. After a most difficult sea voyage in which he was hoping to go to America, he finally arrives in Dunedin, a port city in New Zealand, where many search for gold. Mature readers will empathize with a young man who triumphs despite a demanding mother, a physical handicap, and numerous humiliations.

Rodgers, Frank. *Cómo cuidar a tu primer monstruo. (Looking after Your First Monster)* Translated by Mireia Blasco. Barcelona: Ediciones B, 1992. 32p. ISBN: 84-406-2906-0. $10.95. Gr. 2-5.

Children will enjoy caring for their first monster as they learn about three different types of monsters—wild, imaginary and domestic—and their likes and dislikes. Amusing, colorful illustrations of monsters and their owners participating in various activities are sure to appeal to children eager to play with their "monsters." This is a fluid Spanish translation of the original English version.

Ross, Tony. *Un cuento de hadas.* *(A Fairy Tale)* Illus: the author. Translated by Catalina Domínguez. México: Fondo de Cultura Económica, 1993. 28p. ISBN: 968-16-4115-9. $12.95. Gr. 3-5.

Bessie is bored reading fairy tales; she wishes books would tell about real things instead of inventing things that are not true. Then she meets a kind neighbor, Mrs. Leaf, who tells her about magic moments and enlightens her about fairies and special friends. This is not a traditional fairy tale but rather it is a touching story about friendship and growing up and life. The realistic, full color illustrations depict a most wonderful perspective of life that is sometimes magical and at other times sad and happy at the same time. This is an excellent translation of a story originally published by Andersen Press, London, in 1991.

Sapunar Goic, Jessica. *Travesuras y aventuras.* *(Antics and Adventures)* Illus: Antonio Castell Rey. Santiago: Editorial Andrés Bello, 1992. 24p. ISBN: 956-13-1045-7. pap. $8.95. Gr. 3-5.

Six delightful stories in rhyme tell about a meddlesome rabbit, a handsome mouse, a traveling turtle, a happy kitten, a bad-mannered parrot, and a special dog. The charming, detailed watercolor illustrations are sure to please all readers and listeners, but what makes this collection so unique are the wonderful verses with recurring correspondence of end sounds that can definitely be used as examples of the beauty, symmetry, and rhythm of the Spanish language. These are just right for Spanish-speaking readers or for those eager to practice their Spanish.

Schujer, Silvia. *Las visitas.* *(Visitors)* Buenos Aires: Juvenil Alfaguara, 1991. 94p. ISBN: 950-511-128-2. pap. $10.50. Gr. 7-10.

In a gripping and fast-moving narrative, a young boy relates his feelings upon discovering that his father is in prison. In addition, he has to deal with his sister's troubled adolescence, his mother's new boyfriend, and other problems facing adults in his life. Perhaps the author tried too hard to write a "realistic, problem novel," but some adolescents may empathize and understand.

Seuss, Dr. *El Lórax.* *(The Lorax)* Translated by Aída E. Marcuse. New York: Lectorum Publications, 1993. 64p. ISBN: 1-880507-04-8. $13.95. Gr. 3-6.

Spanish speakers will delight in this joyful translation of the popular, yet unsubtle discourse on ecology, *The Lorax,* in which the heroes *Árboles-Trúfula* (Trufula Trees), fresh air, clean water, green grass—are urged to triumph over money, factories, noise, pollution, and big business. Dr. Seuss's typically bright action-packed cartoonish-style illustrations are as amusing as the originals.

Sierra i Fabra, Jordi. *Banda sonora. (Sonorous Band)*   Madrid:
Ediciones Siruela, 1993. 251p. ISBN: 84-7844-159-X. $11.95.
Gr. 8-12.

Vic, a seventeen-year-old boy, is eager to finish school and to
devote his time and energy to his guitar, his music, and that world
which caused so much pain to his mother. Vic inherited the love of
music from his father, one of the great rock music figures of Spain,
but he hasn't seen him since his parent's divorce. Vic's re-
encounter with his father is set against the trials and tribulations in
the lives of professional musicians. This frank coming-of-age novel
will appeal to rock music lovers.

Sierra i Fabra, Jordi. *Una boda desmadrada. (A Chaotic Wedding)*
ISBN: 84-348-4265-3.

————. *Los mayores están locos, locos, locos.   (Grownups Are
Crazy, Crazy, Crazy)* ISBN: 84-348-4264-5.

————. *Noticias frescas. (Blunt News)* ISBN: 84-348-4263-7.

————. *El rockero. (The Rock Musician)* ISBN: 84-348-4266-1.

Ea. vol.: 125p. (Los Libros de Víctor y Cía) Madrid: Ediciones
SM, 1994. $9.50. Gr. 5-8.

Victor, an engaging adolescent, can't understand why his father
gets upset, his mother worries, his older sister shrieks, and his
brother complains when he embarks on yet another creative, logical,
albeit far-fetched, project. In *Una boda desmadrada*, Victor realizes
that even though most weddings are dull, this one is different. He
has to wear a tie and a jacket, which would ruin anyone's reputation
forever, but the excitement is worth it. Victor's birthday present
becomes a serious issue in *Los mayores están locos, locos, locos*
especially when his mother is considering giving him socks, under-
pants, and undershirts. Victor and his friends are delighted to share
their neighborhood's scandals, frauds, and injustices in *Noticias
frescas*. Even though Victor's mother encouraged him to participate
in a recreational activity, he is surprised to learn that she is not
delighted about his becoming a rock musician, as depicted in *El
rockero*. The concerns, feelings, and language of Spanish-speaking
adolescents are wonderfully depicted in this lighthearted series.

Sierra i Fabra, Jordi. *Dando la nota. (Passing Grades)* ISBN: 84-
348-4521-0.

————. *Noche de paz..., o casi. (A Peaceful Christmas. . . Almost)*
ISBN: 84-348-4734-5.

————. *Tres días salvajes.   (Three Wild Days)* ISBN: 84-348-
4522-9.

Ea. vol.: 125p. Illus: Federico Delicado (Los Libros de Víctor y Cía) Madrid: Ediciones SM, 1995. $9.95. Gr. 5-8.

Like the previous eight titles in this series about Víctor, an engaging adolescent who always seems to get in trouble, these relate in an easy-going style his misadventures with his family, teachers, and friends. Víctor's efforts to do well in school and thus be rewarded by his father with a record player, a radio, two cassettes, and two speakers are depicted in *Dando la nota*. In *Noche de paz..., o casi*, Víctor realizes that spending Christmas with distant aunts isn't really much fun. And *Tres días salvajes* recounts Víctor's experiences during a three-day trip to the country. These lighthearted stories can get repetitive, but their approach to the concerns of adolescents is honest and generally amusing.

Sierra i Fabra, Jordi. *Jamalají-jamalajá. (Jamalají-jamalajá)* Illus: Federico Delicado. Madrid: Ediciones SM, 1995. 133p. ISBN: 84-348-4652-7. $10.95. Gr. 7-10.

Sixteen-year-old Víctor is desperate. His idol, Bruce Springsteen, is in town and his parents won't allow him to go to the concert. His close friends see the injustice and together they decide that the next best thing is to meet their idol and ask for his autograph. Despite several far-fetched incidents such as an unlikely encounter with Yasmina, an Arabian princess, and an appearance on a TV game show, adolescents will enjoy the action and Víctor's success in obtaining Springsteen's autograph.

Sierra i Fabra, Jordi. *Malas tierras. (Badlands)* ISBN: 84-348-4265-3.

Ea. vol.: 125p. (Los Libros de Víctor y Cía) Madrid: Ediciones SM, 1994. 143p. ISBN: 84-348-4357-9. pap. $8.95. Gr. 9-12.

Toni, Cristo, and Cati are looking forward to a Bruce Springsteen concert at the Palau Sant Jordi in Barcelona. Concurrently, the parents of another teenager are anxiously waiting for a heart donor which could save their daughter's life. The joy of a music concert and a fun evening with friends result in a tragic car accident in which Cati loses her life and becomes a heart donor. This fast-paced novel definitely portrays the emotions and interests of contemporary adolescents—in Spain and elsewhere.

Sierra i Fabra, Jordi. *Noche de viernes. (Friday Night)* Madrid: Alfaguara, 1994. 167p. ISBN: 84-204-4762-5. pap. $8.95. Gr. 9-12.

One Friday evening, five young men in search of excitement end up involved in the tragic death of Mohamed, a young man from Morocco. Alcohol, drugs, gang violence, and racism complicate the personal problems of young men who seem to have nowhere to go. The contemporary urban setting and fast pace of this realistic novel may appeal to Spanish-speaking adolescents in search of rash action.

Singer, Isaac Bashevis. *Cuando Shlemel fue a Varsovia y otros cuentos. (When Shemiel Went to Warsaw and Other Stories)* Illus: Margot Zemach. Translated by Ramón Buckley. México: Alfaguara/Consejo Nacional para la Cultura y las Artes, 1993. 103p. ISBN: 968-29-5026-0. pap. $6.95. Gr. 6-9.

Singer's collection of eight short stories about crafty fools, kind rabbis, wise men, and others will charm Spanish speakers with their freshness and ingenuity. Zemach's original black-and-white line illustrations add a humorous touch to this zesty translation.

Singer, Marilyn. *En el palacio del Rey Océano. (In the Palace of the Ocean King)* Illus: Ted Rand. Translated by Aída Marcuse. New York: Simon & Schuster/Atheneum, 1995. 32p. ISBN: 0-689-31983-5. $15.00. Gr. 2-5.

Mariana, a brave young woman, is the heroine in this original fairy tale for the 1990s in which the traditional roles are reversed. Silvio, a shy, passive prince is a prisoner of the evil Ocean King, but Mariana overcomes her own fear of the ocean and rescues her beloved. Like the English version, the fantasy goes on much too long with too many details about underwater action. But the double-spread ink-and-acrylic paintings in swirling colors and the romance between the timid prince and the dazzling blond woman may hold some kids' attention.

Soto, Gary. *Beisbol en abril y otras historias. (Baseball in April and Other Stories)* Illus: Mauricio Gómez Morín. Translated by Tedi López Mills. México: Fondo de Cultura Económica, 1993. 149p. ISBN: 968-16-3854-9. pap. $7.49. Gr. 5-9.

Spanish-speaking adolescents will rejoice in this translation of Gary Soto's popular collection of eleven short stories that tell about the trials and tribulations of growing up. The everyday worries and anxieties of preteen Latino boys and girls in Fresno, California, are sensitively depicted as they deal with such concerns as lack of money, embarrassing moments at school, obstinate parents, and other difficult situations. Of special interest because of their universal themes are *"Primero de secundaria"* ("Seventh Grade"), *"Madre e hija"* ("Mother and Daughter") and *"La bamba"* ("La Bamba"). Unfortunately, the stale, black-and-white illustrations are unpleasant detractors.

Speare, Elizabeth George. *El estanque del mirlo.* *(The Witch of Blackbird Pond)* Translated by Ana Cristina Werring Millet. Barcelona: Editorial Noguer, 1995. 190p. ISBN: 84-279-3229-4. pap. $10.50. Gr. 9-12.

Speare's 1959 Newbery Award winner, *The Witch of Blackbird Pond*, is now available to Spanish speakers in this fluid rendition. Kit Tyler, the courageous protagonist from warm and colorful Barbados, will affect teenagers as she deals with the bleak, somber Puritans who arrest her for witchcraft. Fortunately, friendship and honor prevail.

Steig, William. *Doctor de Soto.* *(Doctor De Soto)* Translated by María Puncel. Madrid: Altea, Taurus, Alfaguara, 1991. 30p. ISBN: 84-372-6616-5. $15.95. Gr. 2-5.

Doctor de Soto, a mouse, is a most competent and friendly dentist. He is eager to help all patients except animals who are dangerous to mice. In this wonderful translation with the original, witty pastel illustrations, Spanish-speaking young readers will delight in how Doctor and Mrs. de Soto outsmart a crafty, mean fox.

Steig, William. *Dominico.* *(Dominic)* Illus: the author. Translated by María Luisa Balseiro. New York: Mirasol/Farrar, Straus, and Giroux, 1994. 152p. ISBN:0-374-41827-6. pap. $4.95. Gr. 3-6.

Dominic, a generous and likable dog, sets off to see the world upon the advice of a witch-alligator. Steig's original and humorous black-and-white line illustrations will certainly appeal to Spanish speakers. This wonderful Spanish translation was done in Spain; hence it maintains peninsular Spanish inflected verbal forms and their corresponding pronouns. These conjugations and pronouns, however, are definitely recognizable and, as they only appear a few times at the beginning, they should not deter Spanish speakers in the United States from enjoying Dominic's lighthearted, albeit somewhat rambling, adventures as he fights a wicked gang, receives a fortune from an aged pig, and encounters many animals who need his assistance.

Steig, William. *La isla de Abel.* *(Abel's Island)* Translated by María Luisa Balseiro. New York: Mirasol/Farrar, Straus, and Giroux, 1992. 125p. ISBN: 0-374-34286-5. $14.00. Gr. 3-6.

This enchanting Spanish translation, originally published in Spain in 1977, of Steig's beloved story about a fastidious Edwardian dandy who gets swept away in a driving rainstorm while rescuing his wife's scarf and winds up stranded on a river island for a year, has maintained all the feelings of courage, affection, and determination. The author's pen-and-wash drawings are as touching as the originals. What a treat for Spanish speakers!

Steig, William. *El verdadero ladrón.* *(The Real Thief)* Illus: the author. Translated by Sonia Tapia. New York: Mirasol/Farrar, Straus, and Giroux, 1993. 57p. ISBN: 0-374-30458-0. $15.00. Gr. 3-5.

Steig's endearing story about an honorable goose who only has his king's best interests at heart but is accused of theft on the basis of circumstantial evidence is now available in the United States in this Spanish translation, originally published in Spain. This is a joyful translation that maintains Steig's captivating style and tongue-in-cheek humor. Some readers, however, may object to Spanish inflected verbal forms and pronouns never used by Hispanic Americans. In addition, this translation is enriched by a stylized Spanish vocabulary. Selectors should note, relax, and enjoy.

Suárez, Maribel. *Miguel y el pastel.* *(Miguel and the Cake)* Illus: the author. ISBN: 970-05-0148-5. Mexico: Editorial Grijalbo, 1992. 22p. pap. $4.95. Gr. 2-4.

Miguel, a young baker, tells about the secret ingredients, preparation, and unforeseen results of a chocolate cake. The lighthearted watercolor illustrations and amusing, rhyming text make Miguel's baking experiences a joyous unexpected treat.

Teixidor, Emili. *Corazón de Roble.* *(Heart of Oak)* Madrid: Ediciones SM, 1995. 187p. ISBN: 84-348-4526-1. pap. $9.95. Gr. 8-12.

Through Tinco and Viana, two courageous adolescents, readers will be exposed to the last moments of the third Carlist War (1872-1876), a Spanish civil war between pretenders to the Spanish throne. The conflicts and issues of the times are set amid Tinco's personal tribulations about his own parents and Viana's down-to-earth attitude in this engrossing historical novel full of adventure and excitement.

Thomas, Ruth. *¡Culpable!* *(Guilty!)* Translated by Pilar León Fiz. Madrid: Ediciones SM, 1995. 208p. ISBN: 84-348-4665-9. pap. $7.95. Gr. 6-9.

The problems of crime, racism, and unemployment in a big city are poignantly depicted in this novel full of adventure and intrigue. Adolescents will empathize with twelve-year-old Kate who, in addition to having a difficult time in school, is rejected by her friends and family. Originally published by Hutchinson Books, London, this fast-paced novel received the British *Guardian* Award.

Thomas, Valerie. *La bruja Gertrudis.* *(Winnie the Witch)* Illus: Korky Paul. Translated by Néstor Busquets. Barcelona: Editorial Lumen, 1992. 26p. ISBN: 84-264-3665-X. $16.95. Gr. 2-4.

Gertrudis the witch lives in a black house that has a black carpet, black chairs, a black bed, and even black walls. Naturally her cat, Jeremías, is also black, creating numerous problems which Gertrudis finally solves with her magic wand. The engaging full-page watercolor spreads of this amusing story, originally published by Oxford University Press in 1987, make this a most eye-catching story to read to a group of eager listeners.

Traven, B. *Puente en la selva.* *(Bridge on the Jungle)* Illus: Manuel Ahumada. Translated from the English by Esperanza López Mateos. México: Fondo de Cultura Económica, 1991. 258p. ISBN: 968-16-3662-7. pap. $7.95. Gr. 9-adult.

B. Traven, pseudonym of the American author Traven Torsvan Croves, gives evidence of his love for his adopted country in this touching novel set in one of Mexico's perilous jungles. In a heart-warming manner, Traven depicts the feelings, customs, and values of the people of rural Mexico through the grief of a mother and the funeral of her beloved child. Sophisticated readers will empathize and understand.

Traven, B. *El visitante nocturno.* *(The Night Visitor)* Illus: Claudia de Teresa. Translated from the English by Rosa Elena Luján. México: Fondo de Cultura Económica, 1991. 128p. ISBN: 968-16-3669-4. pap. $7.95. Gr. 8-adult.

B. Traven, pseudonym of the American author, Traven Torsvan Croves, who lived for many years in Mexico, wrote these two short stories after his trips to the jungles of Mexico. In them, he expresses his fascination with the native people of Mexico and with Mexico's turbulent and glorious history. Sensitive, two-tone illustrations perfectly convey the mood of rural Mexico.

Treviño, Elizabeth Borton de. *Yo, Juan de Pareja.* *(I, Juan de Pareja)* Translated by Enrique R. Treviño Borton. New York: Farrar, Straus, and Giroux, 1994. 218p. ISBN: 0-374-38699-4. $16.00. Gr. 6-10.

The wonderful Newbery Award-winning novel about a black slave boy, Juan de Pareja, and the greatest Spanish painter of the seventeenth century, Diego Velázquez, is now available in Spanish. Spanish-speaking readers, like English readers since 1965, will be touched by the author's sensitive treatment of the affectionate relationship between two great men. This is indeed an ode to the brotherhood of man.

Van Allsburg, Chris. *El higo más dulce. (The Sweetest Fig)* Illus: the author. Translated by Francisco Segovia. México: Fondo de Cultura Económica, 1995. 30p. ISBN: 968-16-4619-3. $10.99. Gr. 2-4.

Like other Van Allsburg's fantasies, this fluid Spanish rendition will appeal to all young Spanish speakers. The powerful three-tone illustrations and the direct text provide the perfect background to this compelling story about Monsieur Bibot, a demanding dentist, and his patient dog, Marcel.

Van Allsburg, Chris. *Jumanji. (Jumanji)* Illus: the author. Translated by Rafael Segovia Albán. México: Fondo de Cultura Económica, 1995. 30p. ISBN: 968-16-3666-X. $10.99. Gr. 3-5.

This 1982 Caldecott Medal fantasy will delight Spanish-speaking children as they experience the dangers of a jungle with a lion, two monkeys, two rhinoceroses, a boa, and other excitements in their own living room. Van Allsburg's outstanding sense of mass and play of light and shadow are just as evident as in the original black-and-white illustrations.

Vázquez Montalbán, Manuel, and others. *Breve antología de cuentos 4: Latinoamérica y España. (Brief Anthology of Short Stories 4: Latin America and Spain)* Buenos Aires: Editorial Sudamericana, 1993. 85p. ISBN: 950-07-0897-3. pap. $8.90. Gr. 9-adult.

Seven short stories by Latin American and Spanish authors are included in this collection. They tell of incredible marketing strategies to sell a live elephant with easy payments, offers to exchange old wives for new blondes, the King of Tin's trip to hell, Martín Fierro's last duel, and a suitor's efforts to win the love of a beautiful and arrogant woman. Sophisticated readers will enjoy these stories which vary in length from two to fifteen pages by Manuel Vázquez Montalbán (Spain), Juan José Arreola (Mexico), Jorge Luis Borges (Argentina), Virgilio Piñera (Cuba), Isabel Allende (Chile), Joao Guimaraes Rosa (Brazil), and Augusto Céspedes (Bolivia). Brief biographical sketches about each author as well as a glossary and notes add to the interest of this collection. It is unfortunate that the prosaic cover and cheap paper will discourage most readers.

Waber, Bernard. *Quique duerme fuera de casa. (Ira Sleeps Over)* Translated by Teresa Mlawer. ISBN: 968-6579-15-X. Mexico: Sistemas Técnicos de Edición, 1991. 48p. $16.95. Gr. 3-5.

Delightful translation of *Ira Sleeps Over*, originally published in 1972 by Houghton Mifflin. Quique is looking forward to spending the night at his friend's house, but his sister wonders what he is going to do about going to bed without Chi Chi, his beloved teddy bear. After much thought, Quique decides to leave Chi Chi at home; however, listening to a story about ghosts makes him reconsider. Children of all ages will certainly empathize. The unaffected four-tone illustrations certainly convey the tone and spirit of this charming story.

Walsh, María Elena. *El diablo inglés y otros cuentos. (The English Devil and Other Stories)* Illus: Nora Hilb. Buenos Aires: Editorial Sudamericana, 1992. 93p. ISBN: 950-07-0745-4. pap. $11.50. Gr. 3-6.

Six stories are in this collection by the outstanding Argentine author, María Elena Walsh, originally published in 1974. The first three—*"El diablo inglés," "La sirena y el capitán," "El país de la geometría"*—are old-time favorites. In a fast-moving and amusing manner, they tell about the English devils who appeared in Argentina in 1806, a beautiful mermaid who was captured by a Spanish captain, and the King of the Compass who finally found his beautiful round flower. The other three lack the author's usual reader appeal and charm. Another disappointment is the tiny black-and-white illustrations that serve merely as decorations.

Westall, Robert. *Cielo negro sobre Kuwait. (Gulf)* Translated by Javier Franco Aixelá. Madrid: Santillana, 1995. 151p. ISBN: 84-204-4824-9. pap. $6.95. Gr. 8-12.

Through Tom and Andy, two British adolescents, readers will experience the emotions of rugby, a game from which American football developed, and a strong negative view against the United States position in the Gulf War. Originally published by Methuen Children's Books, London, in 1992, this fast-paced novel has been most popular with British adolescents. Despite its anti-American slant, this fluid Spanish rendition will appeal to Spanish-speaking readers.

Wilder, Laura Ingalls. *A orillas del Río Plum. (On the Banks of Plum Creek)* Illus: Garth Williams. Barcelona: Editorial Noguer, 1993. 191p. ISBN: 84-279-3208-1. $9.95. Gr. 6-9.

The wonderful courage and admirable persistence of Laura, her sisters, Mary and Carrie, and their parents as they settle on the banks of Plum Creek are beautifully rendered in this fluid Spanish translation. Garth Williams's soft, black-and-white pencil illustrations provide a charming glimpse of the lifestyle and vicissitudes of this spirited family.

Wilder, Laura Ingalls. *Un granjero de diez años. (Farmer Boy)* Illus: Garth Williams. Translated by Josefina Guerrero. Barcelona:

Editorial Noguer, 1994.   199p.   ISBN: 84-279-3224-3.   pap. $9.50.   Gr. 8-12.

Like other Wilder novels that beautifully describe the impact of isolation and self-sufficiency on pioneers on the frontier, this excellent Spanish rendition will captivate Spanish speakers.   In addition, Garth Williams's black-and-white illustrations bring immediacy to the dream of Almanzo, the youngest in the family, who is eager to own a colt of his own.

Williams, Margery. *El conejo de terciopelo. (The Velveteen Rabbit)*
Illus: Michael Hague.   Translated by Juan González Alvaro. Madrid: Editorial Everest, 1992.   40p.   ISBN: 84-241-3337-4. $13.50.   Gr. 3-5.

The ever-popular story of the velveteen rabbit who became real because of a little boy's love is now available in Spanish in this well-done translation.   Hague's tender watercolor illustrations together with the excellent quality of the paper and the appealing cover will make this touching story as popular with Spanish speakers as it is with English speakers.

Wilson, Eric. *El desenmascarado de Ksan.   (The Unmasking of Ksan)* 127p.   ISBN: 84-348-4525-3.
————. *Detectives de Tejas Verdes. (The Green Gables Detectives)* 144p.   ISBN: 84-348-4524-5.
————. *Espíritus en el bosque. (Spirit in the Rainforest)* 128p. ISBN: 84-348-4523-7.
Ea. vol.:   Illus: Samuel Velasco.   Translated by Emilio Ortega. (Tom y Liz)   Madrid: Ediciones SM, 1995. $9.95.   Gr. 5-8.

Fast pace and lots of action characterize these mystery stories, originally published by Totem Books/Collins.   Dawn and Graham search for a magic mask in *El desenmascarado de Ksan*.   An old cemetery, an enchanted church, and an unoccupied lighthouse are the setting for Liz Austen's strange happenings as described in *Detectives de Tejas Verdes*.   Tom's and Liz's efforts to protect the environment are ultimately rewarded in *Espíritus en el bosque*. The black-and-white, cartoon-like illustrations are simplistic at best but lovers of this genre will appreciate the exciting plots loaded with easy-to-read dialogues.

Wyllie, Stephen, and Julek Heller. *Los magos: Un mágico libro de hologramas. (The Magicians: A Magic Book about Holograms)* Barcelona: Parramón, 1994.   22p.   ISBN: 84-342-1745-7. $23.95. Gr. 3-5.

The unique appeal of holography—photographic plates which diffract three-dimensional images of genies, goblins, bats, and other fantastic creatures—provides a distinctive touch to this story about two competing magicians. Lovers of magic and special effects will enjoy this well-illustrated book, originally published by Sadie Fields Productions, London, in 1994.

APPENDIX

DEALERS OF BOOKS IN SPANISH FOR CHILDREN AND YOUNG ADULTS

ARGENTINA

Fernando García Cambeiro
Cochabamba 244
1150 Buenos Aires, Argentina
Tel. (541) 361-0473; (541) 300-2797
Fax (541) 361-0493

CHILE

Herta Berenguer L.
Publicaciones
Correo 9 - Casilla 16598
Santiago, Chile
Tel. & Fax (562) 231-7145

COSTA RICA

Editorial Costa Rica
Edificio Central Apartado 10010
San José 100, Costa Rica
Tel. (506) 286-2523; (506) 286-1759
Fax (506) 286-1817

MEXICO

Sra. Carmen García Moreno
Empresa 109
Col. Mixcoac
03910 México D.F., México
Tel. (525) 611-1513
Fax (525) 598-4378

Scripta, Distribución
Copilco 178, 22-D
Copilco Universidad
04340 México D.F., México
Tel. (525) 548-3616

PERU

E. Iturriaga y Cia S.A.
Casilla 4640
Lima, Perú

SPAIN

Crisol
Juan Bravo, 38
28006 Madrid, España
Tel. (341) 322-4800
Fax (341) 322-4770

UNITED STATES

Aims International Books, Inc.
7709 Hamilton Avenue
Cincinnati, OH 45231
Tel. (513) 521-5590
Fax (513) 521-5592

Hispanic Book Distributors, Inc.
1665 W. Grant Road
Tucson, AZ 85745
Tel. (520) 882-9484
Fax (520) 882-7696

Mariuccia Iaconi Book Imports
970 Tennessee Street
San Francisco, CA 94107
Tel. (415) 821-1216
Fax (415) 821-1596

Lectorum Publications, Inc.
111 Eighth Avenue
Suite 804
New York, NY 10011
Tel. (212) 929-2833
Fax (212) 727-3035

VENEZUELA

Ediciones Ekaré
Avenida Luis Roche Altamira Sur
Apartado Postal 5893
Caracas 1010-A, Venezuela
Tel. (582) 263-0080; (582) 263-0091
Fax (582) 263-3291

AUTHOR INDEX

(Including coauthors and editors)

TITLE INDEX

Title Index 239

SUBJECT INDEX

BIOGRAPHY

CHILDREN'S POETRY

ECOLOGY

ENVIRONMENTAL PROTECTION

EUROPE

EVOLUTION

EXPLORERS

FAIRY TALES

HOLIDAYS

HOLOCAUST—Fiction

HOLOGRAPHY

HOME

PICTURE DICTIONARIES

PSYCHOLOGY
> Koplow, *Tanya and the Tobo Man: A Story for Children Entering Therapy/Tanya y el hombre Tobo: Una historia para niños que empiezan terapia* 70

PUERTO RICO
> Nodar, *El paraíso de abuelita* 136
> Santiago, *Cuando era puertorriqueña* 99

PUERTO RICO—Folklore
> Belpré, *Perez y Martina; un cuento folklórico puertorriqueño* 23
> Mohr and Martorell, *La canción del coquí y otros cuentos de Puerto Rico* 31
> Pitre, *Paco y la bruja: Cuento popular puertorriqueño* 140
> Veray, *Villancico Yaucano* 34

PUZZLES
> Clemson, *Mi primer libro de mates* 46
> Davis, *¿Y qué más?: Máquinas desafiantes y labertinos disparatados* 76
> Ramírez and others, *Adivinanzas Nahuas de ayer y hoy* 33

QUICKSAND
> de Paola, *El libro de las arenas movedizas* 48

RABBITS
> Duckett, *No os lo podéis imaginar* 120
> Evans, *Conejo* 52
> Solotareff, *Bebé conejito* 147
> Zolotow, *El señor conejo y el hermoso regalo* 157

RACISM—Fiction
> Ferrer Bermejo, *Silvestre y los ladrones de sueños* 175
> Hagemann, *Lobo Negro, un skin* 180
> Knight, *¿Quien es de aquí?* 184

RAIN FORESTS
> Cowcher, *El bosque tropical* 117
> Mutel, *Las selvas tropicales* 63
> Taylor, *La selva tropical* 55

RECIPES
> Bosch, *Bebidas y helados* 71
> Bosch, *¿Cómo se hacen? Postres* 72
> Drew, *Mi primer libro de pastelería* 103

ABOUT THE AUTHOR

Dr. Isabel Schon was born in Mexico City. She came to the United States in 1972, where she obtained her doctorate in philosophy from the University of Colorado in 1974.

She has received several national and international awards, including the 1992 U.S. Role Model in Education Award presented by the U.S.-México Foundation; the 1992 Denali Press Award from the Reference and Adult Services Division of the American Library Association for "achievement in creating reference works that are outstanding in quality and significance and provide information specifically about ethnic and minority groups in the U.S."; the 1987 Women's National Book Award, as "one of seventy women who have made a difference in the world of books"; the American Library Association's 1986 Grolier Foundation Award for "unique and invaluable contributions to the stimulation and guidance of reading by children and young people"; and the 1979 Herbert W. Putnam Honor Award presented by the American Library Association "to study the effects of books on students' perceptions of Mexican American people."

She is the author of twenty books and over 300 research and literary articles in the areas of bilingual/multicultural education and literature for Latino children and adolescents.

Dr. Schon has been a consultant on bilingual/bicultural educational materials to schools, libraries, and ministries of education in Mexico, Colombia, Guatemala, Argentina, Venezuela, Chile, Spain, Italy, Ecuador, and the United States.

Currently, she is a member of the founding faculty and founding director of the Center for the Study of Books in Spanish for Children and Adolescents at California State University, San Marcos.